Critical Issues in Educational Leadership Series

Joseph Murphy, Series Editor

A New Agenda for Research in Educational Leadership
WILLIAM A. FIRESTONE AND CAROLYN RIEHL, EDS.

The Effective Principal:
Instructional Leadership for High-Quality Learning
BARBARA SCOTT NELSON AND ANNETTE SASSI

Redesigning Accountability Systems for Education
SUSAN H. FUHRMAN AND RICHARD F. ELMORE, EDS.

Taking Account of Charter Schools:
What's Happened and What's Next?
KATRINA E. BULKLEY AND PRISCILLA WOHLSTETTER, EDS.

Learning Together, Leading Together:
Changing Schools through Professional Learning Communities
SHIRLEY M. HORD, ED.

Who Governs Our Schools? Changing Roles and Responsibilities
DAVID T. CONLEY

School Districts and Instructional Renewal
AMY M. HIGHTOWER, MICHAEL S. KNAPP,
JULIE A. MARSH, AND MILBREY W. MCLAUGHLIN, EDS.

Effort and Excellence in Urban Classrooms:
Expecting—and Getting—Success with All Students
DICK CORBETT, BRUCE WILSON, AND BELINDA WILLIAMS

Developing Educational Leaders: A Working Model:
The Learning Community in Action
CYNTHIA J. NORRIS, BRUCE G. BARNETT,
MARGARET R. BASOM, AND DIANE M. YERKES

Understanding and Assessing the Charter School Movement
JOSEPH MURPHY AND CATHERINE DUNN SHIFFMAN

School Choice in Urban America:
Magnet Schools and the Pursuit of Equity
CLAIRE SMREKAR AND ELLEN GOLDRING

Lessons from High-Performing Hispanic Schools:
Creating Learning Communities
PEDRO REYES, JAY D. SCRIBNER, AND
ALICIA PAREDES SCRIBNER, EDS.

Schools for Sale: Why Free Market Policies
Won't Improve America's Schools, and What Will
ERNEST R. HOUSE

Reclaiming Educational Administration as a Caring Profession
LYNN G. BECK

A New Agenda
for Research in
Educational Leadership

Edited by
WILLIAM A. FIRESTONE
CAROLYN RIEHL

TEACHERS
COLLEGE
PRESS

Teachers College, Columbia University
New York and London

Published by Teachers College Press, 1234 Amsterdam Avenue, New York, NY 10027

Library of Congress Cataloging-in-Publication Data

A new agenda for research in educational leadership / edited by William A. Firestone, Carolyn Riehl.
    p. cm. — (Critical issues in educational leadership series)
    Includes bibliographical references and index.
    ISBN 0-8077-4630-4 (cloth : alk. paper)
    1. Educational leadership—Research—United States. 2. School management and organization—Research—United States. I. Firestone, William A. II. Riehl, Carolyn. III. Series.
    LB2806.25.N49 2005
    371.2'007'2—dc22   2005051049

ISBN 0-8077-4630-4 (cloth)

Printed on acid-free paper
Manufactured in the United States of America

12   11   10   09   08   07   06   05   8   7   6   5   4   3   2   1

To Peter,

For waiting patiently (most of the time)

—C.R.

To Susan,

For listening to it all (several times)

—W.A.F.

Contents

Preface   ix

1. Introduction   1

   William A. Firestone and Carolyn Riehl

2. What Do We Already Know About Educational
   Leadership?   12

   Kenneth A. Leithwood and Carolyn Riehl

3. What Can Researchers on Educational Leadership Learn
   from Research on Teaching? Building a Bridge   28

   Mary Kay Stein and James Spillane

4. How Can Educational Leaders Support and Promote
   Teaching and Learning? New Conceptions of Learning
   and Leading in Schools   46

   Nona A. Prestine and Barbara Scott Nelson

5. How Can School Leaders Incorporate Communities
   as Contexts for Student Learning?   61

   Mary Erina Driscoll and Ellen B. Goldring

6. How Do Leaders Interpret Conflicting Accountabilities
   to Improve Student Learning?   81

   William A. Firestone and Dorothy Shipps

7. How Does Leadership Promote Successful Teaching
   and Learning for Diverse Students?   101

   Pedro Reyes and Lonnie Wagstaff

8. How Can Educational Leaders Promote and Support
    Social Justice and Democratic Community in Schools?   119

    Gail C. Furman and Carolyn M. Shields

9. What Do We Know About Developing School Leaders?
    A Look at Existing Research and Next Steps for New Study   138

    *Mark A. Smylie and Albert Bennett with Pamela Konkol
    and Carol R. Fendt*

10. What Research Methods Should Be Used to Study
    Educational Leadership?   156

    Carolyn Riehl and William A. Firestone

11. Conclusion   171

    William A. Firestone and Carolyn Riehl

References   185

About the Editors and the Contributors   221

Index   225

Preface

The work leading to the production of this book stretches back several years and embraces the efforts of many individuals. From 1997 to 1999, a task force of Division A (Administration) of the American Educational Research Association (AERA) assessed the quality of research in educational administration. That group examined problems in the field and reported their observations in a special issue of *Educational Administration Quarterly* (Pounder, 2000). As the task force completed its work, Karen Seashore Louis, then vice president of Division A of AERA, appointed us co-chairs of what became a second task force. Our challenge was to help our field respond to the findings of the first task force, and we determined that it might be useful to develop and articulate an agenda for future research on educational leadership. Rather than form a complete task force immediately, we sought additional financial and intellectual support from the University Council for Educational Administration (UCEA) and the Laboratory for Student Success (LSS) in Philadelphia and began a series of preliminary conversations with other scholars.

These conversations suggested both a great variety of research issues and numerous people who could help develop a research agenda. They set the stage for a meeting in Philadelphia in November 2001. We invited people with a variety of backgrounds to the meeting. Those who attended included emerging and established scholars in educational leadership, as well as those who were closer to the world of practicing educational leaders and those whose research was on teaching and learning. In addition to us, participants included Betty Hale, Institute for Educational Leadership; Ken Leithwood, Ontario Institute for the Study of Education; Catherine Lugg, Rutgers University; Melinda Mangin, Rutgers University; JoAnn Manning, Laboratory for Student Success, Temple University; Barbara Scott Nelson, Education Development Corporation; Darlene Opfer, Ohio State University; Penelope Peterson, Northwestern University; Mary Podmostko, Institute for Educational Leadership; Nona Prestine, Penn State University; Pedro Reyes, The University of Texas-Austin; Karen Seashore, University of Minnesota; Mark Smylie, University of Illinois-Chicago; and Nicole Suozzi, Institute for Educational Leadership.

   This group thus included persons whose work is closer to the classroom, some who are more familiar with the external environment of the school, and some who focus on the organizational levels of schools and school districts. We hoped that this group would provide enough diversity but also enough familiarity with what had been done in the past, both in educational leadership and in related fields, to suggest a challenging research agenda.

   After 2 days of reviewing the field and identifying the emerging issues, the group suggested a set of questions that became the core of the task force's work; a later review by the co-chairs of the task force added to the list of questions. The next step was to recruit pairs of people to write working papers developing these question areas. The authors of those papers met in August 2002, with some additional participants from the November 2001 meeting. Chapters had not been fully developed by this time, so there was extensive opportunity to revise in response to critiques of oral presentations of preliminary ideas. Additional review and critique of both the general agenda and specific working papers came through presentations at annual meetings of UCEA and AERA in 2001, 2002, 2003, and 2004. We were fortunate to receive comments on the papers from two discussants at the 2003 AERA annual meeting: Annemarie Sullivan Palincsar, University of Michigan, and Karen Seashore Louis, University of Minnesota. Also, we solicited additional individuals to critique the papers in written reviews; these persons included Eric Camburn, then at University of Michigan; Robert Crowson, Vanderbilt University; Larry Cuban, Stanford University; Michael Dantley, Miami University (Ohio); Steve Jacobson, State University of New York-Buffalo; Barbara Levin, University of North Carolina at Greensboro; Catherine Lugg, Rutgers University; and David Mackinnon, Acadia University (Canada). We are very grateful to all of the individuals who contributed ideas, text, and feedback to the work of the task force. We are also grateful to Terri Hawkes of Rutgers University who orchestrated the several meetings and managed the manuscript development process that made this book possible.

   Our goal in producing this book is to enhance the quality and impact of research on school leadership and to strengthen the field's efforts toward building knowledge to inform practice. In doing so, we draw on other activities within educational administration that have been intended to consolidate knowledge and promote understanding. The two *Handbooks of Research on Educational Administration* (Boyan, 1988b; Murphy & Louis, 1999) have helped to draw together the best examples of research knowledge. Volumes such as the recent National Society for the Study of Education (NSSE) volume on leadership have attempted to articulate new directions for practice (Murphy, 2002a). What distinguishes our current effort is its emphasis on future directions for research and ensuring that future research informs practice and policy. We believe that future research will be more effective if it consistently focuses on how leadership contributes to student learning. We recognize that leaders are called upon to support student learning in many ways, some more direct than others, and we think it is important to understand how all of them work and can be improved. This task force will be successful if a decade from now, it will have spurred both more research on educational leadership in general, as well as more focused efforts to address critical problems of practice.

While we seek more focus, we do not expect a consensus to form that precludes other research topics from being addressed. Because educational research in general and research on educational leadership in particular are applied fields that draw on the social and behavioral sciences, agreement on critical research questions is especially difficult to achieve (Becher, 1989). In addition, although we sought and benefited from a wide spectrum of perspectives and experience among those who helped with this work, the persons who contributed to the task force as authors simply cannot reflect the full range of demographic diversity or scholarly orientation that characterizes the educational leadership research community. Different research questions and methods will continue to be raised in the study of educational leadership. Our hope is that this agenda will reduce the diffusion and inconsistency of discourse about the research needs of the field. Even if this particular agenda is not taken up by a substantial number of researchers, the conversation itself should prompt a constructive discussion about where research on educational leadership should go and—we hope—lead to more focused and effective efforts to improve our knowledge about constructive educational leadership.

We have not engaged in a formal consensus-building process, though we have tried to solicit broad involvement in this project. Thus, this book is not intended to be a sanctioned directive or a straitjacket. New developments will emerge that are not within the current scope of this project, and some of the directions proposed may not pay off as we hope. That is the risk of trying to see into the future. Nevertheless, we believe that the ideas proposed here suggest a direction that, if followed, will help research on educational leadership become more useful to educators and better grounded than it is now.

CHAPTER 1

Introduction

William A. Firestone and Carolyn Riehl

How can educational leaders increase student learning, and how can they foster equity in educational outcomes? The educational leadership research community must address these primary questions if research is to help improve practice.

In stating this simple but bold claim, we also make two important observations. First, the relationship between leadership and learning is exceedingly complex and requires attention to many detailed subquestions. Second, while nearly all research on educational leadership has at least some potential relevance to these basic questions, the impact of research has been weakened by a lack of overall focus and by the frequent failure to articulate how a given instance of research addresses the linkages among leadership, learning, and equity.

With these thoughts in mind, this book is intended to inspire and support researchers as they study leadership in schools and school systems. We present here a broad agenda for research on educational leadership that, we hope, can galvanize and give coherence to the efforts of many investigators. In this chapter, we provide a context for the development of a new research agenda and introduce the primary questions that form the agenda. In the chapters that follow, these questions are discussed in detail. Our intention is to encompass, as much as possible, the depth and range of knowledge about educational leadership, while seeking to establish strong connections between any discrete aspect of leadership and the primary concerns for learning and equity.

WHY EMPHASIZE LEADERSHIP FOR LEARNING?

In the last half of the 20th century, the broad legitimacy that public schools had enjoyed for many decades declined with the erosion of confidence that schools were educating children appropriately (Tyack & Cuban, 1995). Concerns in the United States surfaced in the 1950s amidst national dismay when Russia released its Sputnik spacecraft, reached a new level in the 1980s with the release of *A Nation at Risk* (National Commission on Excellence in Education, 1983), and have been fueled more recently by troubling evidence from national and international assessments of educational achievement. Observers have questioned the merits of these criticisms of educational quality (e.g., Berliner & Biddle, 1995). Nonetheless, both serious observers and pundits continue to diagnose many different problems with American education, and the quest to improve schooling continues.

One domain that has consistently been part of the reform agenda is the search for better educational leadership (e.g., Murphy & Datnow, 2002). Following closely on the heels of *A Nation at Risk*, another commissioned report, entitled *Leadership for America's Schools* (National Commission on Excellence in Educational Administration, 1987), suggested a rationale for improving the preparation and performance of school administrators. Since then, other organizations have devoted much attention to framing standards and expectations for school leadership (for example, the National Policy Board on Educational Administration, the Interstate School Leaders Licensure Consortium, and the Council of Chief State School Officers). Similar efforts worldwide are described by Hallinger (2003). In addition, the foundations currently providing funding to improve the knowledge about and the practice of educational leadership are a testament to the high level of interest in the potential of leadership.

In the past, educational leaders were judged routinely on their effectiveness in managing fiscal, organizational, and political conditions in their schools and school systems. In essence, they were expected simply to set the stage for student learning. Now leaders are increasingly being held accountable for the actual performance of those under their charge. With new assessment instruments and data-processing technologies, educational institutions and systems have much greater capacity for measuring outcomes, reporting them at the school and student level, and using them as indicators of leaders' effectiveness. Given growing expectations that leaders can and should influence learning, it is important to understand how leadership, learning, and equity are linked.

LEARNING, EQUITY, AND LEADERSHIP

Expectations for who should be schooled and for how long have changed dramatically. In 1900, most children attended elementary school, but only about 6% graduated from high school. A century later, a high school diploma has become a minimum educational credential, guaranteeing very little in the way of social or economic opportunity.

Expectations for what children should actually learn in school have also risen. Content requirements have expanded, as evidenced by state curriculum guidelines and increased course-taking requirements. Students are expected to go beyond rote memorization of information to master deeper forms of understanding. In language arts, they must be able to read critically and understand complex texts. In mathematics, science, and technology, expectations go well beyond the capacity to apply algorithms for basic mathematical operations or memorize scientific facts. Students should understand the basic concepts and major ideas in these fields and be able to use their knowledge to solve problems, communicate their reasoning, and generally participate productively in society (National Council of Teachers of Mathematics, 2000; National Research Council, 2002a). By most accounts, public schools still have a long way to go to help all children attain these ambitious learning goals.

Local, state, and national educational standards, especially those related to the federal *No Child Left Behind* legislation, hold schools accountable for ensuring that students from diverse demographic backgrounds achieve at equally high levels. Still, educational achievement and attainment continue to differ dramatically depending on students' backgrounds, especially their race/ethnicity and family socioeconomic circumstances. In 2000, the national dropout rate was 7% for White students, 11% for African-Americans, and 27% for Hispanics. While showing some irregular declines, achievement disparities persist between African-American and Latino children on the one hand and White children on the other, as measured by the National Assessment of Educational Progress. Disparities are especially dramatic when income is taken into account. Meanwhile, the country's student population has become increasingly diverse, with the numbers of Hispanics and Asian-Americans growing much more rapidly than the population as a whole (Reid, 2001). This diversity makes the responsibility for providing equal educational opportunities and achieving equal educational results even more challenging.

Rising standards for educational equity and excellence place new demands on teachers, educational systems, and educational leaders. Teachers need deeper understandings of the subjects they teach and greater expertise in appropriate instructional methods. Organizational arrangements in schools must be reoriented to new teaching and learning standards; new technologies and forms of assessment must be incorporated into routine pedagogical practice. The challenges of gathering resources, developing capacities, and orchestrating action to achieve increasingly challenging standards often fall on the shoulders of educational leaders. Leaders must have new knowledge, not only about teaching, learning, and school organization, but also about the leadership competencies and practices that are associated with increased performance and effectiveness.

Many thoughtful critiques have been offered for why the current directions of education reform are ill conceived, inadequate, or even dangerous for students in the public schools. Scholars, policymakers, educators, and members of the public debate whether the current educational system is oriented too much toward a materialistic culture, valuing students only for their potential for economic productivity. Some question whether current curricular goals and accountability pressures are dehumanizing to both teachers and students. Others question whether students are being prepared adequately to confront the moral, cultural, political, and spiritual challenges of contemporary life. Still others ask whether the quest for equity is a thinly masked effort to preserve the status quo. Educational leaders should and do participate in and even lead these debates from their vantage points as stewards of education at local, state, and national levels. We think the questions raised are significant; we endorse the importance of these critiques; and we hope that careful scholarship will continue to inform the debates. But we also assert that however its general contours and specific requirements take shape, the educational system will continue to require competent and agile leaders who can influence and respond to the challenges they, their teachers, and their students face.

THE NEED FOR RESEARCH

Demands for more and better educational research are on the rise. They come from practitioners, policymakers, private and governmental funders of education and research, and of course from researchers themselves. Some demands seem to be politically motivated, using the rhetoric of science to cover ideologically driven reform agendas (Shaker & Heilman, 2004). But others seem quite genuine, decrying the sorry condition of education research when compared to research in other domains of science, technology, medicine, and human affairs (Lagemann & Shulman, 1999). Educational leadership research is not alone in receiving this criticism. Many subfields of education have long-standing research traditions that have been more comprehensive, better coordinated, and better received than could be said of research on educational leadership. One such area is mathematics education. Yet even there, leaders in the field argue that "the absence of cumulative, well-developed knowledge about the practice of teaching mathematics and the limited links between research and practice have been major impediments to creating a system of mathematics that works" (RAND Mathematics Study Panel, 2003, p. 5).

Why the demand for more research? What is it expected to accomplish? Research should provide a clarifying antidote to the welter of hunches, opinions, casual observations, and traditions that often guide practice and policymaking in education. Much practice is rooted in common sense, but common sense can be dangerous—as when the common understanding has been that certain groups of students cannot learn challenging subject matter. It can also be contradictory, leading to the polarization and even politicization of debates about how to teach subjects like reading and mathematics (Loveless, 2001). Research, it is hoped, will provide the most reasonable justifications possible at any given time for assertions about how things are or how the world works (Phillips, 1990). While some doubt that such certainty can ever be attained in a field as complex and contested as education, others hold out that research can lend clear and unequivocal weight to conclusions that can guide practice and policy.

An extensive debate is currently raging about what research methods are most appropriate for developing more strongly warranted assertions about effective educational practice. One strand of opinion, reflected in the *No Child Left Behind* legislation, advocates the use of randomized experiments for developing generalizable knowledge to guide practice (Olson & Viadero, 2002). However, many researchers question the practicality and utility of experiments and the validity of the postpositivist epistemological reasoning that undergirds such methods (St. Pierre, 2002). Debates about the appropriateness of different research methods—i.e., randomized or natural experiments, quasi-experimental surveys and statistical analyses, ethnographies and case studies—have a long history in education and are not likely to be resolved soon.

In this book, we argue that high-quality empirical research can provide guidance about the nature of educational leadership and how it impacts learning, and we make specific suggestions about potentially valuable research questions and directions. We also describe a variety of research methods that are appropriate for the study of educational leadership.

Research alone cannot guide practice. Some issues, like the questions about the fundamental purposes of education noted above, require deliberative processes to which research is mostly tangential. Beyond that, many educational decisions are highly contingent because problems and their contexts are complex and constantly changing. Decision makers, from teachers to policymakers, must consider more factors when deciding how to proceed than can be covered in any one research study or synthesis of many studies (Shavelson & Towne, 2002). Thus, well-designed and strongly warranted research conclusions will inform, but not determine, educational practice.

This is as true in educational leadership as it is in other areas. Historically, school administrators have relied heavily on their own practical knowledge and judgment (Riehl et al., 2000). What is not clear is whether this is because administrators' reasoning often may be informed more by sensitive inquiry into specific circumstances than by referring to a general body of knowledge or because the research base is not yet strong enough to guide practice.

School administrators also face recurring problems and situations in which the most important dynamics and challenges are consistent even if specific details vary from event to event. These are the kind of problems that well-designed programs of research can enlighten. If research provided well-developed and broadly accepted principles and tools for understanding and addressing those problems, many benefits would follow. Leaders could become more effective, training and development programs would be enhanced, and more individuals could be successful leaders.

RESEARCH ON EDUCATIONAL LEADERSHIP

Research on school leadership has led to few robust conclusions, and it has not yet reached broadly or deeply enough to account sufficiently for the extensive variations that leaders face in the contexts they serve, the people and organizations they lead, the actions they take, and the outcomes they pursue. The community studying educational leadership has never developed a solid focus of attention. It has often moved from one idea to another without persisting in studying any specific problem or testing any particular formulation long enough to yield strong results (Ogawa, Goldring, & Conley, 2000). Even the most productive scholars disagree on what the critical problems are or which ones are most likely to improve practice if they become the focus of an extended research program (Tschannen-Moran, Firestone, Hoy, & Johnson, 2000).

Most importantly, educational leadership research has rarely investigated the impact of leadership on learning outcomes. In the 1970s, research on effective schools suggested that strong leadership contributed to student achievement, but it provided little guidance about what leaders did to make a difference and it was heavily criticized on methodological grounds (Purkey & Smith, 1983). Subsequently, the design of research on how educational leaders contribute to student learning has improved enough to suggest that better-designed and executed research could yield important benefits (Hallinger & Heck, 1996b). Yet we have a long way to go, and many questions remain. For example, since most of the research focuses mainly on building-level educational leaders, we know very little about how leaders in other roles impact student learning. A vigorous research agenda is needed to help educational leaders maximize their contributions to achieving the twin goals of educational equity and increased student learning.

THE VALUE OF A NEW RESEARCH AGENDA

A strong and well-accepted agenda can make three contributions to the improvement of research on educational leadership. First, it can focus the research. Few people spend most of their life doing research on educational leadership, and the community of scholars is poorly organized. (For a comparison to mathematics education, see Romberg, n.d.) When relatively little research is undertaken, it is important that there be agreement on what major problems the field should address, and a research agenda can help achieve that end. In other areas, considerable progress has been made through long-term, programmatic research. The fact that at least some of these research programs successfully integrated researchers, developers, and school-based educators into a common effort probably contributed to their impact (Greeno et al., 1999; Lehrer & Schauble, 2000). In some instances, cross-role collaborations and at least partial consensus on the big questions in a field have been influenced by intentional planning. For example, the National Council of Teachers of Mathematics held two "catalyst conferences"—the most recent in September 2003—to develop a research agenda focusing on important aspects of mathematics education and build interest among researchers and funders in pursuing that agenda.

Still, trying to build consensus around a research agenda is unusual. We do not expect this agenda to drive out other issues or establish a research straitjacket. Knowledge development in many domains proceeds from the margins to the center. At the least, we could have left important considerations out of this agenda; at most, we could be dead wrong about some things. Our hope, however, is that this agenda will stimulate more focused discourse about the research needs of the field of educational leadership.

The second contribution may be to increase the amount of research on educational leadership. The fact is that relatively little research is conducted on educational leadership. Typical professors of educational leadership or administration actually publish very little scholarship of any sort during their careers (Tschannen-Moran et al., 2000). If researchers can agree on a common set of problems that are tractable and have the potential for increasing more equitable educational outcomes, that consensus will attract new researchers and researchers from related fields. The latter is especially likely if the agenda developed makes both conceptual and methodological links to those fields. Agreement on an agenda and the beginnings of evidence that research on that agenda is having practical as well as theoretical payoffs may also increase the amount of funding available for research in the area.

Finally and most importantly, a clear agenda, if well executed, will benefit education. If researchers continue working on an agreed-upon agenda that has a high promise of providing well-supported answers to questions about what leaders do to help schools become more meaningful learning settings, teachers become better instructors, and students learn more, their results are bound to become more useful over time. Of course, this payoff is more likely if ways are also found to engage the community of school leaders in active consideration of the research (not simply accepting its premises or advice), and if the research also leads to the development of mediating tools to help leaders do their work. Moreover, as Willinsky (2001) has suggested, high-quality educational research can also stimulate substantive public deliberation about educational policies and practices, which may be the most important route of all to educational improvement in a democracy.

THE PROPOSED AGENDA

In framing our broad research agenda, we began by asking questions about the relationship among leadership, learning, and equity. These questions quickly oriented in two directions. Leaders devote much of their time to developing the context where intellectually challenging teaching can contribute to improved and equitable learning. This work is focused inward toward the classroom. Simultaneously, they must work with external constituencies to obtain resources and support for the learning enterprise while ensuring that the work of the schools responds to the needs and demands of those constituencies. This looks outward. This boundary-spanning nature of leadership has influenced the agenda that we propose and the chapters included in this volume.

Following this introduction, the text begins with a synthesis of what is already known about school leadership, written by Kenneth A. Leithwood and Carolyn Riehl. The authors begin by defining leadership as *the work of mobilizing and influencing others to develop shared understandings and intentions and to achieve the school's goals.* They describe a core of basic leadership practices that are useful in almost all contexts; these encompass the functions of setting directions, developing people, and redesigning the organization. Leithwood and Riehl also describe leadership responses that are useful in schools serving highly diverse student populations.

Two chapters then explore what we need to know about how leadership contributes to student learning. Both draw on the substantial progress in understanding teaching and learning that has come from the constructivist turn in psychology and instruction. Mary Kay Stein and James Spillane ask what can be learned from recent developments in research on teaching. They suggest that just as classroom teachers create settings for children to learn, leaders can create opportunities for teachers to learn. By examining the questions that researchers on student learning have fruitfully addressed to suggest more effective teaching processes, they suggest an agenda that can be used to explore how leaders can contribute to teacher learning, which they argue is central to reforms that promote more equitable student outcomes.

Nona A. Prestine and Barbara Scott Nelson ask how educational leaders can support teaching and learning. They argue that new constructivist conceptions of teaching and learning require reconceptualizations of instructional leadership. The time has come to shift from analyzing norms and formal procedures to focusing on leadership practices. This shift will require greater attention to how leadership is distributed across leaders, followers, and the teaching situation. Like Stein and Spillane, they believe that this new focus will require greater attention to how leaders support teachers' learning about practice. They also call for exploration of educational leaders' content knowledge, which should be similar to, but different from, teachers' pedagogical content knowledge. Ultimately, new theories of learning require co-participation in the learning act by teachers and formal leaders. These new conceptualizations of what leadership are like suggest an array of new questions to be addressed.

Leadership that supports learning takes place in complex environments. Two chapters explore how different aspects of the environment create challenges and opportunities for leaders. Mary Erina Driscoll and Ellen B. Goldring believe that exploring relationships between the school and the community can have special benefits for diverse students. To question the current school-centric view of school-community relations, they propose moving in three directions. First, drawing on new cognitive perspectives, leaders should recognize that learning takes place in the community and that transfer between community-based and school-based learning is crucial. Such recognition requires extending the school into the community, taking advantage of more elements in the community to support learning, and working with sources of leadership outside the school that can support improved learning. Second, researchers need to clarify the networks and social capital that exist in communities, clarify how that capital can support student learning, and identify what leaders can do to build and take advantage of such social capital. Finally, researchers need to explore how leaders can contribute to community development. In many contexts, it is helpful to ask how a school's strategy for school improvement contributes not only to student achievement but also to a wider range of desirable outcomes in the community.

William Firestone and Dorothy Shipps explore the interplay of accountability, leadership, and teaching. They argue that past researchers have mis-specified the accountability problem. For leaders, the challenge is to cope with multiple accountabilities that create contradictory pressures; some press for increased and more equitable learning and others do not. They argue that leaders enact their environments by attending more to some parts than others. They call for more research on how leaders negotiate an interpretation of the environment. They further hypothesize that external accountability—that coming from bureaucratic, political, and market forces—is less crucial for improved student learning than internal accountability, a shared sense that improved outcomes for all children is important.

Two chapters address issues of equity. Pedro Reyes and Lonnie Wagstaff ask how leaders can contribute to the success of schools serving students from diverse backgrounds. They first develop a broad conceptualization of diversity and then present a perspective on the forms of leadership that may serve diverse students well. Both leadership values—the substantive directions that leaders pursue—and leadership ability—the process skills for working effectively—are significant. Moreover, leadership must be context-specific. Given the dearth of empirical literature linking leadership to the achievement of students from diverse backgrounds, the chapter concludes with suggestions for new research: needed are intensive case studies of settings where students of diverse backgrounds are educated well, as well as studies that test different constructs of leadership and studies that examine the development of leadership capacity.

Gail C. Furman and Carolyn M. Shields propose an agenda that explores how leaders improve learning by pursuing social justice and democratic community in schools. They argue that leadership grounded in democratic community and social justice is, at its core, instructional leadership. It pursues a socially just pedagogy that is created and sustained through the processes of deep democracy. The authors suggest directions for research on leadership for social justice and democracy. Such research must begin with consideration of the voices being heard and reflection on how to ensure that the powerful are not having undue influence on the conduct of the research or the interpretations that result. Research on leadership for socially just and deeply democratic communities will be fundamentally relational and interventionist, done in close partnership with those in schools who share an interest in this question.

The contribution of leaders to educational equity and increased learning depends in part on who is recruited to leadership roles. Mark A. Smylie, Albert Bennett, and their associates describe the need for a diverse and well-qualified leadership workforce, focusing on the demographics, value orientations, and competencies that must be present among the next generation of school leaders. They also describe innovative ways in which potential leaders can be identified, recruited, prepared, and supported throughout their careers. Finally, they suggest a number of directions for research that will both promote and evaluate new initiatives in leadership workforce development.

To help operationalize this research agenda, Carolyn Riehl and William A. Firestone summarize suggestions for methodologies that can be used to produce significant and robust knowledge about educational leadership that informs policy and practice. These suggestions address concerns for systematic, cumulative research with wide applicability, although needs for more local and targeted forms of research also are acknowledged. The chapter argues for more sophistication in research methodology, more coordination of activity across settings, and more interconnection among research questions being pursued.

CONCLUSION

Research-based knowledge about educational leadership has potential impact through multiple pathways—not only by influencing the practice of principals, superintendents, and other leaders in the trenches, but also by building the knowledge base of others with whom leaders work. This includes policymakers who encode understandings of leadership in various educational initiatives and structures, representatives of governmental and private funding agencies who support the development of new knowledge about leadership, teachers and consultants who are engaged in preservice preparation and in-service professional development for leaders, and of course researchers themselves, whose work directly determines the quality, range, and relevance of general knowledge about educational leadership.

Ten years from now, when the research agenda we are proposing has been pursued, the knowledge that results will be used in a world that is likely to be even more complex and diverse than the one we live in now. New knowledge will help school leaders respond to stronger demands, cope with organizational designs for schools that might be quite different, and address governance, institutional, and organizational contexts that are more complex, interrelated, and challenging than now and where accountability looks completely different. The situations will be different then, and the research needs may be different also. Nonetheless, we hope that our work will help stimulate a wide-reaching and vigorous conversation about research within the educational leadership community; motivate a variety of our current and future colleagues in educational leadership and related fields to focus a significant part of their attention on important questions with a high potential for improving the quality of American education; and encourage those who provide the resources for educational research—foundations and government—to consider these issues when they are making investments in their educational improvement agenda.

CHAPTER 2

What Do We Already Know About Educational Leadership?

Kenneth A. Leithwood and Carolyn Riehl

School leadership is currently the object of almost unprecedented attention. The continually evolving educational reform agenda appears to have seized upon leadership as both an important target for reform and a vehicle for making other changes happen. In such a climate, it is important to be able to turn to a compelling and well-grounded body of knowledge for information and guidance about leadership. Knowledge about leadership comes from many different sources, including the wisdom of experience; philosophical, conceptual, and critical analyses; and empirical research. The chapters in this book present a broad agenda to help strengthen the extent, quality, and clarity of the latter source of knowledge—empirical research on leadership. In this chapter, we set the stage for that agenda by reviewing well-established, research-based conclusions about educational leadership. We ask: What do we believe that we know right now about educational leadership? What empirical findings and interpretations can qualify as robust knowledge that can be applied in many different contexts? We address these questions at a fairly general level of abstraction, developing conclusions that provide a comprehensive but not deeply detailed portrait of leadership. Our framework and conclusions form a starting point for the chapters that follow.

Leadership exists at many different junctures in the complex arena that comprises most educational systems. In this chapter, we focus on the leadership of school principals or heads. While the study of other leadership roles is expanding (e.g., Spillane, 1998b; Stein & D'Amico, 2002a), the research base on formal leadership at the school level is presently more extensive, and conclusions are firmer.

Because the purpose of this chapter is to present research-based knowledge about school leadership, it is important to describe what we did and did not include in this review. One main source of evidence was quantitative research studies that reflected accepted methodological standards sufficiently well to be published in refereed academic journals and books. We also used evidence from published or publishable-quality multiple-case studies or from systematic single-case studies in which the results either supported or explicitly did not support evidence from other sources.

We did not include the findings of journalistic stories, testimonials, or informal case accounts in which data collection and analysis methods either were not described or did not conform to widely accepted procedures for arriving at reliable and valid conclusions. We did not use evidence from procedurally competent individual case studies that introduced findings as yet unsupported by additional research. There are aspects of school leadership that may be significant, even crucial, for success, but that have not yet been the subject of much formal research; thus, they are not addressed in this chapter.

These decision rules reflect a traditional view in the social sciences that some knowledge can be generalizable and that knowledge claims become more robust as the quantity of acceptable evidence accumulates. This view clearly leans toward the epistemological perspective of "soft positivism" or realism. We recognize its limitations, and we also gratefully admit that our understandings have been much informed by other types of knowledge and inquiry. Nonetheless, we have adopted this approach in order to make our conclusions as clear and straightforward as possible and to document how they are warranted.

A WORKING CONCEPTION OF SCHOOL LEADERSHIP

Leadership is difficult to define, and too narrow a definition might unduly restrict thought and practice. Nonetheless, a broad working conception will help to ground this review. Our approach to leadership incorporates the following understandings, drawn from empirical, conceptual, and normative sources:

> *Leadership exists within social relationships and serves social ends.* Although leaders are individuals, leadership is embedded in social relationships and organizations and is expected to accomplish something for a group. It is not an individual or personal phenomenon.
>
> *Leadership involves purpose and direction.* Leaders pursue goals with clarity and tenacity and are accountable for their accomplishment. In some views, it is the leader's role to develop and champion group goals. In other views, it is a more inclusive process, but one in which the leader is a key player. In still other cases, leadership may consist of the focusing of effort around a vision that originates elsewhere.

In the past, educational leaders were rewarded for pursuing the efficient technical management of schools or school systems (Rosenblum et al., 1994). Increasingly, educational leadership that purports to serve any end other than student learning is viewed as illegitimate and ineffectual. This explicit learning-focused goal for leadership does not narrow school leaders' purview to the instructional system per se, as did older notions of instructional leadership. Rather, it assumes that leaders will direct their attention to ensuring that all components and actions within the educational system support the learning of students.

Leadership is an influence process. Leaders sometimes do things that have a direct effect on the primary goals of the collective, but more often their agency consists of influencing the thoughts and actions of other persons and establishing the conditions that enable others to be effective. This influence may be targeted, helping people to accomplish something specific; or quite broad and transformative, lifting the aspirations and actions of others in expansive, often unpredictable ways (Burns, 1978).

Leadership is a function. Many observers of leadership acknowledge that leadership encompasses a set of functions that are not necessarily equated with a particular office or formal appointment. Persons in many different roles may do the work of leadership, although they often have different resources, abilities, and proclivities for doing so.

Leadership is contextual and contingent. Most contemporary theories of leadership suggest that leadership is practiced differently depending on the nature of the social organization, the goals being pursued, the individuals involved, resources and time frames, and many other factors, including characteristics of leaders themselves (Hallinger & Heck, 1996a; Leithwood & Duke, 1999). No one formula of effective leadership is applicable in all contexts.

Given these general orientations, we can define school leadership as *the work of mobilizing and influencing others to articulate and achieve the school's shared intentions and goals.* Leadership work can be accomplished by persons occupying various roles in the school. Formal leaders—those persons in formal positions of authority—are genuine leaders only to the extent that they fulfill these functions. Leadership functions can be carried out in many different ways, depending on the individual leader, the context, and the nature of the goals being pursued.

FOUR STRONG CLAIMS ABOUT SCHOOL LEADERSHIP

In this chapter, we portray the complex body of research about school leadership as an argument for four claims. In the discussion that follows, we intend "successful" school leadership to refer to leadership orientations and practices that have been demonstrated to have a positive impact on student learning, whether directly or indirectly through school conditions or the actions of others.

Claim 1: School Leadership Makes Important Contributions to the Improvement of Student Learning

In the long-standing quest to identify malleable influences on student learning, it has been no simple task to parse out the contributions of school-related factors, student background factors, and other contextual factors. These factors are not independent of each other, and methodological approaches to measurement and analysis can influence the relative weighting of effects. Nonetheless, in many studies, student characteristics persistently emerge as having the strongest effects on student achievement. School-related factors explain a much smaller but still important portion of the variance in achievement (Coleman 1966; Jencks et al., 1972; van de Grift & Houtveen, 1999). And they are, of course, the factors most amenable to change and improvement by educators. Some studies have shown that schools can significantly reduce the effects of student demographics on learning (e.g., Knapp & Associates, 1995).

Among school-related influences, classroom practices matter a great deal. Students tend to learn more when their teachers have strong formal qualifications and when they use appropriate, high-quality pedagogical techniques and a well-crafted curriculum (Brophy & Good, 1986; Monk, 1994; Wang, Haertel, & Walberg, 1992). School leaders also have an effect on student learning. The effects of leadership on student learning are properly conceived as mostly indirect effects (Hallinger & Heck, 1996a).

Claims about the effects of leadership on learning are justified by two sources of research evidence. Qualitative case studies often examine "outlier" school settings in which student learning is significantly above or below normal expectations. These studies have reported very large effects of leadership on student learning (e.g., Gezi, 1990; Levine & Lezotte, 1990; Mortimore, 1993; Scheurich, 1998). Effective leadership appears to encompass functions and characteristics such as a "maverick" orientation, the vigorous selection and replacement of teachers, buffering the school from non-learning-focused distractions, frequent monitoring of school activities, sense-making, high expenditure of time and energy for school improvement, support for teachers, and superior instructional leadership. In addition, principals presumably have some effect on other factors that matter; these include parent involvement, monitoring of student progress, successful student grouping patterns and other organizational arrangements, curriculum coordination, and rigorous and equitable student promotion policies and practices (Cotton, 1995; Sammons et al., 1995; Scheerens & Bosker, 1997). Case studies that do not begin by looking for leadership effects but end up concluding that leadership does matter for the improvement of teaching also provide convincing evidence (e.g., Coburn, 2001; Hamilton & Richardson, 1995).

The second broad source of evidence is quasi-experimental quantitative studies. A chief problem with this research is that many quantitative studies examine the relationship between school organizational conditions and student achievement without explicitly including measures of leadership. These include studies of school mission and goals (Hallinger, Bickman, & Davis, 1996); culture (Nias, Southworth, & Campbell, 1989); structural alternatives such as school size, the academic nature of the curriculum, or the assignment of qualified teachers to classes (Ingersoll, 1999); participation in decisionmaking (Smylie, Lazarus, & Brownlee-Conyers, 1996); and relationships with parents and the wider community (Epstein, 2001). Since these are conditions on which school leaders can have considerable impact, one might infer that leadership could exert indirect influence on learning through them.

In two early studies, Barr and Dreeben (1983) and Bidwell and Kasarda (1980) demonstrated the value of tracing an extended chain of influence across district, school, and classroom contexts to impact student learning, but this approach has not been used much to examine the direct and indirect impact of leadership on student learning. Even when such a method is employed, it is sometimes difficult to quantify leadership effects. An example of this problem is the research reported by Burns and Mason (2002). These researchers compared the achievement of students in single-grade versus multi-grade classes in elementary schools and found that the composition of classes helped to explain the higher achievement in multi-grade classes. The researchers reported firm evidence that principals deliberately assigned particular students to multi-grade classes (Burns & Mason, 1998, 2002), thus establishing a clear linkage between principal actions, class composition, and student achievement. But the principal behaviors themselves were not included in the quantitative model, so an effect size could not be estimated.

There are, however, some promising examples of research that specifies a reasonably complete model, incorporating contextual and leadership variables and using some form of student achievement as an outcome. Hallinger and Heck (1996a, 1996b) identified forty-odd such studies from a 15-year period. Quantitative studies of school effectiveness that included leadership in their models were also reviewed by Scheerens and Bosker (1997).

Hallinger and Heck concluded that in studies using the most sophisticated modeling, the effects of leadership on pupil outcomes were inconsistently present and generally small, but educationally significant. The most common mediating variable through which leadership effects were evident was school goals, although the construct of goals (or vision) was not always consistently defined across studies. Scheerens and Bosker (1997) reached similar conclusions. Their comprehensive review of quantitative evidence suggested that classroom and instructional factors have clear warrants for their impact on student achievement, and organizational conditions such as "high expectations" and "parent involvement"—factors over which school leaders clearly have some influence—have moderate empirical support. Other factors related to leadership, such as "pedagogic leadership," school climate, and organizational structure, have what Scheerens (1992) deemed "doubtful empirical confirmation." In general, factors and conditions closer to student learning—like instructional variables—have stronger effects than more distant factors such as school organization, policy-related conditions, or school leadership. Scheerens and Bosker found a small, though statistically significant, effect for school leadership. They also concluded that when contextual factors were taken into account, leadership effects emerged more clearly. For example, contextual studies indicate that "controlling educational leadership" is associated with effective schooling in low-SES schools more than in high-SES schools, and that strong leadership appears to be more important in urban rather than suburban elementary schools (1997, p. 288).

Other reviews of research, mainly from the international tradition of quantitative school effectiveness studies, have concluded that while leadership explains only 3 to 5% of the variation in student learning across schools, this is actually about one quarter of the total variation (10 to 20%) explained by school-level variables after controlling for student intake factors (Creemers & Reetzigt, 1996; Townsend, 2001).

Different results regarding leadership effects reported by these sources of evidence can be explained, at least in part, by sampling decisions. Most qualitative case studies examine the effects of exceptional leadership in schools most in need of it. In contrast, large-scale quantitative studies report average leadership effects across schools that range from being very needy to already highly productive, perhaps underestimating leadership effects in schools where leadership is likely to be of greatest value.

Despite these conceptual and methodological problems, the impact of educational leadership on student achievement is demonstrable. Leadership effects are mostly indirect, and they appear primarily to work through the organizational variable of school mission or goals and through variables related to classroom curriculum and instruction.

Claim 2: Leadership in Schools Is Exercised Primarily by Principals and Teachers and May Be Distributed to Others as Well

Principal and Teacher Leadership

Most research on school leadership focuses on leadership exerted by administrators and teachers and has documented a wide range of leadership responsibilities, styles, and functions. A recent review (Leithwood & Duke, 1999) described 20 distinct forms of principal leadership that the reviewers classified into 6 generic leadership approaches: instructional, transformational, moral, participative, managerial, and contingent forms of leadership.

Teacher leadership may be even more varied in form and function. Teachers assuming formal leadership roles (including lead teacher, department head, special program coordinator, or mentor) are expected to carry out functions such as representing the school in district-level decisionmaking (Fullan, 1991); leading subunits of schools (Cooper, 1993); stimulating the professional growth of colleagues (Wasley, 1991); being an advocate for teachers' work (Bascia, 1997); and improving the school's decisionmaking processes (Malen, Ogawa, & Kranz, 1990). Teacher leadership can also exist in a more informal sense, for example in teachers' supportive roles with each other in professional learning communities or in school change efforts (Grossman, Wineburg, & Woolworth, 2001; Wolf, Borko, Elliott, & McIver, 2000).

Empirical evidence concerning the effects of either formal or informal teacher leadership is limited in quantity and reports mixed results. For example, Hannay and Denby's (1994) study of department heads found that they were not very effective as facilitators of change because of their lack of knowledge and skill in effective change strategies. Firestone and Fisler (2002) found that conflicts among informal teacher leaders undermined shared vision. Several researchers have demonstrated that teachers' ability to function as leaders can be hampered by the principal's reluctance to share authority (Brown, Rutherford, & Boyle, 2000; Scribner, Hager, & Warne, 2002; Smylie, Conley, & Marks, 2002).

On the other hand, Duke, Showers, and Imber (1980) found that increased participation of teachers in school decisionmaking resulted in a more democratic school. Marks and Louis (1997) concluded that teacher participation in site-based governance impacted both teaching quality and student performance. In their study of special education initiatives, Mayrowetz and Weinstein (1999) found that teachers and other persons not in formal leadership roles had important leadership functions with regard to promoting inclusive education for students with special needs, and that the leadership functions of many different persons tended to overlap, a finding consistent with Heller and Firestone's (1995) earlier research.

Both principal leadership and teacher leadership entail the exercise of influence on the beliefs, values, and actions of others (Hart, 1995). What may be different is how that influence is exercised and to what end. Teachers and administrators often attempt to exercise leadership in relation to quite different aspects of the school's functioning, although teachers often report a strong interest in expanding their spheres of influence (Reavis & Griffith, 1993; Taylor & Bogotch, 1994). Their resources for leadership differ as well. In a traditional school, for example, persons in formal administrative roles have greater access to positional power in their attempts to influence classroom practice, whereas teachers may have greater access to the power that flows from technical expertise about teaching and learning. In a study of eight elementary schools, Spillane, Hallett, and Diamond (2003) found that teachers tended to consider other teachers to be real leaders if they employed human, cultural, and social capital in their work with others, while administrators were constructed as real leaders primarily on the basis of cultural capital, especially supportive interactional styles. When teachers considered principals to be leaders on the basis of human capital, it was generally because they displayed instructional expertise grounded in experience with a particular subject matter domain.

Distributed Leadership

Organizational restructuring initiatives stimulated inquiry about distributed conceptions of leadership as flatter, team-based, more organic structures began to replace hierarchical structures (Banner & Gagné, 1995; Chrispeels, Brown, & Castillo, 2000; Day & Harris, 2002; Murphy & Beck, 1995). Recent interest in distributed leadership has been supported by "substitutes for leadership" theory (Jermier & Kerr, 1997), situated and distributed cognition theories (Brown & Duguid, 1991; Wenger, 1998), and institutional theory (Ogawa & Bossert, 1995). Recent understandings of "learning-focused leadership" suggest that it requires an interrelated set of roles and functions across the school or system, especially in the context of complex policy initiatives (Gronn, 2000; Knapp et al., 2002; Spillane, Halverson, & Diamond, 2001). Empirical evidence concerning the nature and effects of distributed leadership is at an early stage of development, but research activity in this area is on the rise.

Wilson and Corcoran (1988) observed that in the successful secondary schools they studied, the source for leadership shifted as problems and issues shifted. Similarly, Spillane et al. (2001) found that the configuration of distributed leadership in high-poverty elementary schools differed depending on the curriculum area. With science education, for example, school principals exerted minimal leadership, ceding that role to highly involved teachers or to outside consultants or curriculum facilitators. With language arts instruction, however, principals and teachers with formal leadership designations (such as literacy facilitator) were more likely to exert leadership influence.

As interest in the idea of distributed leadership grows, it becomes increasingly important to research its specific nature and effects and to identify the contexts in which this orientation to leadership is most productive. In addition, it may be important to examine whether the total amount of leadership from all sources in a school may account for significant variation in school outcomes and effectiveness (Bryman, 1992). This hunch has yet to receive empirical testing in school contexts.

Claim 3: A Core Set of Basic Leadership Practices Is Valuable in Almost All Contexts

Evidence from many different kinds of schools supports the idea that some leadership practices are valuable in almost all contexts (Day et al., 2000; Leithwood, Jantzi,

& Steinbach, 1999; Southworth, 1998). Such practices ought to be considered a necessary but not sufficient part of a successful leader's repertoire. Describing the practices common to most successful leaders in most contexts is easier than one might imagine, because many large-scale quantitative studies have identified a rather stable set of findings. This evidence, from school and nonschool contexts, points to three broad categories of leadership practices that contribute to success. Hallinger and Heck (1999) label these categories "purposes," "people," and "structures and social systems." Conger and Kanungo (1998) speak about "visioning strategies," "efficacy-building strategies," and "context-changing strategies." Using Leithwood's (1994) labels, we briefly describe the categories and illustrate some specific practices.

Setting Directions

A critical aspect of leadership work is helping a group develop shared under-standings about the organization and its goals that can frame a sense of purpose or vision. The practice of setting directions is enacted through several means.

Identifying and articulating a vision. Educational leaders help identify new opportunities for the school and articulate a vision of the future that can inspire others. When visions are value-laden, they can lead to increased commitment from organizational members and provide compelling purposes for continual professional growth (e.g., Hallinger & Heck, 2002).

To identify and articulate visions well, leaders must be skilled communica-tors, able to focus attention and frame issues in ways that will lead to productive discourse and decisionmaking (Bennis, 1984; Fairhurst & Sarr, 1996). Leaders must understand their environmental context and work effectively with all constituen-cies to foster shared understandings (Bennis & Nanus, 1985; Daft, 1992). People act on the basis of their understandings of things; thus, by managing meanings, leaders influence how others view the world and how they choose to act. Leaders also must monitor performance and use that information as goals are developed and refined. This requires astute skills for gathering information and turning it into useful knowledge (Fuhrman, Clune, & Elmore, 1988; Mohrman et al., 1994).

Some would argue that a key element in developing vision in education is having a critical perspective toward schooling (e.g., Foster, 1989). Such a perspec-tive enables leaders to identify school practices that support injustice and inequity and to strengthen the school community's willingness and ability to resist these tendencies (Moore et al., 2002). To date, however, there is little empirical evidence to describe how this is enacted by local school leaders.

Fostering the acceptance of group goals. Leaders help set direction by encour-aging staff to develop goals that are shared. People are motivated by goals that they find compelling and challenging but achievable (e.g., Ford, 1992). Having such goals helps people make sense of the organization and craft an identity within their work context (Pittman, 1998; Thayer, 1988). Shared goals also help to orient organizational activity in common directions for maximal impact. Important leadership practices involve knowing how to sustain democratic processes and how to use conflict productively (Beck, 1994). Although this strategy contradicts some of the norms of individuality that have characterized teaching practice (Lortie, 1975), it is consistent with newer models of schools as collegial learning communities (Little, 1982).

Creating high performance expectations. Leaders help provide direction through actions that demonstrate their expectations for quality and high performance from staff. High expectations can help organizational members see the challenging nature of the goals being pursued, while also making it clear that the expectations are feasible (e.g., Podsakoff et al., 1990).

Developing People

Leaders promote effectiveness by influencing the capacities and motivations of key organizational workers (Lord & Maher, 1993). In schools, the ability to do so depends partly on leaders' knowledge of the "technical core" of teaching and learning, often invoked by the term "instructional leadership." But this ability also depends on what is referred to as leaders' emotional intelligence, or the leader's capacity to connect emotionally with others and to help others develop and deploy their own emotional resources in the service of their work (Goleman, Boyatzis, & McKee, 2002).

Offering intellectual stimulation. Educational leaders help generate the questions and ideas that prompt change in people by challenging staff to examine assumptions about their work and rethink how it can be performed. Leaders offer intellectual stimulation by providing opportunities for in-depth conversations about teaching and schooling, making informational resources available, supporting well-organized programs for professional development, and introducing new ideas for the school to consider (Leithwood, 1994).

Providing individualized support. Educational leaders support staff by showing respect and concern about their personal feelings and needs. This assures staff that the problems encountered while changing their practices will be taken seriously and that help will be offered (e.g., Louis, Toole, & Hargreaves, 1999). Recent evidence suggests that a leader's personal attention to employees increases levels of enthusiasm and optimism, reduces frustration, transmits a sense of mission, and indirectly increases performance (McColl-Kennedy & Anderson, 2002).

Providing an appropriate model. Principals exert leadership for developing people by setting examples for others to follow that are consistent with the organization's values and goals. Modeling provides a clear guide for growth and action; it also enhances staff beliefs about their own capacities and their sense of self-efficacy.

Redesigning the Organization

Successful educational leaders develop their schools as effective organizations that support and sustain the performance of teachers as well as students. Three specific sets of practices are typically associated with this category:

Strengthening school cultures. Leaders influence organizational culture through practices aimed at developing shared norms, values, beliefs, and attitudes and promoting mutual caring and trust among staff. A strong school culture draws members together around the goals being pursued by the school and the values and beliefs underlying the goals (e.g., Leithwood & Jantzi, 1990; Skalbeck, 1991).

Modifying organizational structures. Leaders redesign organizational structures through changes in staff and task assignments, the scheduling and design of time and space, routine operating procedures, and the deployment of technology and other material resources, all of which can hinder or enable individual performance and the accomplishment of organizational goals. Successful educational leaders direct structural changes to the establishment of positive conditions for teaching and learning (Louis, Kruse, and Associates, 1995).

Building collaborative processes. Leaders work to enhance school performance by providing opportunities for staff to participate in decisionmaking about issues that affect them and for which their knowledge is crucial. Such involvement assures staff that they can shape the organizational context to meet their own needs relative to goal accomplishment (e.g., Sleegers, Geijsel, & van den Borg, 2002).

Claim 4: Successful Leaders in Schools Serving Diverse Student Populations Establish Conditions That Support Student Achievement, Equity, and Justice

Many educational leaders serve student populations with diverse social backgrounds and characteristics. This includes students who live in poverty or whose race/ethnicity, mental or physical characteristics, cultural background, or native language abilities fall beyond the cultural mainstream. Such students often have not experienced much success in school.

Leadership appears to be especially important in schools serving diverse students and to be practiced differently as well. For example, leadership effects on student achievement have been found to be stronger in low-SES schools than in high-SES schools (Hallinger & Heck, 1996a). Unfortunately, experimental research indicates that aspiring school leaders may be especially reluctant to serve in such contexts, further exacerbating leadership challenges in these schools (Winter & Morgenthal, 2002).

Evidence suggests that successful leaders of schools focus their efforts on four priorities that, while important in all contexts, take on additional significance in schools striving to improve their ability to serve diverse students well.

Building Powerful Forms of Teaching and Learning

In schools that show impressive achievement gains, educational leaders maintain a clear and consistent focus on improving the core task of teaching, and they accept no excuses for failure. They help teachers to understand how they can work more effectively with their students, and this improves teachers' certainty that they can make a difference (Louis & Smith, 1992; Rosenholtz, 1985).

Building powerful forms of teaching and learning requires attention to both classroom and school-level issues. For example, leaders emphasize the necessity of all staff having ambitious learning goals for all students. They express high expectations in part by making careful decisions about student promotion policies (McCoy & Reynolds, 1999; Westbury, 1994) and about the size and composition of classes (Finn, 2002; Nye, Hedges, & Konstantopoulos, 1999).

Successful school leaders have high standards for the curriculum to which students are exposed. Unfortunately, the curriculum in schools serving diverse and disadvantaged students often is narrowly focused on basic skills and knowledge and lacks much meaning for students. Knapp and associates (1995), Gamoran et al. (1995), Reyes, Scribner, and Scribner (1999), and Scheurich (1998) are among the researchers who have begun to explicate the dimensions of challenging curricula that can be effective with low-achieving or marginalized students.

Children in diverse contexts may benefit from culturally responsive teaching, in which instruction is adapted to build on the norms, values, knowledge, skills, and discourse patterns associated with students' cultural backgrounds (Foster, 1995; Ladson-Billings, 1994). School leaders promote culturally responsive teaching by demonstrating a culturally responsive approach themselves in their relations with parents, teachers, and students (Riehl, 2000).

Student learning in schools serving diverse populations also appears to increase when there is instructional program coherence; this requires strong leadership to select and adopt a common framework and make it a priority for the school, to encourage teachers to work collaboratively, and to provide sustained training for staff in the use of the framework (Newman et al., 2001).

Finally, evidence is mounting that student achievement is lower in schools serving diverse and disadvantaged populations because, at least in part, these schools receive the least qualified teachers and are unable to retain qualified teachers (Darling-Hammond & Youngs, 2002). In these schools, teaching and learning are enhanced when school leaders adopt any means possible to attract and retain good teachers.

Creating Strong Communities in School

Effective leaders in schools serving diverse groups of students promote a sense of community among all of the school's members, including students, teachers, parents, and others.

A small but impressive body of evidence also suggests that pupils benefit when teachers in a school form a "professional learning" subcommunity (Bryk & Driscoll, 1988; Newmann & Associates, 1996). Professional community stimulates growth in teachers' instructional skills, supports instructional program coherence, and enhances teachers' sense of responsibility for and control over student learning. School leaders, whether administrators or teachers, help develop professional community through attention to individual teacher development and by creating and sustaining the structural conditions and human and social resources that support community. Structural conditions include school size and staffing arrangements that facilitate collaboration, additional time for teacher planning, and opportunities for teacher decisionmaking. Human and social resources include supportive leadership, policies and practices that create an atmosphere of openness to innovation, feedback on instructional performance, and professional development opportunities (Louis, Marks, & Kruse, 1996).

Nurturing the Development of Families' Educational Cultures

Social conditions associated with poverty, such as residential mobility, family breakups, and poor health, certainly are likely to affect students' ability to focus and do well in school (e.g., Dillard, 1995; Englert, 1993; Gezi, 1990; Natriello, McDill, & Pallas, 1990; Portin, 2000). Beyond that, however, other family conditions and interactions provide more powerful explanations for family background effects on student learning (Lee, Bryk, & Smith, 1993). These conditions and interactions constitute what is known as a family's educational culture.

At the core of family educational cultures are the assumptions, norms, and beliefs held by the family about intellectual work in general and schoolwork in particular. Other basic dimensions include family work habits, academic guidance and support, parents' or guardians' academic and occupational aspirations and expectations for their children, adequate health and nutritional conditions, and physical settings in the home conducive to academic work (Henderson & Berla, 1994; Walberg, 1984). These conditions are related to school success, as evidenced by a substantial body of research (e.g., Finn, 1989; Rumberger, 1987; Scott-Jones, 1984). When schools support families to develop strong educational cultures at home, children from low-income families and diverse cultural backgrounds approach the grades and test scores expected for middle-class children. They are also more likely to take advantage of a full range of educational opportunities after graduating from high school (Henderson & Berla, 1994).

School leaders help families develop strong educational cultures by championing parent education and coordinated services. Parent education helps families acquire resources and competencies to support their children's education; it can be provided through group meetings and classes, newsletters, home visits, neighborhood meetings, phone consultations, and the provision of audio, video, and print resources (Epstein, 1996, 2001).

Research on the effectiveness of parent education programs suffers from various methodological weaknesses (Mattingly et al., 2002), but there is reason to believe that promising interventions provide useful information, material supports, emotional encouragement, therapeutic guidance, and/or skill development (Gorman & Balter, 1997). Well-designed parent education programs seek to reach all parents and acknowledge that most parents are more involved in their children's education than educators assume (Epstein, 2001). They enable families to share their expertise about their children with schools and provide schools with information about family "funds of knowledge" that can be used to strengthen home–school connections and increase student learning (Delgado-Gaitan, 1991; Moll et al., 1992). They are culturally sensitive and culturally specific, explicitly showing acceptance of different childrearing practices, unique family structures, or preferred forms of social interaction within families.

School leaders also support family educational cultures by helping to coordinate social services designed to meet a full range of children's and families' needs (Dryfoos, 1994). Integrated social services can enhance families' access to and control over the services they receive and can help ensure that social assistance is congruent with the cultures and needs of families and communities. Evidence suggests that educational leaders can help such efforts by developing with all stakeholders a common vision and set of goals; distributing leadership flexibly across roles and stakeholder groups; ensuring adequate communication and resolving conflicts proactively; awarding power to pupils, parents, and community members to make decisions about their needs and services; and incorporating parents' home language into the provision of services (Smrekar & Mawhinney, 1999).

Expanding the Amount of Students' Social Capital Valued by the Schools

Social capital consists of the "assets" accrued by persons through their families and their relationships with others (Coleman, 1988; Driscoll & Kerchner, 1999). Assets such as knowledge and information, norms, and opportunities sustained in extensive social networks provide resources to help children and their families navigate more successfully through the challenges of schooling.

Some students have family educational cultures and social capital resources that are strong and well-developed but different from what schools typically expect (Heath, 1983; Moll et al., 1992). Other students may have limited access to social capital assets. Successful school leaders help students in several ways to employ the social capital they have and acquire more, thereby enhancing their potential for success in school.

First, leaders can increase the proportion of students' social capital that is valued by the school. Ignorance and prejudice can cause educators to deny the value of the knowledge and other forms of social capital that are brought to school by students. Second, leaders can help create meaningful partnerships with parents and communities. These partnerships can help strengthen the social networks that provide capital for students. Partnerships are much more likely to occur when educators work explicitly to help create them (Epstein, 2001).

Third, school leaders can increase students' social capital by helping to enact nondiscriminatory and socially just practices in schools through antiracism education and similar programs for teachers and students (Dei, 1996; Solomon, 2002). At the individual level, such education attempts to eliminate behaviors that impact negatively on persons who experience discrimination. At the organizational or institutional level, antiracist education critically examines and alters the structures and policies that entrench and reproduce inequity and injustice. There is some evidence that antiracist education is effective. For example, Lawrence and Tatum (1997) found that, after participating in voluntary antiracist professional development, over half of their sample of 84 white suburban educators (including teachers, administrators, and other professionals) altered their practice in three substantive ways: by improving interpersonal relationships with students, teachers, and parents with regard to issues of race and culture; by transforming their curriculum; and by helping to improve support services and placement practices for students of color in their schools.

CONCLUSION

Efforts to improve educational leadership should build upon the foundation of well-documented and well-accepted knowledge about leadership that already exists. In this chapter, we have reviewed robust research-based evidence about leadership functions and effects, as well as research findings about key educational leadership challenges. The chapter does not begin to exhaust all that is already known about leadership; much more could be written, and yet there also are still many gaps in our knowledge about effective educational leadership. Research needs in a variety of areas will be delineated more fully in the chapters that follow. Ideally, this chapter and the entire volume will stimulate further inquiry and vigorous conversation among the practitioners, policymakers, and scholars who are part of—and who support—the educational leadership profession.

CHAPTER 3

What Can Researchers on Educational Leadership Learn from Research on Teaching? Building a Bridge

Mary Kay Stein and James Spillane

We take seriously the charge to "set profitable directions" for research on educational leadership in this chapter. Rather than providing an exhaustive review of the literature, we've shaped our selection of research studies and our commentary with an eye toward how research on educational leadership can benefit from the successes and pitfalls experienced by other fields of educational scholarship—fields that have traveled similar paths but that have had longer histories of attending to issues of teaching and learning. By comparing other fields' approaches and contributions to those in educational leadership research, we aim to highlight useful approaches that research on educational leadership might pursue; we also aim to identify blind alleys to avoid.

The direction that we suggest builds on the very long history of research on student learning and a complementary, although less lengthy, body of work on teaching and teacher learning. Our claim is that research on educational leadership has, for too long, remained isolated from these bodies of work and that now is the opportune moment to build bridges between them.

We base this claim on two observations. First, educational administration is in the process of reexamining its foundations and future directions, with a developing consensus that leaders should take as their primary responsibility the improvement of student learning (Chapter 2, this volume; Murphy, 2001). Yet past research in educational leadership is silent on how students learn, how teachers can help students learn, and—most important—*how educational leaders can help both students and teachers to learn.* This is especially critical in the current climate of high standards for all, including the need for students to learn—and for teachers to learn to teach—much more complex forms of thinking and reasoning than have been demanded in the past (e.g., critical interpretation of texts, problem-solving, and thoughtful discourse). Throughout this paper we refer to this as ambitious teaching and learning.

Second, we contend that establishing connections to research on teacher learning will invigorate educational leadership much as research on teaching took a giant leap forward when it connected to the "cognitive revolution" that was occurring in research on student learning (Shulman, 1986a). In the 1980s, after decades of research that focused on classroom management and other structural features of instruction, teaching researchers began attending to research on student learning—research that focused on the knowledge and skills associated with students' acquisition of competence in particular subject matter domains. Using these research findings, teaching researchers began to shift their focus away from studies of *what teachers did* to studies of *student thinking* and how student thinking was or could be impacted by what teachers did. The overall impact of these shifts was to revitalize research on teaching, making it more powerful and more relevant to the core of education: helping students learn academic content.

Similarly, we believe that research on educational leadership can be propelled forward by connecting to what is known about teaching and teacher learning. For example, we know that teachers cannot teach concepts well that they themselves know only superficially. Their presentation is brittle, their examples preformulated and rigid, and their responses to students' questions unfulfilling (Brophy, 1991). We also know something about the conditions under which teachers learn the kind of subject matter knowledge needed for effective teaching (Borko & Putnam, 1996; Kennedy, 1999). This research base has direct implications for the questions researchers could ask about the roles and functions of educational administrators. For example, how do principals assess their teachers' subject matter capabilities and orchestrate opportunities for more and deeper learning for those who need it? Questions such as this will align research in educational administration more closely with core issues of improving teaching and learning.

Our argument is framed by reference to four broad categories of research that cut across research on teaching and learning and research on educational leadership. We first examine research that aims to identify causally relevant connections between educational practice and student achievement. For teaching researchers this involves the search for correlates between teacher behaviors and student learning outcomes (e.g., Brophy & Good, 1986; Rosenshine & Stevens, 1986). For researchers in educational administration, this involves the examination of relationships between what principals do and student outcomes (Pitner, 1988).

We then consider the mediational paradigms that have developed in both fields to fill in the "black box" of processes that lie between what a teacher or principal does and what students learn. In the section on teaching research, we focus primarily on the cognitive mediational model. In the section on research in educational administration, we cover a broader swath of research, as the amount of territory lying between principal actions and student learning is much larger.

Third, we examine learning through interaction with others, including the role of the teacher/administrator in orchestrating interactive learning opportunities. This work further complexifies the relationship between teaching and learning. It derives from the idea that learning is as much a social process as an individual one. For researchers of teaching, this idea has led to increasingly sophisticated examinations of how knowledge is socially constructed by students in the classroom. For researchers in educational administration (where teachers can be viewed as the learners), this idea has steered attention toward teacher–teacher collaboration and professional learning communities.

We end with a brief look at the transition from behavioral to cognitive frames of research with respect to both teachers and educational leaders. This section addresses research on teachers' and educational leaders' thinking processes and how these processes impact their actions in classrooms and schools.

LINKING EDUCATIONAL PRACTICE AND STUDENT LEARNING OUTCOMES

Looking for characteristics of teaching or educational leadership that lead to changes in student learning has a venerable history in educational research (Gage, 1963; Hallinger & Heck, 1996a). This work has been fueled by national concerns about the low levels of achievement of American students, first in the early 1980s (with the release of *A Nation At Risk*) and more recently by international comparisons and the standards and accountability movement, most recently exemplified in the *No Child Left Behind* legislation. It continues to have great appeal to practitioners, researchers, and, especially, policymakers, as illustrated by recent calls for studies to certify effectiveness of interventions that claim the label of "research-based" to qualify for federal funding. In addition, research on educational practice and student learning attempts to provide empirical verification to commonsense notions that instruction matters and that principals make a difference.

The earliest research in this area attempted to link educational practice to student learning outcomes via direct correlations between what teachers or principals did and student scores on standardized achievement tests.[1]

Research on Teaching

Most work on teacher effectiveness fell under the process-product approach, an extremely productive program of research during the 1970s and 1980s (Dunkin & Biddle, 1974; Mitzel, 1960). Essentially, the purpose of process-product research was to define the relationship between what teachers do and how students perform on standardized achievement tests. The data on "what teachers do" consisted of observable, discrete behaviors such as the number of times that teachers dispensed praise, the length of wait time allowed for answering a question, and the number of higher- versus lower-order questions asked during a lesson. During analysis, the behaviors were treated independent of the context in which they occurred, with researchers summing variables across many contexts and then conducting correlational analyses to determine if the prevalence of certain behaviors was more versus less associated with student achievement gains. Findings generally took the form of propositions that described the kinds of teacher behavior associated with gains in student achievement.

This approach has been criticized on a number of grounds. Perhaps most serious was the observation that the propositions did not represent naturally occurring behaviors but rather composites that were created by synthesizing across hundreds of correlations involving many teachers and different contexts (Shulman, 1986a). Hence, the propositions did not represent the exemplary teaching of any single individual and thus had questionable validity when individuals attempted to adopt them (Gage, 1978; see also Gage & Giaconia, 1981 for an interpretation of studies that attempted to train teachers to use the composites). Other criticisms pointed to the profoundly atheoretical tenor of the research (Dunkin & Biddle, 1974; Good, Grouws, & Ebmeier, 1983).

Research on Educational Leadership

Researchers in educational administration have searched for direct effects of principals on student learning (e.g., Bridges, 1982; Hallinger & Heck, 1996a; Pitner, 1988). The purpose is to account for variation in student achievement by uncovering differences in what principals in high- versus low-achieving schools did do. According to Hallinger, Bickman, and Davis (1996), much of this work can be traced to research on school effectiveness, the summaries of which have consistently pointed to the importance of the principal's role as an instructional leader (Edmonds, 1979; Purkey & Smith, 1983). Like the process-product studies of teaching, research on principal effectiveness examines the relationship between observable actions of school leaders and student outcomes using cross-sectional designs to search for significant correlations between decontextualized behaviors and student achievement.

The findings from this research have been called weak and conflicting (Hallinger & Heck, 1996a, 1996b) or suspect in terms of validity (Rowan, Dwyer, & Bossert, 1982). In a recent review, Hallinger and Heck (1996a, 1996b) conclude that the direct effects model is much too simple a representation of an exceedingly complex phenomenom. Despite the prevalence of the direct effects studies in the educational administration literature, they note that:

> The process by which administrators achieve an impact (if one is found) is hidden in a so-called black box. A relationship is empirically tested, but the findings reveal little about how leadership operates. Thus, these studies do little to advance our theoretical or practical understanding of the school processes through which the principal achieves an impact on school effectiveness. (p. 18)

Looking across the teaching and leadership studies, then, we see similar concerns. First and foremost, the resulting body of knowledge is exceedingly atheoretical, seeking causes in behaviors, not in meaningful mechanisms or explanations (Shulman, 1986a). Second, the decontextualized nature of the findings limits their usefulness. Stripped from the contexts that gave rise to teachers' or principals' decisions to enact such behaviors, future practitioners have little guidance about when, where, and how to enact "effective behaviors." Finally, there is a serious mismatch in some studies between the intention to establish causally relevant connections and the use of correlational methods.

MEDIATIONAL PARADIGMS

Largely in reaction to the above criticisms, researchers in both fields began to fill in the "black box" of actions/interactions/processes that lie between what a teacher or principal does and what students learn. In research on teaching, the first systematic efforts to fill in the box occurred largely through the establishment of deep linkages to cognitive research on student learning. In research on educational administration, although it has been recognized that principals influence student learning through their interactions with teachers, most research has focused on how principals influence student learning by shaping features of the school organization more broadly (Cuban, 1988; Hallinger & Leithwood, 1994; Heck, 1993).

Research on Teaching

Influenced by the cognitive revolution in research on student learning, researchers of teaching began to rethink their notions of how teachers influence student learning. Rather than impacting student learning through students' passive reception of incoming information, teaching researchers began to explore whether the consequences of teaching could be better understood in terms of *what occurs in students' minds as a result of instruction*. In this view, teaching does not directly influence student learning; rather, teaching acts are mediated by how students cognitively process what they have seen and heard. Early work in the cognitive mediational paradigm retained the focus on the teacher, but added the question of how students interpreted teachers' actions and statements. While sociologists focused on meanings that students attached to social interactions occurring during instruction (e.g., the way turns were distributed, cues that signaled opportunities to participate—see, for example, Mehan, 1979), cognitive psychologists focused on the ways in which students attached meaning to academic work (e.g., the strategies they employed, the ways in which they interpreted classroom tasks—see, for example, Anderson, 1984; Doyle, 1983).

Later work began to anchor teaching research in what was known about *how students learn*, specifically how students learn the school subjects of reading, mathematics, science, and history. Some of this research was based on very fine-grained understandings of how students learn (see, for example, Carpenter and colleagues' research on teaching that grew out of basic research on how children learn to add and subtract [Carpenter & Moser, 1984; Carpenter, Fenemma, Peterson, & Carey, 1988]). Other research was based more broadly on the cognitive processes that expert students tended to use across subject areas to build knowledge (actively connecting new knowledge to prior knowledge, the use of high-level thinking and reasoning skills, and the transfer of newly learned knowledge to novel situations [Hiebert & Wearne, 1988]). The distinguishing feature of this later research was that it asked questions that originated in research on how students acquire complex knowledge and skills, which then led to questions regarding how teachers could assist students to learn in cognitively competent ways.

Both kinds of teaching research shared methodological similarities that set them apart from the process-product research described earlier. Rather than sampling many teachers periodically over time, they focused more intensively on a few teachers teaching specific curriculum units or sometimes even individual lessons. Detailed information about classroom processes was recorded, using field notes and/or videotape rather than checklists. Instead of relying on achievement tests, researchers began interviewing students, asking them to solve tasks that represented an extension of what was presented during instruction and devising other novel ways to assess their understanding.

These studies also yielded findings that were very different from the earlier process-product findings. As summarized by Brophy (2001) in the eighth volume of *Advances in Research on Teaching*:

> . . . these studies highlighted the importance of such factors as coaching the teaching of content within application contexts, emphasizing conceptual understanding of knowledge and self-regulated application of skills, providing explicit explanations

and elaborating on these in ways that are responsive to students' questions or learning difficulties, connecting input with students' existing ideas and correcting their misconceptions and scaffolding their learning efforts by initially providing a good deal of explanation, modeling, and cueing, but gradually fading these supports as the students develop expertise and become capable of more independent and self-regulated learning. (p. x)

Three features stand out about the cognitive mediational paradigm. First, the move to focusing on student thinking paralleled a much larger shift in education from a basic-skills, behaviorist paradigm to one that focused on the teaching and learning of complex, high-level knowledge and skills. As such, new teaching and learning variables assumed ascendancy, including knowledge, especially subject matter knowledge. Second, researchers found two ways to incorporate student thinking into their models: (a) looking at the effects of teachers' actions on students; and (b) beginning with student thinking and asking questions about how teaching could assist powerful forms of learning. Third, in many cases, researchers had to create particular instructional conditions in order to have something to study. Although research on student learning had revealed significant differences between deep versus superficial ways of understanding content, few teachers routinely established the conditions necessary to develop higher-level learning. Thus, some researchers (e.g., Magdalene Lampert, Deborah Ball) became classroom teachers themselves to try out new approaches; others (e.g., Paul Cobb, James Hiebert) formed alliances with teachers and then collaboratively designed and reflected on lessons that aimed to encourage the development of deep understanding and reasoning skills.

Research in Educational Leadership

Most research on educational leadership that falls within the mediational paradigm tends to focus on how principals influence student learning by shaping the school environment. This research shows that schools do matter when it comes to improving student learning and that certain organizational structures, leadership roles, and conditions of schools contribute to instructional innovation (Hallinger & Heck, 1996a). We know, for example, that schools with shared visions and norms about instruction, norms of collaboration, and a sense of collective responsibility for students' academic success create incentives and opportunities for teachers to improve their practice (Bryk & Driscoll, 1988; Little, 1982; Newmann & Wehlage, 1995) and that principal leadership is important in promoting these conditions (Lieberman, Darling-Hammond, & Zuckerman, 1991; Rosenholtz, 1989). A recent synthesis of the research confirmed a strong positive relationship between effective principal leadership behaviors (including developing and communicating school goals, monitoring instruction, mobilizing incentives for teachers, supporting professional development) and teacher commitment, openness to innovation, and professional involvement (Sheppard, 1996). Finally, evidence suggests that principal leadership, as mediated through the development of these school-level conditions and processes, has an effect on student learning (Hallinger & Heck, 1996a, 1996b).

While these studies provide a rich conceptualization of the many ways that principals exert influence, few, if any, have examined the influence of principal actions and policies on teachers' thinking. In research on teaching, the portrayal of students as active interpreters of teachers' lessons represented a noteworthy advance. However, most studies of principal leadership do not portray teachers as active interpreters of principals' actions or policies. When teachers are surveyed, they typically are asked questions aimed at identifying school-level variables such as teacher perception of school climate (e.g., Hoy & Woolfolk, 1993; Lee, Dedrick, & Smith, 1991). However, they are rarely asked what sense *they* have made of the principal's policies or actions.

Research that has looked at teacher sense-making can be found in the implementation and school improvement literatures. This research asks how teachers make sense of broad policies, not just principal actions. It suggests that teachers' beliefs about subject matter, teaching, students, and learning influence how they interpret reforms intended to change their practice. Differences in interpretation predicted the level of implementation rather than teachers' outright rejection of reform (Educational Evaluation and Policy Analysis [EPPA], 1990; Firestone, Fitz, & Broadfoot, 1999; Jennings, 1992; Spillane, 1998a). Further, case study research shows that teachers often miss the unfamiliar and more fundamental transformation in teaching sought by reformers (Cohen, 1990; EEPA, 1990). This happens because teachers notice and attend to familiar ideas, such as group work and the use of manipulatives; however, lacking a mental framework to connect and explain the unfamiliar ideas, they devote less attention to them and often overlook them altogether (Spillane, 2000a; Spillane, Reiser, & Reimer, 2002). These findings provide provocative glimpses into the importance of attending to how teachers construe principals' actions and policies.

Research on educational administration could incorporate attention to teacher thinking in two ways. First, it could ask questions directly of teachers regarding how they interpret principals' actions and statements. Researchers could focus more on the meanings that teachers make of the social context of the school (e.g., the ways in which teachers are selected to participate in certain activities, the access that teachers have to resources) or the ways in which teachers make sense of academic directives (e.g., how they interpret the task of textbook selection or writing curricula). For example, some recent work (Spillane, Hallett, & Diamond, 2003) explores why teachers construct school administrators and other teachers into the role of instructional leader.

Second, similar to how some teaching researchers have anchored their studies in what is known about how students learn, researchers of educational leadership could anchor investigations of instructional leadership in what is known about how teachers learn. The explosion of research on learning to teach in the past few decades (Borko & Putnam, 1996) could provide the foundation for a new set of questions for research on educational administration. As with research on student learning, research on teacher learning has taken a decidedly cognitive turn over the last few decades, with emphasis on what effective teachers know and understand, how their knowledge is organized, and how they use their knowledge to create powerful learning opportunities for their students. For example, we now know that effective teachers have an overarching conception of the purposes for teaching their particular subject matter and that they possess knowledge of student understandings and potential misunderstandings of that subject, of the curriculum and curricular materials associated with that subject, and of the strategies and representations for teaching particular topics in that subject (Grossman, 1990). Moreover, attention has increasingly been devoted to the conditions that facilitate meaningful and deep teacher learning. These include the opportunities to address (and perhaps challenge) teachers' existing knowledge and beliefs, to experience the learning of subject matter in new ways, and to ground their learning in classroom practice (Borko & Putnam, 1996).

Beginning with these findings, research on educational administration could ask how principals and district leaders assist their teachers to learn. For example, on what content do they typically focus when arranging professional development for their teachers (does it align with what research tells us regarding what teachers need to know)? Or, what features do they attend to when designing both formal and informal learning opportunities for their teachers? Are they concerned with *how* teachers learn, as well as *what* they learn? That is, do they provide opportunities for their teachers to confront well-established but perhaps ill-informed beliefs? Do they provide opportunities to learn subject matter in the same ways that teachers will, in turn, be expected to teach their students? Such research would open up a new range of methodologies, as well as different foci. We'd expect, for example, more in-depth focus on the opportunities that are arranged for teacher learning in a school, as well as more attention to principals' goals for teacher learning. Some research has begun to address these issues. For example, a study of administrative support of literacy reform in Community School District 2 in New York City examined ways in which principals assisted teacher learning in meaningful ways by regularly observing their classrooms, conversing with them, and arranging for in-classroom support that was tailored to their specific needs (Stein & D'Amico, 1999).

Our sense is that we have not seen more research in educational administration that examines how principals impact teacher learning because (a) the emphasis has instead been on social and organizational conditions; and (b) principals are just beginning to assume roles as instructional leaders, so there are few schools in which learning opportunities for teachers are routinely available to study, especially subject-specific learning opportunities. There have been instances, however, in which researchers have created situations that were, in turn, studied. For example, Nelson and her colleagues at the Educational Development Center have designed and carried out a set of professional development experiences for administrators that focuses on ways to understand and improve the mathematics instructional programs in their schools (Grant, Nelson, Davidson, Sassi, Weinberg, & Bleiman, 2002). Nelson and others have then followed these administrators back into their schools and observed and interviewed them as they used their newly acquired knowledge and skills to perform administrative tasks such as designing professional development for their teachers or leading a curriculum selection committee (Driscoll, Nelson, Sassi, & Kennedy, 2000).

LEARNING IN A SOCIAL AND INTERACTIVE CONTEXT

If the advance represented by the mediational approach was the recognition that students (and teachers) learn by actively constructing knowledge, the advance represented by this paradigm is recognition that learning occurs in interactive, social contexts. Rather than assuming that learning occurs in individuals' minds, interactive theories of learning assume that learning is "something that happens *between* people when they engage in common activities" (Bredo & McDermott, 1992, p. 35, italics added). As individuals exchange views, listen to and critique others' contributions, and expose their own beliefs and assumptions, they together create a shared new understanding. In research on teaching, the interactive view of learning contributed to studies that investigate the role of the teacher as a creator of communities of learners in the classroom. In research on educational administration, hints of a more interactive view can be found in research that points to the importance of social relations in schools (Lieberman & Miller, 1984; Lortie, 1975; Purkey & Smith, 1983; Rosenholtz, 1989). For a tighter link to this paradigm, however, one needs to look beyond mainstream educational administration research toward research on teacher professional communities of practice and the implementation of change.

Research on Teaching

Studies that examine the social construction of knowledge in the classroom draw on a variety of disciplines, ranging from sociolinguistics (Cazden, 1986) to sociology (Mehan, 1979) to ethnography (Lightfoot, 1983) to sociocultural theory (Newman, Griffin, & Cole, 1989). The uniting feature of such work is its emphasis on the shared creation of meaning by all participants in the classroom—students as well as the teacher. As noted by Shulman (1986a):

[Individuals are viewed as] actively engaged in "making sense" in the setting, taking both senses of that phrase. They both discern the meanings intended by other actors and they engage in the continuing invention and reformulation of new meaning. (p. 20)

Most of this research begins with a focus on how student interaction is associated with student learning (broadly defined) and then asks how teachers can foster those processes associated with positive student learning. For example, after finding that students learned mathematics most effectively when provided with opportunities to first understand, and then to critique, alternative interpretations or solutions (Wood & Yackel, 1990), Cobb and his colleagues began investigating how teachers could promote such interactions. Similarly, Palinscar and Brown's early work (1984) focused on how students can learn to read with understanding by participating in discussions in which their peers supported their attempts to ask questions, clarify, predict, and summarize. The Fostering Communities of Learners Project (Brown, 1994) built on this early work by helping teachers to create environments in which students supported one another in their quest to develop new knowledge.

Methodologically, studies in this paradigm channel researchers' attention away from the cognitive attributes of students toward the social interaction among students and between students and the teacher. Learning is viewed not as the acquisition of knowledge, but rather as a process of becoming a member of a community (Lave & Wenger, 1991). This involves learning how to communicate using the language of the community and learning how to act according to its particular norms. As such, much work in this genre highlights the role of the teacher as an "expert" member of the community and as the facilitator of classroom discourse. Often, researchers analyze a single classroom discussion in great detail in order to understand how students are socially constructing meaning.

Responding to concerns that "knowledge" and "concepts" appear to have disappeared from research that views learning as participation (Cobb, 1994; Sfard, 1998), some researchers blend attention to the academic tasks with which students are engaged with a focus on how students talk and participate in the classroom. For example, O'Conner and Michaels (1993) focus on "revoicing," a method used by teachers that creates participant frameworks that facilitate students' "alignment" with various positions in classroom academic debates and their socialization to roles and identities in the classroom discourse.

Two things stand out as noteworthy about this body of research. First, it often begins with detailed observations of how students actively construct knowledge as they work together in dyads, small groups, or whole-class discussions and then moves to questions of how the teacher can assist such learning. Second, researchers recognize the tendency for "academic knowledge" to fade into the background in analyses that focus on student interaction. Attempts have been made to raise the profile of what students are working on and how their knowledge of central academic ideas and concepts is gradually built up as they interact with one another and their teacher.

Research on Leadership

Smylie and Hart (2000) point to three bodies of literature that support the vital role of social interaction in teacher learning: research on teachers' collegial relations in schools, studies of teacher collaboration in improvement initiatives, and research on teacher professional communities. Research in each area has tended to progress by first examining how school processes are related to teacher learning and then looking at how leaders (mostly principals) can foster the social processes that are routinely associated with teacher learning. We now know that principal leadership is important in promoting the conditions that are required for teachers to interact with one another in positive ways (Lieberman et al., 1991; Rosenholtz, 1989).

In general, however, this research has made little contact with what is known about teacher learning. As with our critique of the mediational paradigm in research on educational leadership, we note again the absence of reference to research on *what* teachers need to learn and *how* they can learn it. For example, one finds references to the importance of reciprocity, interdependence, egalitarianism, mutual trust, and a common focus on teaching in the "collegial relations" research (e.g., Little, 1982); to trust, common vision and values, open communication, shared responsibility, and accountability in the teacher collaboration for school improvement literature (e.g., Lieberman et al., 1991); and to a shared focus on student learning, norms of collective responsibility, mutual support, and high levels of professional normative social controls in the teacher professional community literature (e.g., Talbert & McLaughlin, 1994). Most of this research examines the social dimensions of teacher–teacher collaboration, with little attention to *what* teachers are collaborating about. While important, findings that primarily focus on the process and conditions for social interaction fail to connect with what is known about the content and kind of learning that is important for teachers to achieve if they are to provide more ambitious forms of student learning in the classroom.

Ideally, researchers in educational leadership would be able to turn to their peers in research on teaching for insights into how teachers learn ambitious content and pedagogy in interactive settings with their peers and others. Unlike research on *individual* teacher learning, however, research on the interactive learning of teachers is less abundant. Conventional ways of viewing teacher learning take the individual teacher as the unit of analysis, assuming that learning consists of changes in the ways knowledge is organized and represented in individual teachers' minds (see, for example, Brown & Borko, 1992). In contrast, an interactive view of teacher learning would need to focus on communities in which teachers participate and how teachers' participation patterns in those communities change over time (Cobb, McClain, Lamberg, & Dean, 2003; Lave & Wenger, 1991).

Some studies have adopted this perspective. For example, Stein and her colleagues examined how middle school teachers' capacities to enact a complex mathematics reform increased as their participation moved from peripheral to more central forms of participation within a community of like-minded peers (Stein, Silver, & Smith, 1998), or from assisted to unassisted performance (Stein & Brown, 1997). Similarly, Coburn (2001) has shown how teachers' professional communities can be especially influential in what teachers learn from policy and other sources. In particular, she showed how teachers who participated in different formal and informal groups within the same schools learned different things. Another study (Spillane, 1999) found that teachers' social circumstances—their enactment zones—influenced their sense-making about reforms. Teachers whose enactment zones extended beyond their individual classrooms to include frequent and ongoing deliberation with fellow teachers and other experts about the policy proposals and their implications for practice understood standards in ways that resonated with policymakers' proposals. While the above studies use different theoretical frames, they all assume that teacher learning occurs interactively, and all attempt to make contact with what needs to be learned, by whom, and with what kind of assistance.

These studies open up new territory for researchers in educational leadership. If we know, for example, that teachers learn content and pedagogy crucial to the improvement of their practice through regular interaction with a peer who is just slightly ahead of them in their learning more readily than by observing a "master practitioner" (see Stein & D'Amico, 2002a), it may suggest new dimensions to instructional leadership. For example, a principal or district leader may need to move beyond conventional notions of teachers learning from observations of recognized experts to the intentional fostering and use of variability in teacher expertise throughout one's building or district (see Stein & D'Amico, 2002b).

Our sense is that we have not seen more research in educational administration that examines such issues because few schools or districts have routinely created conditions that foster interactive teacher learning of content and pedagogy. While many schools have created the structures for teacher interaction (e.g., shared planning times, coaches), little emphasis has been placed on the content of learning within these structures and the kinds of expertise needed to ensure learning (Kennedy, 1999). Even when administrators recognize the need for expertise in, for example, a coaching staff, the pool of individuals from which to select is often of lower-than-optimal capacity (Stein, Hubbard, & Mehan, 2004). This suggests the need for studies of how administrators can build the capacities of teachers and teacher leaders so that pools of expertise are available in a school or district.

RESEARCH ON THE THINKING PROCESSES OF TEACHERS AND EDUCATIONAL LEADERS

Lastly, we turn to research that involves the characterization of teachers and educational leaders as "thinking individuals" rather than simply "doers" or actors. Whereas the research discussed in the sections on mediational paradigms and learning in a social and interactive context has focused on the cognitive underpinnings of individuals on the receiving end of teaching or leadership (students and teachers respectively), the research to which we now turn examines those on the initiating end. For research on teaching, we will examine what is known about how teachers' knowledge and cognitive processes impact what they do in the classroom. For research on educational leadership, we will focus on what is known about how principals' knowledge and cognitive processes impact what they do in the school.

Research on Teaching

According to Shulman (1986a), early work on teacher cognition focused on three types of cognitive processes: judgment, problem-solving, and decisionmaking (Shavelson, 1983; Shulman & Elstein, 1975). In general, researchers focused on how teachers planned their lessons or on their thinking processes during the delivery of a lesson. Researchers would interview teachers as they prepared for the next day's lesson, asking them why they made particular decisions. Interactive decisionmaking (decisionmaking *during* lessons) was typically studied using stimulated recall. The researcher and teacher would view a videotape of the lesson together; at predetermined points, the tape was stopped so that the researcher could ask the teacher what she was thinking when she made particular instructional moves. In this way, the thinking behind teacher actions was probed and studied.

This early work did not develop into a robust or productive line of inquiry. Shulman (1986a) suggests that a primary reason was that it attended to a limited range of teaching activities. Rather than probing teachers on a range of potentially interesting maneuvers (e.g., why a teacher may have chosen to highlight a part-icular misconception or how the teacher selected a specific counterexample), researchers focused on the same behaviors attended to by process-product researchers—behaviors without theoretical import or explanatory power. Overall, distance grew between research on teacher decisionmaking and the more central cognitive-psychological work on student learning in specific subject areas. As cognitive psychologists focused more and more intensely on the subject matter specificity of student learning and delving into the intricacies of learning school subjects, researchers on teachers' thinking—influenced by cognitive-psychological research in noneducational areas like the college admissions judgment processes—remained locked into explaining why teachers decided to dispense praise or other generic behaviors (Shulman, 1986a).

Later research on teacher cognition focused on how teachers understood their subject matter and how to best teach it. Beginning in the late 1980s, with Shulman's identification of subject matter knowledge as the missing paradigm in research on teaching (1986b), a whole new field blossomed, including the creation of a new and powerful construct: pedagogical content knowledge. Teachers, it was argued, needed a different kind of subject matter knowledge than that possessed by mathematicians, scientists, or linguists. Rather than needing more (and more advanced) knowledge of subjects, teachers need a qualitatively different kind of knowledge—one that would enable them to help others to learn it. So, for example, elementary teachers do not need knowledge of advanced calculus or linear algebra; they need to understand how to make place value understandable to children who are learning subtraction with regrouping. The construct of pedagogical content knowledge was thus created to highlight that subject knowledge must be transformed for the purpose of teaching.

The most productive research on teacher thinking for the past two decades has centered on what teachers know about the subjects they teach and the ways in which their knowledge is accessed and used in the classroom. Studies have focused on elaborating the construct of pedagogical content knowledge (Gudmondsdottir, 1991; Marks, 1989), as well as establishing linkages between teachers' knowledge of content and their instructional practice (e.g., Brophy, 1991; Stein, Baxter, & Leinhardt, 1990). In addition to its generativity, another noteworthy feature of this work is the extent to which it has further strengthened the synergy between research on student learning and research on teaching. For example, much of what is now considered important for teachers to know comes from research on how students learn in particular domains.

Research on Educational Leadership

Over the past decade, it has been increasingly recognized that studies of principals' behaviors are an inadequate basis upon which to build a theory of educational leadership or training programs for new principals:

> An almost exclusive focus on overt behaviors left unanswered important questions about why and under what conditions educational leaders performed the observed behaviors. Increasingly those involved in research and training in educational leadership have acknowledged the need for better information on how expert school leaders *think* about what they do. (Hallinger, Leithwood, & Murphy, 1993, p. 72, emphasis added).

Researchers of educational leadership, most notably the program of studies at the Ontario Institute for Studies in Education under the direction of Leithwood, have gradually incorporated studies of principal thinking into their repertoires.

Sometimes there has even been explicit recognition of the dividends that accrued with the application of a cognitive psychological lens to the analysis of teacher thinking, and that similar dividends may accrue from research on how principals think about their practice (Hallinger, Leithwood, & Murphy, 1993, p. xiv).

Most cognitive psychological investigations into principals' thinking have focused on differences in problem solving between expert and novice principals. Noting that problem-finding and problem-solving are core functions of educational leadership, Hallinger et al. (1993) contend that there is much to be gained by applying a cognitive perspective to better understand how leaders exercise vision, that is, where and how they focus their attention in a problem-strewn environment. Under the general heading of problem-solving, there have been cognitive psychological investigations of principals' "multi-frame thinking" (Bolman & Deal, 1993), strategic thinking in the context of everyday problem-solving (Kerchner, 1993), and the values that superintendents bring to problem-solving (Raun & Leithwood, 1993).

With respect to administrator expertise, some work from the broader management field has been cited as applicable to school leadership (e.g., Wagner, 1993). However, significant work in schools and districts has been conducted by Leithwood and his colleagues. Their analysis of data associated with principals' thinking and problem-solving surrounding a particular improvement project provided extensive insight into how "expert" versus "typical" principals interpret problems, frame goals, hold values, view constraints, and undertake various solution strategies (Leithwood & Steinbach, 1990).

Interestingly, the research on educational leaders' thinking, to date, has not touched upon administrators' thinking about what teachers need to know and be able to do in order to teach in more ambitious ways, or their thinking with respect to how teachers learn. One would expect that administrator thinking in this regard might be different in, for example, mathematics versus literacy. Despite Ohde and Murphy's (1993) identification of the important role that domain knowledge plays in cognitive expertise (p. 76), however, the mainstream educational administration literature has not addressed what content knowledge is needed for instructional leadership. Do effective leaders of literacy and mathematics reforms think about different things? Some recent work suggests that the subject does indeed matter. In a study of urban elementary school leaders, Burch and Spillane (2003) found that while most of the leaders studied identified reading and mathematics as the primary focus of their school improvement efforts, their mental scripts for the work of instructional improvement differed depending on the subject matter. Eighty percent of the school leaders in the study viewed their own school community as the primary source of expertise for improving literacy. In contrast, leaders viewed the curriculum and/or training associated with an external program as central in their school's efforts to improve mathematics. While school leaders understood the expertise for leading change in literacy instruction to be home-grown, the expertise for leading change in mathematics was outside the schoolhouse.

Studies of administrators' knowledge of the content of the reforms they are being asked to lead (and being held accountable for) constitute a useful addition to research on educational leaders' thinking. Stein and Nelson (2003) have argued for the creation of a new construct, leadership content knowledge, the kind of knowledge that would equip administrators to be strong instructional leaders. Standing at the intersection of subject matter knowledge and the practices that define leadership, this form of knowledge could be viewed as the special province of principals, superintendents, and other administrators charged with the improvement of teaching and learning. In short, it would involve the transformation of subject matter knowledge for the purposes of providing intellectual leadership for instructional reform. It is *not* an argument that administrators know or should know the subject matter in the same way as do mathematicians or historians—or even to the level that they expect their teachers to understand them. It is an argument that administrators should know strong instruction when they see it, know how to encourage it when they do not, and know how to set the conditions for continuous academic learning among their teaching staffs.

Similarly, studies of administrators' knowledge of how teachers learn to teach in more ambitious ways would add to our understanding of expertise in educational administration. Along these lines, Spillane found that most administrators hold behavioristic views of teacher learning, that is, they expect that teachers will learn new ideas through being told what to do and receiving appropriate sanctions and rewards. Few, if any, held constructivist notions, that is, beliefs that acknowledge the cognitive reorganizations inherent in learning to teach new and complex forms of knowledge (Spillane, 2000a).

Both research on the kind of content knowledge needed to lead reform and research on how principals conceive of teacher learning will bring the field of research on educational administration into closer contact with research on teaching and with the current political pressures for administrators to improve instruction and student achievement.

CONCLUSION

All indications point to the need for a thorough transformation of our schools—from administrative bureaucracies to organizations for the learning of teachers as well as students—if we are to pull public education out of its current undistinguished status. Although a slight rise in student achievement might be attained by more time on task, a stronger focus on the content tested, and incentives and sanctions, everything that we know about how students and teachers learn suggests the need for a much larger investment in the gradual building of the capacity of our schools and districts to continuously improve teaching and learning. The argument that we have advanced in this chapter is that research in educational administration can and should contribute to the knowledge base that underlies such capacity-building. To do so would entail recognizing and building upon the research base of what teachers need to know and be able to do and how they learn it. Making contact with this body of work, we argue, will open new questions, new methodologies, and new ways of framing studies of instructional leadership.

NOTE

1. Later work (not reviewed herein) has focused on more complex interventions such as whole-school reform models and strategies for teaching reading (see, for example, the National Reading Panel's report on effective strategies for teaching reading). Readers are referred to Floden's chapter in the most recent *Handbook of Research on Teaching* (2002) for a review of this work.

CHAPTER 4

How Can Educational Leaders Support and Promote Teaching and Learning? New Conceptions of Learning and Leading in Schools

Nona A. Prestine and Barbara Scott Nelson

For all its complexity, schooling revolves around just two basic functional domains: teaching and learning, and organizing for teaching and learning. Over time these functions became largely segregated by role, with teachers assuming nearly all responsibility for the former and administrators taking responsibility for the latter (Callahan, 1962; Tyack & Hansot, 1982). While there have been some overlaps between the two,[1] they have remained relatively separate, discrete domains with little interface.[2] Because of this decoupling of management from teaching and learning, administration (and, by inference, leadership) in schools "has come to mean not the management of instruction but the management of the structures and processes around instruction" (Elmore, 2000, p. 6).

Elmore's sharp observation is well taken. Much research on educational leadership has only indirectly addressed issues of teaching and learning. However, with the advent of reforms that call for more intellectually demanding subject matter content for *all* students, stringent accountability demands (Goertz & Duffy, 2001; Luhm, Foley, & Corcoran, 1998; NCTE, 1996; NCTM, 1989; National Research Council, 1996), and the growing consensus around constructivist understandings of learning (Bransford, Brown, & Cocking, 1999; Bruner, 1960; Piaget, 1977;

Vygotsky, 1978), today's schooling context demands different approaches to and different questions about the nature of educational leadership and its connections to teaching and learning. How educational leaders can support teaching and learning is influenced by two critical factors: (1) how one understands what constitutes teaching and learning and (2) how one understands what constitutes leadership in schools. Recent research developments in both these areas suggest new conceptualizations that may bring them closer together

This chapter first explores current understandings about teaching, learning, and leadership. We then examine some issues, problems, and challenges that arise at the nexus of these ideas. In doing this, we suggest questions that can frame a research agenda for the future. This work joins and extends previous calls to focus leadership research more directly on teaching and learning (see, for example, Elmore, 2000; Heck & Hallinger, 1999; Rowan, 1995). Our contribution is to more systematically develop an agenda by linking current work on leadership with recent research on teaching.

CURRENT UNDERSTANDINGS

Technically, everything school leaders do could be construed in one way or another as providing support for teaching and learning. In this chapter, we focus on aspects of leadership that are most directly connected to instruction. We ground our discussions and conceptualizations of teaching, learning, and leadership in a constructivist framework centered on three major tenets of cognitive learning theory (Resnick, 1989): (1) Learning is a process of active knowledge construction, not something that can be given or handed to some else. (2) Learning is knowledge-dependent, and current understandings are used to construct new understandings. (3) Learning is a social activity situated in specific contexts. This constructivist framework gives us a stance from which to examine possible connections of leadership to teaching and learning and provides parameters for our investigation. There is already a growing interest in constructivist perspectives on leadership (Spillane, Halverson, & Diamond, 2001) and a burgeoning literature investigating and advocating teaching and learning based on a constructivist view of knowledge development. However, connections between the two are neither obvious nor immediate (Elmore, 1995a, 1995b). We look for evidence of close connections, which we call "critical interfaces," between educational leadership and the core technology of schools.

The Nature of Teaching and Learning[3]

In America, the theories of learning that inform instruction have changed over time (Bransford, Brown, & Cocking, 1999; Cohen, 1988; Gardner, 1985; Greeno,

Collins, & Resnick, 1996). Behaviorist theories, which view knowledge as fixed and objective, learning as a matter of knowledge accumulation, and teaching as a matter of telling students about this knowledge, dominated the field of education for many decades.

The behaviorist tradition provides the foundation for curricula in which learning tasks are arranged in sequences of increasing complexity, as determined by task analysis studies (e.g., Gagne, 1968). It also undergirds direct instruction, the form of instruction administrators are most familiar with, and which most were trained to supervise. First promulgated in the 1970s and 1980s, direct instruction is a structured lesson format that begins with a review of prior learning and a statement of goals, presents new material in small steps, offers detailed explanations and extensive opportunities for guided practice, and gives students systematic feedback and correction (Rosenshine & Stevens, 1986).

In contrast, the newer cognitive tradition supports curricula that start with students' prior knowledge of a subject and develop instructional tasks that provide them with the opportunity to refine and extend their initial understandings and grasp the major unifying principles of the domain. Teaching based on a constructivist view of learning consists of gauging what students currently understand and creating social and material environments (problems to be solved, investigations to be undertaken, discussions to be had, etc.) in which students think through new ideas and build ever more complex knowledge structures. Such teaching requires that teachers know the subject well, and understand how children's knowledge of it develops (Ball, 2000; Bransford, Brown, & Cocking, 1999; Shulman, 1986b).

More recently, education researchers working within the cognitive tradition have come to understand that students' sense-making is situated in particular communities that have material and social characteristics (Greeno, 1998). The level of analysis, then, is not the individual, but the activity system—interactions among people, in conjunction with physical and technical systems. Knowing, in this perspective, is both an attribute of groups that carry out cooperative activities (communities of practice) and of individuals who participate in those communities. This view of learning leads to a focus on instruction that provides students with the opportunity to learn to participate in classroom discourse that is characteristic of a domain and to use the representational systems and tools of the domain (cf. Lampert, 2001). Also corresponding to this view of learning is project-based learning, in which students engage in complex, real-world tasks, with subject matter concepts and principles embedded in the activity setting (Greeno, Collins, & Resnick, 1996). In this view, learning is a function of curriculum, instruction, and organizational resources rather than the knowledge and skills of the teacher alone (Cohen & Ball, 1999; Knapp, Copland, Ford, Markholt, McLaughlin, & Milliken, 2003).

Each school of thought has expanded (and redefined) the range of activities considered as learning and teaching, and thus has increased the explanatory power of learning theory.[4] However, schools originally were designed to support behaviorist forms of teaching, and educational administration has grown up around that image of the core technology of schooling (Elmore, 1996; Rowan, 1995). A major task for educational leadership research is to trace out the implications of these dramatically different views of the nature of learning and teaching for the design of school organization and the definition of educational leadership.

The Nature of Educational Leadership

Two different yet complementary approaches to educational leadership have emerged that appear to resonate with the basic assumptions of this chapter. These two approaches include recent work on instructional leadership and recent work on distributed leadership.

Instructional leadership. The concept of instructional leadership gained prominence in the effective schools movement in the late 1970s and early 1980s as one attribute of schools where academic achievement appeared to be independent of students' social class or race (Edmonds, 1979). In this incarnation, instructional leadership referred to the work of principals who were exhorted to improve their schools by setting high expectations for all children, maintaining an orderly environment, instituting a regular testing program, and focusing on basic academic learning. The effective schools movement represented a critical turning point, marking an early effort to clarify the relationship between leadership and student outcomes and, to a lesser extent, teaching and learning.

Since then, there has been steady growth in the number and design sophistication of studies that attempt to define the characteristics of school leaders (e.g., beliefs, behaviors, management skills) that are linked to school success.[5] This work has substantiated the observation that principal leadership appears to have an important, if indirect, effect on student outcomes by shaping a variety of internal school processes (Hallinger & Heck, 1996a).

However, most studies have focused on variables associated with school policies and norms. Few examined principals' influence on the practices of teachers. For the most part, the focus remained on the relationship of principal leadership to overall school effectiveness as measured by student outcomes and not on exploring the relationship of leadership to classroom teaching and learning.

By the early 1990s, as the push for standards-based reform and accountability for improved student performance landed squarely on the shoulders of the building principal, numerous authors (Elmore, 1995b; Rowan, 1995; Ubben & Hughes, 1996) argued that if the main business of schools is instruction and student learning, then leadership of this arena must be the primary task of school leaders.

Calls for instructional leadership came to dominate the literature, but the term remained conceptually weak and ill-defined. Most descriptions incorporated general management strategies to create a context that could facilitate instruction, but few offered direct connections to instructional practice, descriptions of how leaders were to enact such practices, or the role that interpersonal/group, organizational, and/or environmental factors play in determining the outcome of such behaviors. What appears to be lacking is an underlying theory of action that drives such leadership practices. Without such a framework, it seems likely that instructional leadership will remain little more than a fragmented list of behaviors and admonishments for "best practice" that are not clearly connected to instructional improvement and that are largely detached from administrators' day-to-day life.

Distributed view of leadership. The idea that leadership is distributed among individuals in organizations as well as incumbent within certain roles is not new. Only the narrowest, most hierarchically oriented of perspectives equate positional authority with leadership (Weber, 1947). The human resources literature long advocated for meaningful participatory decisionmaking to promote cooperation and engagement with organizational tasks (Barnard, 1981; Miles, 1965). Political analysts also recognized that power is distributed across the span of organizational participants and rises from different sources (Mechanic, 1962; Pfeffer, 1981).

Leaving behind the organizationally based literature that grounded these previous perspectives on leadership, Spillane, Halverson, and Diamond (2001) argued for a distributed theory of leadership practice. They drew heavily on sociocultural approaches, appropriating major ideas from distributed cognition and activity theory and translating these to the realm of educational leadership. The authors argued that leadership practice is best understood as socially distributed across an organization and constituted in the interaction of formal leaders, teachers, and the activity being undertaken. This perspective holds two important ideas. The first is a reconceptualization of the notion of leadership as "stretched over" the practice of multiple leaders in interaction with their followers and, thus, an organization-wide phenomenon available to all participants (Ogawa & Bossert, 1995).

The second major tenet is the identification of activity as the appropriate unit of analysis for studying leadership. Because leadership is evident only in social interactions or activities with others, using available cultural tools and artifacts, it exists "in between" participants, rather than residing within a given individual or individuals. In this sense leadership becomes more than the sum of the contributions of individual participants (Smylie, Conley, & Marks, 2002).

This collective property of distributed leadership holds especially profound implications for linking leadership with teaching and learning. It suggests that we might think of both teaching and leadership in terms of communities of practice. Administrators can be seen as playing a role, with teachers, in communities of practice centered around instruction; and teachers can be seen as playing a role, with administrators, in school or district-based communities of practice centered around leadership for instruction. Further, it suggests that a common conceptual framework can be developed to examine both teaching and learning and how leadership contributes to the improvement of teaching and learning. Rather than holding leadership practice as separate from instructional practice and understood in different ways, there might be coherent understandings that stretch across both and provide an explanatory and analytic framework for understanding both.

The conceptual framework for distributed leadership rests on situated cognition and sociocultural perspectives that are also used to study teaching and learning. These perceptions offer an appealing linkage between the ambiguous, atheoretical field of leadership and the relatively more grounded, substantive theories of cognitive science. Research on teaching that is based on constructivist views of learning is already achieving solid payoffs.[6] Distributed perspectives now seek to ground conceptions of leadership in the same fertile soil.

ISSUES AND QUESTIONS

Perspectives on teaching and learning that emphasize constructivist and socially mediated learning, paired with perspectives on leadership that emphasize its cognitive and sociocultural dimensions, may constitute a conceptual bridge between leadership and the core technology of schooling. In this section, we set forth some issues that must be addressed as the field explores the robustness of this conceptual bridge.

Rethinking Leadership—What Counts as Leadership for Learning?

New directions in leadership inquiry will likely encompass two major directions: exploring and explicating ideas of distributed leadership and expanding understandings of learners and leaders in schools. Each has implications for understanding different facets of leadership for learning. We explore these below.

Distributed leadership. The distributed leadership perspective is consistent with previous research (Smylie, Conley, & Marks, 2002), but it points further toward the development of a social theory that could encompass conceptions of both leading and learning in schools. This view highlights administrators and teachers as arrayed in complex collegial networks that form and re-form around specific tasks or issues—for example, principals and teachers in a school working on how to improve math scores on standardized tests; principals in a district figuring out how to ensure that students with the right to change schools have the opportunity to do so; teachers, principals, and district subject matter coordinators evaluating new curricula for adoption; and so on. It then asks how leadership is shared by several people and what and how ideas about learning and teaching influence their work.

While distributed leadership is an appealing construct, clear conceptions remain elusive. Part of this may be due to its heavy grounding in sociocultural and sociocognitive perspectives—territory largely unfamiliar to most educational leaders as well as educational leadership researchers. There may be a real danger in appropriating concepts or theories developed as explanatory frameworks for specific phenomena in one field and applying them to seemingly analogous but perhaps only distally related phenomena in another (see Sprio, Feltovitch, Coulson, & Anderson, 1989). It is not clear how analogous and applicable notions of distributed cognition are to leadership. As Lea and Nicoll (2002) noted, in a related area, Lave herself has "expressed concern at how the broader concept of 'communities of practice' . . . has been taken up and imposed in a top-down way in educational settings as a sort of model of 'good pedagogy'" (p. 10), a use for which it was not intended. Distributed leadership is neither a collection of best practices nor a management strategy, though already it is being referred to as such. Notions of distributed leadership offer a way to understand leadership and learning and the connections between the two in organizations, specifically educational ones. To avoid misappropriation, clearer understandings of distributed perspectives on leadership need to be developed.

Along with this, the role of individual agency in distributed leadership needs to be explored. The agency of individuals may shape how they engage in and the degree to which they participate in a given activity (Cobb, 1998; Engestrom & Middleton, 1996). There is little evidence that individuals unhesitatingly and unquestioningly engage in any practice, let alone leadership practice, simply because the opportunity is afforded them. Rather, the relationship between leadership practices that individuals engage in and the individuals themselves may be co-constituted. In other words, there is likely a fairly strong interdependence and reciprocity between how leadership practices invite individuals to participate and how (to what extent) individuals decide to engage in these practices. Further, how opportunities for participation are offered (and to whom) and certainly individuals' decisions on how they will participate are not likely to be uniform across or even within organizations or work groups (Billett, 2002).

While all these questions about distributed leadership are quite theoretical, they can be investigated in educational settings, and were such investigations to happen, the findings would shed light on both the construct of distributed leadership and the ways in which teachers and administrators work together to improve schools.

Expanding understandings of learners and leaders. Instructional practices associated with constructivist orientations toward teaching and learning present a fair departure from traditional classroom practice and may be especially dependent upon principals' active support (Elmore, 2000; Spillane, 2000b). This support is not likely without a solid understanding of the beliefs and principles of constructivist ideas (McLaughlin & Mitra, 2001). As Spillane and Louis (2002) contend, "Without an understanding of the knowledge necessary for teachers to teach well—content knowledge, general pedagogical knowledge, content-specific pedagogical knowledge, curricular knowledge, and knowledge of learners—school leaders will be unable to perform essential school improvement functions such as monitoring instruction and supporting teacher development" (p. 97). Principals who do not understand or value such teaching and learning practices may create, albeit inadvertently, structures, policies, and procedures that compete or conflict with practices associated with a constructivist orientation to teaching and learning.

Administrator learning will need to be continuous, reflective, and focused on improving student outcomes and teaching and learning practices (Mohr & Dichter, 2001; Zederayko & Ward, 1999). Examining three different theory-based constructivist change efforts, McLaughlin and Mitra (2001) concluded that those schools able to sustain the reform after external assistance ended had principals who became learners themselves. That is, administrators who themselves adopt an orientation of learning about student learning and instructional practice become part of the school community in a different way and permit the power of their position to be harnessed for the improvement of student learning. Writing from a sociocultural perspective, Tharp (1993) notes:

> A basic condition for effective activity settings is "jointedness." Without it, . . . [p]rofessors, teachers, principals, curriculum specialists, and other authorities direct their pupils/subordinates to accomplish a task but do not participate in the productive work itself. It means that they lose the opportunity to develop joint understanding, even that minimal understanding that would allow them to assess their subordinates adequately. (p. 277)

Co-participation in professional development activities appears essential if leaders are to develop the jointedness and shared understandings that Tharp (1993) refers to and thus be able to engage in a meaningful dialogue with teachers about instructional practice. Such co-participation also can symbolically communicate the importance and value the leader attaches to the work of teachers by engaging with them in such work (McLaughlin & Mitra, 2001).

The importance of learning in leadership points to several important questions. What incentives are there for leaders to learn about teaching and learning from a constructivist perspective? How much of this learning needs to happen jointly with teachers in the school, and what can happen individually, or in other contexts? How are principals' efforts to learn regarded by the teaching staff? How does their knowledge affect their practice?

Rethinking Teaching and Learning—What Do Leaders Need to Know and to What Depth/Level?

If we conceptualize instructional leadership as a complex function enacted by groups of people rather than individuals acting alone, it becomes necessary to consider what knowledge leaders and others need to work effectively together.

Theory-based understandings. While constructivist-oriented learning theories do not specify particular instructional techniques and strategies, they do suggest a framework or scaffold for the design of learning environments. Over 5 years McLaughlin and Mitra (2001) examined three explicitly constructivist learning theory-based change efforts: Fostering a Community of Learners (FCL), Schools for Thought (SFT), and the Child Development Project (CDP)[7]. Across these theory-based change efforts, McLaughlin and Mitra identified five areas critical to the sustainability of these constructivist teaching and learning reforms—resources, knowledge of first principles, a supportive community of practice, a supportive principal, and a compatible district context. Interestingly, two of these directly relate to administrators and the other three are, to greater or lesser extents, related to administrative actions and decisions.

McLaughlin and Mitra (2001) argued that without understanding the theory upon which new practices are premised, the "first principles," as they call them, teachers will be unable to see the "big picture" of constructivist change and will be susceptible to focusing on the "concretes"—fragmented activities and practices that they can immediately put to use in their classrooms. Also, without understanding the foundational theory, reflection, critique, and growth though dialogic means are not likely to occur.

> The experiences of these three theory-based reforms underscore the point that the relevant "it" that needs to be embedded in practice is not the particular activity structures, materials, or routines, of a reform, but rather the first principles. The problem for implementation, then, is not only teachers "learning how to do it," but teachers learning the theoretical precepts upon which participant structures and activity structures are based. Absent knowledge about why they are doing what they're doing, implementation will be superficial only, and teachers will lack the understanding they need to deepen their practice or sustain new practices in the face of changing contexts. (p. 10)

This deep understanding of the theoretical precepts underlying constructivist practices in classrooms also clearly applied to principals. Promoting and sustaining such constructivist-based changes in teaching and learning required a supportive principal who understood and actively endorsed the values and perspectives underlying the project (McLaughlin & Mitra, 2001).

The notion that principals need to know the theory that underlies the design of particular reform efforts needs further investigation. One challenge will be to investigate how knowledge of first principles and leadership capacity intersect within the embedded contexts of the school even as practices and context change over time. Another will be understanding in what ways informed judgments can be made about the extent to which practices at all levels adhere to the core principles.

Deep content knowledge. A second question about what leaders need to know focuses on the subject matter itself. Since instruction is subject-specific and is centered on students' subject matter thinking, what do instructional leaders need to know to carry out such responsibilities as observing classrooms, supervising teachers, selecting curricula, developing programs of professional development, selecting assessment instruments, and communicating about the instructional program to key stakeholders?

There is some evidence that administrators who profess to be instructional leaders must have a degree of understanding of the various subject areas under their purview and how they are learned and taught. Further, it appears inadequate for administrators to generalize from what they know about learning and teaching in one subject to another (Stein & D'Amico, 2000; Stein & Nelson, 2003).

In a conceptual analysis of "leadership content knowledge," Stein and Nelson (2003) show that administrators at several levels of school organization (principals, associate superintendents, instructional leaders in central offices) use varying degrees of subject matter knowledge in their work. By examining several cases of administrators' work, Stein and Nelson show that such knowledge gives administrators a significant advantage in supporting teaching and learning. The authors report that the closer these administrators are to the classroom and the narrower their administrative function, the more fine-grained and detailed their knowledge of subject matter and how children learn it appears to be. Work that is further removed from the classroom and involves a wider range of administrative functions requires less fine-grained, concrete subject matter knowledge, knowledge of how children learn that subject, and how it is best taught. Importantly, if their work is further away from the classroom, knowledge about subject matter and how children learn it does not disappear, and what administrators need to know does not become more generic. It remains anchored in knowledge of the subject, how students learn it, how it is best taught, and ways to best support it from an organizational perspective. But it tends to focus more on the ways in which teaching and learning in different fields are similar and different. For example, administrators need to know the similarities and differences in the nature of the curricula that are available in different fields, and they need to know the implications of this for the nature and design of professional development for teachers.

Stein and Nelson (2003) propose that once administrators have developed the requisite subject matter knowledge, they will be well served in their subsequent administrative work in relation to these subjects by others in the district who may have deeper and broader subject knowledge—teachers, instructional leaders, department chairs, subject matter supervisors, and so on. Distributed leadership or communities of practice for instructional leadership may be anchored in the distribution of subject matter knowledge itself. The notion of leadership content knowledge is still largely unexamined. There has been as yet little empirical work on the nature of leadership content knowledge in different subjects, or as used by leaders in different organizational positions. While Stein and Nelson (2003) propose a method for administrators to gain sufficient content knowledge in most subjects, it is not yet clear just how detailed such leadership content knowledge needs to be, or whether it can be different for different administrative tasks. Nor is it clear how administrators' content knowledge would be similar to or different from teachers' knowledge, how administrators would learn this knowledge, nor how much they would need to know about all school subjects. There have as yet been no studies of the comparative content knowledge of administrators and teachers working together in communities of practice. One also might ask how Stein and Nelson's "leadership content knowledge" relates to McLaughlin and Mitra's "first principles." Do these constructs overlap? Is either sufficient? Are both necessary?

Rethinking Communities of Practice—Is There an Advantage in Viewing Schools as Communities of Practice?

Currently, much reform literature talks about the importance of communities of practice or professional learning communities that support and foster teacher collaboration in a collegial environment as both a means for and goal of sustainable and significant school improvement efforts (e.g., DuFour & Eaker, 1998). Much of the optimism about this rests on the assumption that teachers working collectively and reflecting on their practice will ratchet up the overall quality of teaching and learning. Yet not all strong professional communities exhibit an orientation to practice that is conducive to change or concerned with improvement (Murphy & Prestine, 2001; Wenger, 1998).

While the instructional and learning benefits of communities of practice are widely extolled, the basic construct and pragmatic workings of such arrangements are elusive. How a school, and especially a leader, goes about creating, nurturing, and sustaining learning communities focused on instructional improvement is not clear-cut. Further, few studies have examined the dynamics by which a community of practice supports and promotes teacher learning and improvements in practice (Little, 2001; McLaughlin & Mitra, 2001). The number of studies examining the role of leadership in such arrangements is even sparser.

If communities of practice do indeed present promising avenues for improved student learning, there is a pressing need to explore the conditions necessary to support and sustain them. Numerous studies have suggested that there must be some degree of compatibility between the values, beliefs, and norms of the change initiative itself and the host school context (e.g., Kruse & Louis, 1995; Wasley, 1995). Yet the reality of changing embedded and entrenched ways of thinking and doing to accommodate this new concept presents a daunting challenge for school leaders.

Murphy and Prestine (2001) studied a large urban high school that attempted to implement a professional learning communities model over 5 years. They reported that merely assembling all the requisite pieces was not sufficient. The presence of collegial conversations or even the establishment of communities of practice are but outer and visible markers. This raises a number of questions for further research: Is a schoolwide focus on improved student learning and improved teaching requisite if professional learning communities are to have an impact on the quality of instruction? Kruse, Louis, and Bryk (1995) posited five common characteristics of a learning community, including shared values, reflective dialogue, deprivatization of practice, focus on student learning, and collaboration. How can these elements of professional communities be fostered in schools? Are communities of practice appropriate for all teachers or just some? And what is the role of leadership in these processes?

Coherence and consistency of pedagogical theory. We propose that classroom pedagogy and those pedagogical strategies used with the adults in a school should be aligned. Alignment, in this sense, would extend far beyond "program coherence" to a degree of consistency or fit between the values and beliefs undergirding classroom teaching and learning practices and the values and beliefs that govern the learning opportunities for teachers and administrators. Such coherence would promote consistency of *learning* throughout the school. Teachers and principals would experience and see modeled in their own learning activities the same approaches and pedagogical techniques they would be expected to use with students.

The school improvement literature, which has long recognized that changing cultures in schools is central to changing instructional practices (Deal & Peterson, 1998; Fullan, 2001), suggests that such coherence could be an important step in improving instruction. While pedagogical coherence could create strong cultural ties among the learning communities in a school, it remains an empirical question whether adults who experience professional development based on constructivist principles actually do understand constructivist-based instructional practice better. What do they learn that is transferable to understanding instruction for students? What about adults whose experiences in constructivist-based professional development are unsatisfactory? What would such professional development programs for teachers and administrators look like? What is the relationship between change in ideas and change in professional practice for teachers and administrators?[8]

Beyond such questions of feasibility and efficacy, there are organizational implications of such pedagogical coherence. Bureaucratically structured schools may not readily support alternative learning definitions that differ too greatly from the traditional organization of learning in the school (Rowan, 1990). However, we know from harsh experience that simple tinkering with the structures of schooling rarely brings about desired changes in teaching and learning practices (Elmore, 1995a; Prestine & McGreal, 1997). How, then, do we achieve a kind of bottom-up consistency and coherence? Is a critical mass of teachers using a constructivist-based approach needed before attempting to change normative and procedural structures? What might these structures look like in a constructivist-based school? What political and strategic skills are necessary to attempt this?

CONCLUSIONS

School leadership and constructivist orientations toward learning and teaching have substantial research communities and literatures that have exerted considerable influence in their separate spheres of influence. As we consider how ideas about learning, teaching, and leadership can be integrated, what are the implications for research on schooling?

A useful way to explore possible connections is to develop research frameworks based on sociocultural perspectives that encompass and integrate learning, teaching, and leadership. A related task is to focus on activity as the unit of analysis for future studies of leadership and teaching and learning. Finally, as a research community, we should consider using design experiments that have been used successfully in mathematics and science education to understand a phenomenon that currently exists rarely, if at all, but may be emergent. We discuss each below.

Research frameworks that integrate constructivist learning practices with ideas about school leadership could provide a powerful means for drawing these domains together in mutually sustaining and reinforcing ways. This would involve redrawing what counts as a research site to include teaching, learning, and leadership. It would also require methods that are anchored in the co-construction of meaning, the "jointedness," that occurs when teachers and administrators work together in schools as members of communities of practice, as well as methods that examine the structural features of such arrangements. Such frameworks suggest empirical studies of those instances wherein teaching, learning, and leadership are truly integrated, not only to ask if such arrangements improve student learning, but also to see how they work—what works reasonably well, what is difficult, what do both teachers and leaders have to know in order to make these new organizational configurations work, and so on. Coburn's (2002) examination of how principals' beliefs about instruction influence leadership practices and how these in turn influence teacher learning and changes in practice provides an auspicious beginning for such efforts.

Design experiments might be appropriate in some cases. Such experiments create conditions that theory suggests are productive, but that are not commonly practiced or are not well understood. The design, or intervention, is enacted through the interactions of materials, teachers, learners, and leaders, and is a product of the context in which it is enacted. Such experiments progress through continuous cycles of design, enactment, analysis, and redesign and contribute to both successful interventions and predictive theory (Brown, 1992; Design-Based Research Collective, 2003).

Finally, we suggest that a framework that takes activity as the unit of analysis allows one to consider three planes of action—the individual, the interpersonal or group, and the institutional/cultural (Rogoff, Radziszewska, & Masiello, 1995). This seems especially significant for investigations of the interfaces of instruction and leadership. Activity theory has already been used in analyzing attempts at implementing educational innovation (see Nicolopoulou & Cole, 1993) and in analyzing constructive classroom practices (see Roth & Bowen, 1995). It holds promise for studies focusing on the interface of leadership and learning as well.

While there are many unanswered questions, we suggest that investigations of the connections and interfaces between school leadership and teaching and learning be undertaken from a sociocultural stance that emphasizes the interrelated and mutually constitutive nature of activity, context, and social interaction for building shared meanings and understandings. From this perspective, the issues surrounding how leaders promote and support teaching and learning are situated in a culturally defined matrix of purposes and values. In essence, a sociocultural orientation toward the interface between school leadership and teaching and learning sets forth a new way of looking at school improvement by suggesting that significant changes to teaching and learning practices in classrooms based on a constructivist orientation toward learning can only be accomplished when such tenets also guide the learning of leaders and the school organization as a whole.

NOTES

1. The decentralization movement in the early 1990s featured shared decisionmaking and site-based management models designed to draw teachers into arenas that were previously the exclusive province of administration. See, for example, Hannaway & Carnoy, 1993; Weiss, 1993; Weiss & Cambone, 1994.

2. This dichotomy is also reflected in the extant research, as those researchers and studies investigating leadership/management issues and those examining teaching and learning have remained, for the most part, separate and discrete groups.

3. For an extended discussion of the three major theories of learning discussed here, see Greeno, Collins & Resnick, 1996.

4. See Greeno, 1998, for an argument that the situative perspective integrates and synthesizes behaviorist and cognitive perspectives.

5. See Hallinger and Heck (1996a, 1996b, 1998) for extensive reviews of the literature focused on the principal's contribution to school effectiveness.

6. For example, in the field of mathematics education see Carpenter, Fennema, Peterson, Chiang, & Loef, 1989; Fennema, Franke, Carpenter, & Carey, 1993; Schoenfeld, 2002; Senk & Thompson, 2003; Stein & Lane, 1996

7. Fostering a Community of Learners (FCL), designed by Ann Brown and Joseph Campione and using reciprocal teaching techniques, applies cognitive learning theory to the design of innovative classroom learning environments called "communities of learners." The primary goals are to promote the critical thinking and reflection skills that support higher literacy attainment and that are embedded in deep disciplinary content knowledge. Schools for Thought (SFT) is a technology-based reform that uses authentic problems that allow for extended in-depth inquiry in content domains. The Child Development Project (CDP) is based on a philosophy of educating the whole child by emphasizing the social and ethical as well as intellectual dimensions of learning using a constructivist approach and building communities of learners.

8. We note that the professional development literature in mathematics education reports inquiries into these issues to some degree. See Knapp, 2003; Schifter & Fosnot, 1993, and Wilson & Berne, 1999.

CHAPTER 5

How Can School Leaders Incorporate Communities as Contexts for Student Learning?

Mary Erina Driscoll and Ellen B. Goldring

Connecting schools and communities has most often been justified in terms of the broad social and political aims of American public education. Democratic ownership of public education has resulted in traditional systems of financing public education that rely heavily on local sources of revenue. This local support has bred in turn a deep sense that schools should privilege the needs and concerns of their surrounding communities.

The rationale for connecting schools with their communities, however, is not merely political in nature. Recent theories of social cognition and situated instruction suggest that communities can be linked much more integrally to the core mission of schooling, teaching, and learning. Parents and community are central to supporting the development of human, social, and financial capital for schools and their students. Simultaneously, newer perspectives suggest that schools could be and should be the engine for social change *in and of* communities.

In this chapter, we advance the perspective that the new science of learning presents important challenges for linking schools and their communities around issues of student learning. In our introductory section, we discuss briefly the ways in which we have thought about schools and their communities, with a particular focus on the implications of these shifting perspectives for the work of school leaders. We then turn to each of the three bodies of literature we deem central to mapping this new terrain, including research on the "new science" of learning; the literature on social capital and schools; and recent work connecting schools with community development and a sense of place. In each of these sections, we briefly review key findings and identify the critical questions relevant to research on school leadership. Finally, we conclude with a discussion of some of the overarching methodological issues that must be addressed if we are to undertake this new scholarship.

EVOLVING PERSPECTIVES ON SCHOOLS AND COMMUNITIES

Parent Involvement: From Buffering to Bridging

Early work on leadership and school–community relations focused entirely on parents as the important elements within a school's community. Researchers found that principals, facing large amounts of uncertainty and ambiguity from their external environments, tended to develop strong allegiances to their school bureaucracy in an effort to buffer teachers, and the school's academic and professional core, from parent and community influence (Goldring, 1990). Hollister (1979) found that schools with high parental demands adopted rationalistic bureaucratic controls to deflect these demands. Principals often insisted that parents contact them first before confronting a teacher, thus buffering the teachers from the parents. Principals buffered their school organizations to seal them off from parents, striving to make decisions in a "closed system." Principals viewed themselves as "trustees" of the school system, rather than as "delegates" of the school community (Mann, 1976). The goal for most principals was to preserve the school from outside interference, maintaining order and stability. The sense that schools needed to "go it alone" to protect teachers from undue interference was the prevalent view of community and parent participation, as principals strived to maintain a delicate balance between professional autonomy and parent involvement (Saxe, 1983). Referred to as the "four-walls-of-the-school tradition" (McPherson et al., 1986), professional group commitment and cohesion were established by insulating the school from parent and community concerns, especially in relation to low-income and ethnically and racially diverse groups of parents (Cairney & Munsie, 1995).

Changes in the educational landscape spurred on by the effective schools movement and later waves of educational reform fundamentally altered both the closed-system view of school–community relations, and the pervasive notion that principals should buffer between teachers and parents (Goldring & Sullivan, 1996). Furthermore, the very idea that teacher commitment, professionalism, and cohesion would be diminished or lost if schools were more responsive to parents and community was questioned. Thus, educational reformers relied on various efforts to increase community–school linkages: parental involvement, parent empowerment, parental choice, and coordinated services (Beck & Foster, 1999).

The effective schools movement gave credence to the idea that parental participation is central to student achievement. A large body of research linked parental involvement to positive benefits for students, families, and schools, including academic achievement (e.g. Hoover-Dempsey & Sandler, 1997). Effective schools were characterized as providing opportunities for parents to support and participate in their children's education (Smith & O'Day, 1991). In turn, effective principals were those who no longer buffered but rather bridged with the community to facilitate parental involvement. Principals were referred to as "environmental leaders," ". . . operating in the community outside their schools while also bringing the community into their schools" (Goldring & Sullivan, 1996, p. 207).

New Roles for Parents and Community

The effective schools era, however, placed clear limits on roles of parents and the community. Parent and community participation was intended to support the value system of the school (Munn, 1993). Also known as the "protective" or "delegation" model of parental involvement, these models suggested that school professionals have primary responsibility for educational decisions and parent participation is largely ritualistic.

To mitigate the limited roles of parents, restructuring efforts emphasized more parent and community participation in decisionmaking, and tried to reduce the gatekeeping perspective of educational leaders. Reformers believed that it was necessary to alter the relationships between parents and educators to enhance learning and realize more substantial school change. School–based management became a key mechanism to alter these traditional role relationships by empowering parents and other community members to engage in governance and decisionmaking. In Chicago and Great Britain, for example, legal mandates established parent involvement in school decisionmaking forums (Hess, 1991). The shift of parent and community roles from supporter to participant in governance, however, was difficult. Researchers found that parents often lacked the information and skills to participate fully in school governance. Furthermore, the fundamental power relationships between parents and school professionals were not substantially altered, as principals still maintained a stance of formal power and authority (Malen & Ogawa, 1988). Despite the difficulties of changing parent–school relationships, however, research suggests that when parents take on active roles at school there is a substantial benefit resulting in academic and social change in schools (Comer, 1984).

Some research on school choice has shown positive implications for developing a sense of community between home and school. Community is often associated with physical or geographical boundaries, but a broader concept of community takes into account social structures and social relations. Schools of choice, such as magnet schools and private schools, may be characterized by strong value communities, communities united around an educational organization where parents, children, and school professionals share similar beliefs.

Connecting Community Services with Schools

Most of the initiatives mentioned above focus on parents as the core members of a school's community. Realizing that schools need help from their communities in order to meet the needs of children, however, policymakers called for a coordinated approach in service provision. A movement toward coordinated services in schools or "full-service schools" began (Dryfoos, 1994). These schools offer an array of services for children *in schools* from health clinics to employment counseling and parent education. Community-based services may also incorporate a wider array of community institutions, such as clubs and churches, to meet the diverse needs of students (Crowson & Boyd, 1993). These initiatives have been implemented across the country with varying degrees of success. Issues of turf, funding, politics, confidentiality, and trust all caused challenges to the successful implementation of social service delivery in schools (Smrekar, 1996).

Beyond the School as Center: New Directions and Questions

When reviewing the path from parent involvement to community-linked social services, we note the fact that all these initiatives positioned schools as isolated institutions within their communities, typically defined by the school's geographic boundaries. The key members of those communities were defined narrowly as parents. Schools were viewed as receivers of resources in support of a "school-centric" view or notion of learning. "Such a school-centric frame assumes that schools are the primary influences for learning in the lives of children and youth rather than one part of students' broader developmental contexts" (Honig, Kahne, & McLaughlin, 2001, p. 1001).

Despite decades of reform, experimentation, and research on the relationships among parents, families, communities, and schools, the empirical knowledge base is still limited and characterized by this school-centric view. Much of the research pursues the rather narrow view of school–family–community relations and is focused on parents' roles in supporting school's work, such as helping with homework, coming to parent–teacher conferences, or volunteering in the library or office (e.g., Epstein, Simon, & Salinas, 1997).

Accompanying this line of inquiry is a body of research on the principalship that has examined how principals facilitate home–school relationships, negotiate the politics of parent–community involvement, and buffer teachers and the academic core. "The focus remains 'inward,' on the school rather than 'outward,' toward change in the surrounding community" (Crowson & Boyd, 2001, pg. 15). Principals view their role as garnering resources from the community (Goldring & Hausman, 2001) or managing a delicate balancing act of buffering and bridging with parents. Clearly, principals primarily view their roles as leaders inside their schools (Ogawa & Studer, 2002).

Contemporary research suggests fresh perspectives that radically realign our views of schools and communities and carry with them new imperatives for understanding effective leadership. We turn now to a discussion of recent research that can provide us with a framework for understanding communities as contexts for student learning.

THE "NEW SCIENCE" OF LEARNING AND SCHOOL–COMMUNITY CONNECTIONS

Theories of cognitive science that focus on situated cognition suggest new ways to think about relationships between the school and the community. This perspective asserts that the "real-world contexts" of learning are vital to constructing the kind of knowledge that is both generative and useful (Brown, Collins, & Duguid, 1989)

These images of learning are not new; in many respects, they echo the work of John Dewey (1897) over a century ago, which connected learning with the social and physical environment of the child. But while Dewey's understanding of learning rested on a philosophical conception of understanding and experience, this recent work has developed from empirical inquiry. A recent National Research Council report (Bransford, Brown, & Cocking, 2000) provides a concise overview of this "new science." This work presents a vivid portrait of the ways in which schools might be envisioned. Below we summarize a few of the issues we believe are particularly provocative with respect to making the connection between school and communities.

The Importance of Preexisting Knowledge for Understanding New Learning

Perhaps the most central tenet of the new science of learning is that all new knowledge is scaffolded onto preexisting knowledge. Building on earlier work of Piaget and Vygotsky, Bransford et al. note that "the contemporary view of learning is that people construct new knowledge and understandings based on what they already know and believe" (2000, p. 10). This means that "teachers need to pay attention to the incomplete understandings, the false beliefs, and the naïve renditions of concepts that learners bring with them to a given subject" (Bransford et al., 2000, p. 10).

The lion's share of preexisting knowledge that learners bring to school is likely to be shaped by the home and community contexts in which they find themselves the majority of their time. Active inquiry on the part of teachers is one way of making the connection between what students already know and what they need to know. Even more important is encouraging students to develop the kind of metacognitive skills—for example, thinking about their thinking—that permit them to articulate points of confusion. Making connections to those leaning contexts is vital if learners are to sort out what they already know, what they think they know, and what they need to know.

Understanding That Learning Is Transferred from One Context to Another

A second critical premise is that learning can be transferred from the context in which it is learned to other relevant settings. Context helps to provide both the conceptual framework and the organizing structures that enable the learner to bring the understandings and competencies gained into a new cognitive venue. Bransford et al. (2000) use the example of students who acquire deep knowledge of a geographic phenomenon such as the Mississippi River. Learning may be organized around general principles that allow students to grasp how geographical features affect the development of cities, of trade, and of the creation of borders. Such a conceptual framework makes it much more likely that learners will be able to transfer these implicit theories to any study of another river in a different setting. It is particularly important, then, that subjects be taught across multiple contexts, with the kind of examples that demonstrate "wide application" and encourage a "flexible representation of knowledge" (Bransford et al., 2000, p. 62).

School and community connections that support transfer of learning must link that learning to the real-world contexts in which such knowledge must be used (Wehlage, Neumann, & Secada, 1996). Understanding some of the key differences between school and nonschool settings is important in constructing optimum learning environments that are likely to encourage transfer, especially those that emphasize "problem-based" learning. This means understanding the nonschool environments in which children learn. Citing the work of Resnick (1987), Wehlage and associates note that schools "put more importance on individual work than most other settings." Nonschool settings make much more use of tools as aids in problem-solving, as opposed to schools, which emphasize "mental work." Finally, real-world settings use more contextualized reasoning than do schools, which often stress abstract reasoning (Bransford et al., 2000).

Dewey's (1897) insight that "The school must represent life, life as real and vital to the child as that which he carries on in the home, in the neighborhood, or on the playground" captures the critical nature of this connection. Such real-world contexts are vital because they permit learners to develop the kind of robust conceptual knowledge that transfers across a broad array of contexts.

Communities as the Contexts for Learning

Finally, another implication of the new science of learning for our understandings of schools and communities is the importance of community itself in this literature. Bransford et al. (2000) argue for a " community-centered approach" to learning, where the classroom, and the outside world, support core learning values (p. 25). Teachers must help students to form the kinds of learning communities where they both give and receive assistance in solving problems. Similarly, teachers themselves must be connected in learning communities that focus on developing expertise in pedagogy and curriculum. Equally critical, however, is the imperative to use the broader community as a source of context and experience in learning. Communities not only provide the structures that facilitate learning; they also shape and determine what learning is valued. Thus it is critical to recognize how these out-of-school contexts include nonschool learning communities that shape students' understandings.

Those involved in developing community schools are struggling with making some of these connections as they develop extended rationales for why such schools should be supported. Melaville, Shah, and Blank (2003) argue that active and concrete learning provided in community school settings is critical, and the "effective learning" occurs when schools, afterschool programs, and other organizations use the resources and challenges of the community as a living textbook for learning (p. 27).

Questions Provoked by the New Science of Learning

Taken together, these precepts from the new science of learning press us to examine new questions about the connections between communities and schools, and to imagine the actual and potential effects of such relationships on student learning using a different framework. Among these questions are:

How broadly do we define the outcomes of learning? The most common measure of learning used when assessing the effects of schools and communities on students is scores on standardized tests designed to measure levels of student achievement. Often the form of these tests emphasizes a limited set of skills, with few opportunities for students to exhibit the full range of their cognitive strategies or the ways in which they have transferred knowledge into new contexts.

This research suggests that we must draw the picture of what learning looks like with much broader strokes, encompassing the full range of those abilities that relevant communities identify as valuable. Although traditional academic skills are certainly part of this view, schools and communities also help children form their understandings about citizenship and civic participation.

Moreover, within the academic realm, we need assessments of learning that capture the generative quality of real learning as well as students' metacognitive abilities. Assessments that draw on this broader construction of learning may include, for example, writing tests that are scored using a rubric that requires staff training, or mathematics assessments that credit students for exhibiting estimation skills even when their computations may be inaccurate. These assessments, however, may be costly to administer or require substantial relearning on the part of those who prepare students for them.

If real world contexts are critical to learning, how do schools and school leaders extend the context for learning to include the community? Honig et al. (2001) argue that school and community connections must be constructed in terms of their capacities for both opportunities to learn and opportunities to teach. Honig et al. (citing Cahill, 1993, and Pitman & Cahill, 1992) argue that school and community connections such as integrated services programs have often been constructed as vehicles through which the barriers to learning are removed—thus enhancing the likelihood that students will have adequate nutrition and rest, fewer absences from schools, and even the presence of role models for learning in their communities, which encourages them to succeed in schools. But, they assert, only rarely have we thought about these connections in terms of their abilities to "reinforce and extend youth's opportunity to learn." Much traditional thinking underestimates the importance of the structures and activities outside of schools among the peer groups that provide learning communities of support for students. Moreover, there is insufficient appreciation for "community classrooms" that "are often more meaningful and motivating than those found in school," especially given that "the engagement with learning that is generated in community classrooms often carries back to school" (Honig et al., 2001, pp. 1016–1017).

Similarly, teachers can think about these connections in terms of opportunities to teach. Teachers can extend the space and time for teaching into the community, using the "access to funds of knowledge about their students' provided by connections with communities and families, the involvement of community partners in teaching who also provide resources connected to real world contexts, and the opportunities for teachers as well as students to create expanded professional networks and supports" (Honig et al., 2001, p. 1017). Such engagement is also likely to result in a realignment of the ways in which schools view the funds of knowledge for teaching (Moll, Amanti, Neff, & Gonzalez, 1992) that are available to students in lower-income communities but are often undervalued by schools.

Empirical investigations that study these links, so plausible at the theoretical level, are needed to map the pathways between these community contexts and schools. Some seminal work in leadership theory has begun to delineate these connections and how leaders might help to facilitate them, but we need far more focused scholarship (Knapp et al., 2002).

Our notion of what constitutes "instructional leadership," in its most fundamental sense, will require rethinking. Narrow visions of instruction as the delivery of tightly directed curricula that do not take into account the contexts of student learning will continue to lead us to similarly narrow constructions of instructional leadership, and the knowledge and insight that are needed to exercise it. Instructional leadership may have at its heart the ability to make sense of the school and community connections that are fluid yet essential elements of the learning imagined by this new science.

If we believe that communities of learners are vital contexts for learning, how broadly do we envision the community that defines and values that learning? Schools frequently discount the out-of-school peer and organizational communities that shape students' understandings and provide skills useful in school (McLaughlin, 2000). The communities that define and value the knowledge, skills, and curriculum are increasingly distanced from the local school setting, as federal and state standards for learning replace more locally constructed forms of knowledge. How do we balance the importance of local definition and support of learning with the reality that the broad aims of education and the means by which they are assessed and taught are defined by a community that has little connection with local schools? How does leadership distributed throughout the system develop knowledge about these different contexts and align them to create the best possible conditions for student learning?

The tension between locally identified purposes of education, closely linked with community activities, and the purposes of a broader society, however defined, is hardly new in American education (Proefreidt, 1985). New developments, however, such as the *No Child Left Behind* law, provide even fewer degrees of latitude among the choices permitted by states and localities that wish to remain eligible for federal aid; similarly, states have increased the specificity and intensity of their requirements. Much empirical work is needed that demonstrates the ways in which schools and communities negotiate the various arenas in which resources and policies are formed.

SOCIAL CAPITAL AND SCHOOLS

Social capital has become an important way in which the community supports that benefit student learning are conceptualized. The essential characteristic of social capital is the fact that it resides in the relationships among individuals within a social organization. The educational benefits accrue when the community as a whole values education and shares some degree of oversight for all children.

Much of the research on social capital dates from a seminal study published in 1987 by Coleman and Hoffer, who looked at the academic effects in public and Catholic high schools. The positive effects they found in the Catholic sector were linked, they believed, to the social structures that supported Catholic schools. They posited a set of overlapping norms and relationships that supported educational achievement and greatly enriched the resources available to any individual student. This "social capital," as Coleman termed it, was as vital to student success as the physical, human, and financial capital that supports learning.

Putnam (1993) extends the idea of social capital to the political and civic networks in communities. Overlapping webs of relationships—what he terms "networks of civic engagement" (p. 173)—enrich the quality of life for any individual residing in the society. Such networks foster robust norms of reciprocity, facilitate communication and the development of trust, and "embody past success at collaboration, which can serve as a culturally-defined template for future collaboration" (pp. 173–174). Although dense social networks may not be focused on the exchange of educational information, they still provide a rich context to sustain and support schooling.

The construct of social capital has had significant influence in the past two decades. Orr points out that both "academicians and ordinary citizens embraced" this concept, bringing together individuals from disparate ends of the political spectrum (Orr, 1999, p. 185). The relationship between students' stocks of social capital and their performance on achievement measures continues to be a resilient theme in this research. In a review of nearly three dozen studies, Dika and Singh (2002) found that at least 10 use social capital to predict scores on achievement tests, and 6 use the concept to predict performance as measured by the grade point average.

A second theme in this research has been the effects of social capital on students' persistence in school, as indicated by their level of educational attainment, and their likelihood of dropping out of school. Dika and Singh (2002) find that indicators of social capital and educational attainment are positively linked, although the theoretical base could be strengthened. Croninger and Lee's (2001) review also suggests that there is a positive relationship between social capital and students' ability to stay and to succeed in school.

Yet another body of research has tried to unpack the construct of social capital by looking at the mechanisms through which such networks provide support for students. Using qualitative as well as quantitative methods, studies have looked at how the integration of schools and workplaces helps create the kinds of overlapping networks and oversight that provide coherent opportunities to learn for students (Smrekar, Guthrie, Owens, & Sims, 2001); how effective intervention programs for high poverty students can create social capital, including the building of social trust, the provision of access to information, and the creation of norms and effective sanctions that promote successful academic behavior (Kahne & Bailey, 1999); how intergenerational closure—as measured by parents' knowledge of their child's friends and child's friends' parents—affects student learning (Carbonaro, 1998); and how social capital is created through relationships in school, specifically through the bonds between teachers and their students.

Finally, some of this literature has explored the relationship between social capital and what Dika and Singh term "psychosocial factors related to education" (2002, p. 42). These include parental expectations, parent and child communication about school, and relationships with peer groups and other organizations (Pribesh & Downey, 1999; Smith-Maddox, 1999).

Emerging Questions About Schools and Social Capital

If, as Orr (1999) suggests, social capital has emerged as an orthodoxy that provides some credence to the academic importance of linking schools and community, what are the most critical questions for researchers to explore? The picture is complicated and requires a sophisticated understanding of the fabric of community and institutions.

How firmly can we establish the links between school effectiveness and the existence of social capital in a way that a) does justice to a robust construct of these networks and, b) maps onto the new constructions of learning that we have outlined above? Dika and Singh (2002) note that much of the work done to date has relied on secondary analysis of large-scale panels of data that limit researchers to variables already extant in the data set; in addition to what they term these "measurement" problems, they assert, "The conceptual umbrella of social capital has been stretched to include a variety of social factors that do not coherently hang together" (Dika & Singh, 2002, p. 46). Although careful and increasingly sophisticated qualitative work has been added to the canon on social capital, it is imperative that emerging investigations continue to "unpack" this construct in action, especially as schools and school leaders attempt to create the kinds of networks that have been demonstrated to be of value to student learning.

Similarly, the measures of learning and performance that have been addressed in most of this work are relatively narrow in scope and often summative in nature. Rich social networks may help to create some of the structures that better connect in-school learning with real-world contexts, or improve the degree to which teachers are aware of the knowledge students bring to school. As schools actively seek to use communities as contexts for learning and to bring respect to the cognitive structures that students have already formed, social capital may be an important element in developing the trust and information needed to create these opportunities for teaching and learning.

How can school leaders maximize the social capital already available in the community and co-create the kinds of networks that support educational success with the community? Little of the research to date focuses on what school leaders can do—either by themselves or in concert with teachers—to develop and learn about the connections that exist between community networks and contexts for learning beyond documenting these connections (Sanders & Harvey, 2002).

It is particularly critical that school leaders at all levels attend to the different kinds of networks that are created and assess many aspects of these connections between schools and communities. Putnam (1993) describes both "vertical" and "horizontal" networks among individuals and institutions; as we have already noted, citing the work of Honig et al. (2001), the relationships between schools and their communities have most often been constructed vertically, reflecting an imbalance in favor of the school, the professional community it comprises, and the dominant power structure. This imbalance, especially between dominant educational structures and those who bring different cultural values or knowledge structures, has been discussed at length in the work of Bourdieu (1977), Lareau (1989), and Stanton-Salazar & Dornbusch (1995). What we need is empirical work that specifies more closely the kinds of actions and activities that succeed in creating more horizontal networks. Such connections require the development of culturally responsive communication (Delgado-Gaitan, 1991) in order to be effective.

What opportunity costs are associated with a renewed focus by school leaders on the creation of social capital? At the school level, numerous studies identify the multiple demands on principals' time and efforts, especially in a climate of high-stakes accountability. Significant attention to social capital will require major time and attention on the part of school leaders that may represent a displacement of focus from other critical factors affecting the school. We need better empirical work that sifts through the choices and priorities principals face, and better information on how the distributed leadership of the school works to maximize student opportunities for learning.

Moreover, Orr's (1999) work on African-American social capital in the Baltimore school system cautions that a focus on social capital as the solution to educational problems effectively places the burden for success outside the school, perhaps even encouraging schools to do more with less. Orr reminds us that focusing on social capital should not exempt government from its obligation to provide the necessary resources for education, as voluntary organizations are also inequitably distributed across communities and may be misaligned with the prevailing goals of the system.

What do we need to know about the negative effects of strong networks on children's life chances and educational performance? An affirmative bias characterizes much of the work on social capital. Unexamined assumptions about the positive nature of strong networks and their unambiguously salient effects on school performance need further empirical investigation. Exceptions can be identified, of course; a careful study of the Department of Defense schools by Smrekar, Guthrie, Owens and Sims (2001), for example, makes credible links between the educational values of military culture and the communities of support in DOD schools for minority students. As Carbonaro (1998) notes, much of the work to date on social capital has used databases, which permit researchers to identify the presence of strong networks but do not provide enough information to ascertain the specific values characterizing those networks. Granovetter (1985) has demonstrated the importance of "weak ties" in a strong network in transmitting new information and creating productive cognitive dissonance, yet such connections are often underestimated in current work on social capital. Moreover, evaluations of novel reforms such as the "new" math and spiral social studies curricula of the 1960s provide ample evidence that community preferences and values may effectively bury unfamiliar yet potentially positive school reforms.

We need more attention to these tensions, and we need to explore how community values are shaped and evolve over time in concert with educational institutions. At the same time, as Noguera (2003) reminds us, research needs to help us understand the complexity of the networks and associations that shape students' identities in their dual worlds of community and school, and the ways in which schools can accommodate and interrupt the "negative" cultures that have been documented by some researchers (cf. Fordham & Ogbu, 1986).

THE SENSE OF PLACE
AND COMMUNITY DEVELOPMENT

In a third body of literature that links schools and their communities, schools are construed as the agents of community development. They are rooted in and help to sustain a sense of place. This literature posits schools as proactive institutions that are integral parts of the overall development and growth of the community. Schools are seen as both the most universal and the most stable entity in communities that often face multiple challenges, including the effects of poverty, racism, and disinvestment in urban centers. This view of schools as a vital and central force is not new.

Two elements distinguish this perspective from these early efforts, however. One is the degree to which schools are integrated with other, noneducational institutions as part of a comprehensive community development strategy, a stance termed the "holistic" perspective (McGaughey, 2001, p. 125). Timpane and Reich (1997) call this "an ecosystem—a total environment supporting the healthy growth and development of America's youth," warning that school reform cannot succeed without community development (pp. 465–466).

A second element is the degree to which school reform is informed by non-educational perspectives such as community development. This literature emphasizes economic investment, and education is seen as an investment in human capital (McGaughey, 2001). Educational reform becomes one of many strategies undertaken to improve the life chances of communities as a whole. The Ford Foundation's decade-long Neighborhood and Family Initiative is an example rooted in this strategy (Chaskin, 2000). Collaborative structures across multiple institutions—local foundations; school systems; higher education, health, and other social service providers; and agents of economic development—were developed nationally, featuring local variations and targeting many educational outcomes.

Crowson's (2003) review of models of empowerment provides an overview of different themes in the work linking schools and their reform with community development. For example, the "Alliance" model argues that the existing institutions within a community—of which schools are often the most prominent—work together to build the resources available to the community at large.

The "Production" model, on the other hand, sees neighborhoods as centers of production, and schools as one of the important production centers. Much of this work relies on the views of communities as collections of assets (McKnight & Kretzmann, 1993). Neighborhoods use these assets in their zones of production, and schools function as a "basic industry," both an engine of development for the community and a magnet for the attraction of new resources (Driscoll and Kerchner, 1999; Kerchner, 1997). Boyd, Crowson, and Gresson (1997) elaborate the role of educational institutions in this framework with their description of an "enterprise school," which may help in the "regeneration of the school's neighborhood environment" (p. 10).

The essence of this second model is actually co-production between schools and communities (Crowson, 2001). Grass-roots noneducational professionals are empowered to make decisions affecting schooling, and school professionals bring their ability to join community resources (Crowson, 2003). Urban school principals become "stewards of developing communal civic capacity" (Goldring & Hausman, 2001, p. 194). They build partnerships to secure resources, serve on civic stakeholder groups, and create coalitions of community organizations.

A third model of collaboration and empowerment outlined by Crowson encompasses the perspective of regime theory developed by Stone (1989) and others. This view emphasizes the informal networks and arrangements that, together with formal structures, help to provide support for the development of institutions within a community. Here, understanding the narrative context of community institutions and daily activities becomes critical in understanding how reform and development take place (Crowson, 2003; Crowson & Boyd, 2001).

If it is important to understand the unique ways in which each community shapes and sustains institutions, then detailed and specific knowledge of the locale is essential in deciphering relevant power structures. Driscoll (2001) suggests that restoring a sense of place to our understanding of schools and their communities results in greater attention to the physical settings of schools; attention to the ways in which communities and schools define and expand overlapping boundaries; consideration of the multiple cultures and histories that characterize both the place itself and the lives of those who inhabit it; and the development of sustained engagement that permits students to gain the kind of deep knowledge that will inform their understandings in other locations. Schools may play a particularly crucial role in creating and maintaining public spaces that permit communities to enact and interrogate their values (Driscoll, 2004).

Emerging Research Questions Exploring Schools as Agents of Community Development

Community development as a model for the ways in which schools relate to their communities has grown in significance in both policy and research (Mawhinney, 2001). The literature that documents and examines the educational consequences of such models is characterized, however, by a heavy reliance on evaluation studies that often focus on a small set of projects. Although the cumulative effect of these studies is impressive, there is much work to be done to understand the issues facing school leaders who wish to link community development to the improvement of teaching and learning in demonstrable ways.

What evidence do we have that community development initiatives in which schools are central can be linked to better models for student learning? At the theoretical level, there has been substantial justification for improved student learning through strategies for community development. Smith (2002) details the long history of "place-based" education throughout the 20th century, and describes the links between schools that use the community as a context for learning with the concepts of Dewey and others. A body of case study and evaluation research (Melaville, Shah, & Blank, 2003) has begun to document specific educational effects of schools with significant involvement in their communities. Stronger connective links between student performance in school and community development initiatives are beginning to emerge with greater definition (Shirley, 1997). Other case studies, which focus on more than educational outcomes (Pena et al., 2001), are also beginning to provide useful information. Significant work remains, however, in understanding the pathways that connect a sense of place, strong school links with the community, and improved learning.

What professional knowledge is required of school leaders to engage effectively as developers of civic capacity? What school leadership arrangements facilitate the school's ability to undertake its core educational mission in league with community outreach? In an earlier section we suggested that a revised construction of instructional leadership must take into account new conceptions of learning and how it can be fostered. It is also evident that involvement in community development may require professional skills and knowledge to be distributed within the school system in a manner that is not presently the norm. In underperforming schools located in impoverished communities, however, this may be an essential link to improved school outcomes (Noguera, 2003). Moreover, the challenge may be to understand how these outreach activities—normally not the province of school leaders—can be integrated with the kinds of educational activities likely to have effects on learning. The work in school-linked services has demonstrated how difficult authentic collaboration is.

What gauges for efficacy in community outreach should be developed for principals? Goldring and Hausman (2001) found that given extra time in their day, few principals would increase the amount of time they spend on civic engagement activities, even when they saw those activities as important. Perhaps these choices reflect a realization of the scope of the task at hand when one attempts to intervene in communities, especially those plagued by significant social problems. An evaluation of the Ford Foundation's decade-long multimillion-dollar intervention, the Neighborhood and Family Initiative, noted that despite "rhetoric" embued with ideas of "poverty alleviation, neighborhood transformation, and systems change," neighborhoods with a long history of disinvestment could not be expected to turn around quickly (Chaskin, 2000, p. 21). If a foundation's sustained attention and substantial resources produce less than optimum results in neighborhoods, even when collaborative structures are deliberately and thoughtfully created, what is a reasonable criteria by which to judge the efforts by schools and community leaders as they engage in community development? Research that focuses on the midrange outcomes of development and provides longitudinal insights on successful initiatives is essential if we are to construct detailed understandings of what progress looks like over time when such arrangements work for children.

What do we need to know about the pitfalls of this approach for school leaders? Finally, we caution again that little of the research explores the down side of connecting schools and communities, especially around development initiatives that locate schools more firmly in a sense of place and local culture.

We need to know how principals who invest substantial time in developing community relationships integrate these demands with the work of leading instruction in the school, and which activities yield the greatest rewards for student learning. Absent connections between this community work and the teaching and learning activities in the school, such investment may turn attention away from the important work of creating meaningful contexts for learning.

Moreover, local communities with significant cohesion and connection to schools may represent values that some may find incompatible with those of the larger body politic. A singular characteristic of American schools has been their oversight not just by those who use them as consumers but by all in society who have an interest in democratic and able citizenry. We need to see how these broader goals connect with these local initiatives.

METHODOLOGICAL CHALLENGES FOR SCHOLARS

Clearly, there is a great need to embark on an empirical research agenda that can begin to address the wider questions of resituating learning in community, developing social capital for learning, and understanding schools as a sense of place. These foci are markedly different from previous work on school–community relations and raise numerous complex methodological issues. As a recent committee on scientific research in education claimed, "Citizens, business leaders, politicians, and educators want credible information on which to evaluate and guide today's reform and tomorrow's education for all students. . . . [T]hey seek trustworthy, scientific evidence on which to make decisions about education" (Shavelson & Towne, 2002, p. 22).

The empirical research on school principals has not typically met this need in terms of theoretical and methodological complexity (Hallinger & Heck, 1996b). In related areas, such as parental involvement programs (Mattingly et al., 2002) and social capital development (Dika & Singh, 2002), the state of the empirical research base is equally weak. There are also some unique methodological challenges that emerge as a result of broadening and reframing the research questions in the field of school–community leadership.

Understanding Context

One of the challenges in posing a research agenda to study emerging questions linking leadership and community is the complexity of the community context. In fact, in many cases, since community and its interactive networks are the topic of study, researchers would not want to control context. This complexity raises important issues. The first is how to describe, operationalize, and measure the contexts of schools, of communities, and of leadership. Research must capture the uniqueness and interrelated dimensions of these contexts. Research must also be concerned with replicability, generalization, and testing of alternative explanations. We need to consider the trade-offs for each of these two poles, and how we can develop credible and valid representations of these very complicated relationships. A recent effort in this direction is the Design-Based Research Collective (2003). But, as the authors of the National Research Council report point out, "With so many confounding variables in a design study, can the knowledge claims be warranted?" (Shavelson, Phillips, Towne, & Feuer, 2003, p. 27).

Can we move from the richness of context to explore and test alternative explanations and hypotheses? Research that is serious about broadening both the conceptual frame and measurements of such concepts as social capital and community must wrestle with this issue. Delineating contexts and bounding them to provide adequate understanding of what we are measuring may be possible in a classroom without artificially narrowing the scope of study. As soon as we move to more multifaceted contexts, however, such as the school, the community, or distributed leadership, the boundaries and contexts of study become enormous. An obvious first step will be to identify, examine, and describe explicitly the roles of teachers, principals, and community members both in and out of the school engaged in school–community collaborations. This description will also help define broadly the notion of community collaboration and engagement.

The unit of analysis we use when studying community as context is another thorny issue. Do we conceptualize community as experienced differently by individuals (and thus measure it at the individual student or community member level), or is community context and its elements a shared property at the community unit of analysis? We need to explore how individuals respond to similar contexts, and investigate those elements of context that appear to contribute to or hinder learning (Crowson et al., 2002; Honig et al., 2001).

Links to Student Learning: Acknowledging Indirect and Reciprocal Versus Direct Influence

Ultimately, the importance of studying school, community, and leadership is to better understand how to propel teaching for learning. To pursue this agenda faithfully, we need to develop a clearer conceptual road map to drive empirical analyses. Recall the three models of effects delineated by Hallinger and Heck (1996b) in their review of research on the principal's role. The first and most simplistic is a direct effects model, where principal leadership is hypothesized to "actually exert an influence on students apart from other variables within the school" (p. 732). This "black box" view of both schools and leadership does not help advance our understanding of schooling processes or outcomes because community and context are notably absent from the models. More sophisticated models look at complex articulations of "leader effects." They acknowledge that leaders "achieve results through other people" (i.e., moderated effects) and that the nature of the interrelationships between leadership and complex school and community contexts is highly interactive (i.e., reciprocal effects).

None of these are sufficient for our purposes. A recentered research agenda that focuses on community learning in context and leadership requires new theorizing and conceptual work into the nature of the interrelationships and the directions of the effects we are attempting to understand. The conceptual lenses of learning in context, social capital, and schools embued with a sense of place require that we think anew about how to best articulate these research issues. If we are serious about moving away from a school-centric perspective, vibrant conceptual frameworks to guide inquiry must be developed that reflect this view.

Long-Term Versus Short-Term Perspectives on Learning

The large majority of educational leadership and school–community research is cross-sectional in nature, a snapshot of one point in time. Little research has focused on both the long-term and additive effects of various types of learning in and from community. Certainly, curriculum and developmental specialists have spent decades understanding developmentally appropriate instruction and the sequencing of learning goals, content, and assessments for more traditional, school-based subjects. How do children and youth develop learning in the community over time? How does community-centered learning influence child development over time? What roles do schools and leaders undertake to help children develop relationships with and from community beyond a single school year? These questions require longitudinal studies that follow children across contexts. Simultaneously, such studies should follow leaders and school contexts to understand a reciprocal framework of school, learning, and community in time frames that are consistent with key developmental stages of children and youth.

Context is a fluid and even an unstable dynamic, changing over time and influenced by numerous factors, most of which are out of the direct control of the schools or even individual families. What combinations of interactive context elements (e.g., policy interventions, service interventions, retrained professionalism, community involvement, and district leadership) might positively influence in-school learning? What might successful learners draw from their contexts over time that the unsuccessful do not?

Reconceptualizing Learning

In general, measures of student learning are narrowly conceptualized, poorly operationalized, or totally absent from many research endeavors. Beyond improving and broadening traditional measures of student learning, it is most pressing to conceptualize and develop measures of out-of-school learning as well as in-school learning that is community-centered. For example, Honig et al. (2001) discuss the benefits of service learning and community service, two aspects of out-of school learning that are positively related to academic outcomes. The fundamental questions, however, concern how we conceptualize and measure transfer of school learning to everyday settings of home and community in order to explore aspects of authentic learning. How do we conceptualize and measure "learning from community" as important in and of itself? How does learning from community transfer to academic, school-based learning? Finally, how do we study community contexts as learning environments? Attention to these issues leads toward a research agenda that relies on the development of alternative measures of student learning, in and out of school.

LEADERSHIP BEYOND THE HIERARCHY

"By any reasonable standard, public schools have become highly porous hierarchies. The current era of educational reform consists almost entirely of those outside the hierarchy attempting to change those inside," argue Kerchner and McMurran (2001, p. 43). They suggest that leadership in such a highly porous system presents challenges for people throughout these hierarchies, not just for a few at the top.

The new directions required for leading schools and communities to become joint contexts for student learning also demand scholarship that is committed to probing difficult and messy questions. We believe the research on student learning, social capital, and community development are good places from which to launch this endeavor, armed with methodological tools that are matched to this fascinating and challenging task.

CHAPTER 6

How Do Leaders Interpret Conflicting Accountabilities to Improve Student Learning?

William A. Firestone and Dorothy Shipps

Educational leaders have long juggled conflicting accountabilities, but researchers have not. Researchers have explored how educators cope with specific obligations, that is, the legitimate demands made by specific government agencies, local political constituencies, or other entities. For instance, some researchers examine how educators respond to the demands of state tests (Firestone, Schorr, & Monfils, 2004). Others explore how educators address the expectations of local government leaders (Shipps, 2003), and a few studies have examined how leaders respond to market requirements (Fiske & Ladd, 2000).

Rarely do researchers examine the interaction of multiple, simultaneous accountabilities. Yet this question is critical. Even before the recent rise in expectations, educators received conflicting signals that many simply ignored. Critics argued that teachers needed more guidance to achieve improvements in student learning and increased equity. Recognizing this need, Smith and O'Day (1991) argued that state and federal policy should become more coherent. If anything, in the decade since this call for coherence, guidance to educators has become more contradictory.

HOW DO LEADERS INTERPRET CONFLICTING ACCOUNTABILITIES TO IMPROVE STUDENT LEARNING?

Our analysis has two starting points. First, we argue that the problem for educational leaders is to cope with multiple, conflicting accountabilities. The coherence that some analysts have called for has not been achieved. An important challenge for those who seek to promote learning for all students is to determine how to do so in the face of conflicting accountabilities. Research will not help leaders address student needs until studies are designed recognizing that schools and districts are liable to legitimate claims that pull educators in different directions. Second, we suggest that there is no necessary relationship between any particular type of accountability and student achievement. Political accountability, for instance, responds to the demands of constituents who often promote goals other than closing the achievement gap.

To help future researchers address these practical problems, we begin with a typology that identifies five different kinds of accountability. The conditions under which such cross-pressures can improve student learning, and make it more equitable, are unclear. Most research designs have only looked at one source of accountability at a time and have done so from the perspective of the party seeking to steer leaders' behavior. This section highlights the necessity to understand the mix of accountability pressures leaders face in specific schooling situations.

Next, this chapter asks how district leaders interpret conflicting accountabilities. Educational leaders include district administrators, principals, and teachers, but sorting out how each interprets clashing expectations requires understanding the different responsibilities and sources of information of each role. We focus on districts because they have the legal responsibility to respond to external demands and because much of the rest of this volume addresses school-level leaders. After briefly reviewing evidence on how districts influence teaching and contribute to improved and more equitable learning, we present a framework for exploring how leaders acquire knowledge about external accountabilities. Such acquisition is more than passively responding to external pressure. It requires active decisionmaking about which accountabilities to attend to and how to construe them, as well as requiring that leaders resolve the conflicts among them.

This framework leads to our concluding hypothesis: Leaders can contribute to student learning by interpreting external and internal accountabilities to help educators promote a shared sense of ethical obligation, that is, "internal accountability" (Carnoy, Elmore, & Siskin, 2003). This hypothesis links research on leadership and accountability to the mainstream of research on how leaders support instructional improvement (see chapter 2, this volume). How powerful this approach can be, what it looks like in practice, and how the interpretations of multiple leaders are melded into one common vision are all issues to be addressed by those who find this suggested research agenda persuasive.

Multiple Accountabilities

A long-standing meaning of accountability is the commitment to answer to a constituent, superior, or customer for one's performance, primarily by reporting and/or justifying procedures and results. Since even regular reports that follow strict procedures may not ensure improvement, modern use also emphasizes the consequences attached to the reporting requirement. Implicitly, the power of any accountability demand—its ability to influence behavior—is thought to determine which expectations are attended to.

We adapt these widely held understandings in three ways. First, we focus on leaders' obligations to improve student performance and demonstrate increased equity rather than any other purpose to which accountability might direct them. Second, we examine accountability from the leader's perspective, putting various and conflicting duties in context. Third, we include expectations that are not readily externalized and are rarely reported upon, characterizing them as a combination of external and internal accountability, meaning that leaders have accepted professional or moral responsibilities to account for their actions. Thus, our definition encompasses the felt obligation for student performance and demonstrations of equity, including the willingness to provide a justification of outcomes to external parties and/or to oneself, and to absorb the tangible or intangible consequences.

Discussions of accountability often begin with a typology. Ours is broader than usual (see Table 6.1). It compares three external forms of accountability—political, bureaucratic, and market—some of their typical manifestations, presumed objectives,

Table 6.1. Typology of Leaders' Accountabilities

	Type	Manifestations (examples)	Objectives	Leader's Expected Response
External	*Political*			
	Local	Citizen Pressure	Satisfaction	Coalition-Builder
	State/Federal	Legal Mandates	Obedience	Negotiator
	Bureaucratic			
	Process	Regulations	Compliance	Functionary
	Outcome	Goals/Incentives	Alignment	Knowledgeable Advocate
	Market	Competition	Efficiency/ Creativity	Manager/ Entrepreneur
External and Internal	*Professional*	Practice Consensus	Preferred Practice	Expert Educator
	Moral	Beliefs	Value Commitments	Consistent, Empathic Defender of Justice

and the responses that leaders are expected to learn and display. It also includes professional and moral accountability, which we describe as combining external and internal liabilities. We conceptualize these two types using the same categories: as combinations of external sources of pressure and internal compunction.

The typology and our discussion below are intended to reveal that different sources of accountability have distinct manifestations and anticipate divergent outcomes and leader reactions. We hope this framework spurs interest in going beyond the study of single accountability mechanisms as perceived by the party wishing to hold leaders responsible, to the examination of leaders' reactions to multiple expectations in particular contexts.

Political Accountability

The legal demands of political representatives and the spontaneous concerns of local constituents are the primary sources of political accountability. Public schools are established by state law and governed by various federal, state, and local elected and appointed bodies. Responsiveness to local constituents is reflected in elected school boards, parent advisory councils, and PTAs, but also in requests from individual parents, teachers' unions, and local civic and business groups. Increasingly, school leaders are liable to the legislators, governors, and judges who wield state and federal authority to establish schools, delimit their legal status, and determine taxes. These many sources of political activity are often at odds with one another, but together they constitute a single type of accountability that calls upon educational leaders' skills as coalition builders and as creative negotiators. Principals and superintendents are expected to convince disparate political interests that a compromise will satisfy their goals, even as they obey the letter of the law.

Using these skills in the service of teaching and learning is daunting for many school leaders. Early 20th-century reformers sought to take populist politics out of schooling, install civic elites on school boards, and capture the emerging expertise of school leaders. Modern administrators remain acutely responsive to a complex web of constituent groups, politicians, and civic leaders, many of whose demands are not motivated by improved student performance or increased educational equity.

Movement protests of the 1960s and 1970s engaged the federal courts, bringing civil rights legislation and long-term judicial oversight to some districts, law enforcement intervention to others. After busing and magnet schools became routine, new court rulings replaced earlier mandates with versions based on a definition of equity that assumes common standards for all children, but that creates mixed messages for leaders. Intensified court involvement added a thick layer of oversight to that from local citizens, requiring that school leaders learn to step carefully between legal obligations and constituent demands.

Federal and state oversight have also increased. The federal *No Child Left Behind* law is aimed at bolstering states' abilities to sanction or reward schools depending on student performance in several demographic categories. It addresses performance and equity in one set of expectations. Although representing unprecedented federal intervention, this law operates through the states, which have created their own legal demands: higher standards, strengthened school accreditation and certification requirements, and laws to promote fiscal equity and inclusion. State interpretation of federal legislation means that even centrally authorized legal demands are experienced differently from state to state, working against a common account of school leaders' political responsibilities.

Local political demands have also grown more complex. Citizens seeking changes in the curriculum and/or access to decisionmaking have engulfed some school systems, receded, and reemerged (Tyack & Cuban, 1995). Teachers' collective bargaining rights have been legalized in many states, giving unions the power to counter the coalitions that principals and superintendents help assemble among board members and local citizens. Research on civic engagement substantiates the value of coalitions of local political, business, and community groups in sustaining change in urban districts (Stone, Henig, Jones, & Pierannunzi, 2001). Yet improvements in student performance are indiscernible or uneven, leaving analysts to disagree over whether the reason lies in educators' mismatched skills or the inappropriateness of reform ideas (Shipps, 2003). We know too little about how leaders steer civic engagement toward student achievement and equity goals.

Moreover, leaders rarely meet local challenges well. Few urban superintendents learned to negotiate legal requirements while sustaining local confidence when the two clashed in midcentury (Cuban, 1976), and we know little about their political skills since. Principals' responses to conflicting local and state political demands is a recent focus of study. Those responses rarely promote improved teaching and learning (Bizar & Barr, 2001). And recent surveys suggest that political accountability continues to bedevil school leaders, who report being driven out of the field by the combination of political and bureaucratic demands (Public Agenda, 2001).

Bureaucratic Accountability

When late-19th-century urban school reformers wrested schools from political machines, they reorganized them as bureaucracies in which teachers reported to principals and principals to superintendents, who in turn accounted for the whole system to a board of civic elites. Following a long history of top-down, process-oriented bureaucracy in public schooling, the last decade has seen the development of a second form that imposes outcome expectations.

Just as legal mandates changed local political accountability, federal incentives to alter school programs and curricula changed the bureaucratic accountability structure. New funnels of bureaucratic authority grew up around federal compensatory programs spurred by the civil rights agenda. Specialists working in these bureaucracies generated regulations that challenged the line authority of principals and superintendents. Some states developed their own compensatory programs, further fragmenting bureaucratic accountability between state and federal hierarchies. Often these fiefdoms generated resistance or encouraged leaders to "game the system" to attract more benefits, a condition widely deplored as excessive compliance (McLaughlin, 1987).

More recently, bureaucratic accountability sought to eliminate the gaming by rewarding and punishing outcomes. This "new accountability" has been codified in federal and state regulations and incentives over the last two decades. Student performance measured by achievement tests has clearly been the dominant outcome. Coordinated systems of rules and sanctions that align the major processes of schooling (e.g., curriculum, assessment, professional development, hiring, and induction) are supposed to send complementary and mutually reinforcing signals toward the goal of higher student performance (Smith & O'Day, 1991).

New accountability pressures are created by performance evaluations linked to incentives that reward high-performing schools and increase scrutiny on those that perform poorly (Ladd, 1996). The approach is justified by the lack of knowledge about how various schooling inputs (e.g., certified teachers, class sizes) interact to create the outcomes we want. Without reliable research about how to promote learning, outcome orientations are said to be "reasonable" because they leave the daily decision-making to educators (Hannaway, 1996). This new approach includes penalties that cause principals or superintendents to be removed, school or district staff to reapply for their jobs, or schools (sometimes districts) to be taken over by the state. Bureaucratic rewards often consist of relative autonomy in practice. By the 1990s, most states expected leaders to achieve outcome goals to receive routine government resources or in exchange for additional fiscal incentives. School and district leaders are asked to be advocates of performance targets and the improvement steps they require. They are to explain and defend the reward and punishment structures—including the technically difficult measurement instruments that bedevil this new bureaucratic accountability (Linn, Baker, & Betebenner, 2002), and unintended increases in inequity that have already been decried (Orfield & Kornhaber, 2001).

Market Accountability

Market accountability aims to improve schooling through increased competition: between educators for jobs, educators and external service providers for contracts, and schools for students. Competition with alternative providers is expected to increase teaching and learning efficiency, while competition between schools for students and staff encourages instructional innovation. Leaders are expected to become better managers or learn to function as entrepreneurs.

Competition between educational and private sector leaders draws on the view that school systems should function like corporations, with leaders adopting the techniques of scientific management. With market accountability, leaders are expected to treat parents and students as customers and adopt corporate management strategies to get more effort from school employees for the same (or fewer) tax dollars (Shipps, 2003). Market logic dictates that leaders who show improvements in student performance should receive material incentives, while failure leads to removal. Although the effects of bonuses on leaders has not been systematically researched, similar material incentive systems for teachers have not proven effective except when they are provided collectively (O'Day, 2002).

Experiments in outsourcing special education, school support, and school management services come from similar arguments about market efficiencies. Contracting aims to take advantage of private sector expertise, while encouraging leaders to become more efficient and creative managers. Research has noted a lack of real savings (Hannaway, 1999), but has not yet explained whether the core assumption is the intended performance spur.

Another form of market accountability aiming "to provide signals and incentives similar to those that might emerge from a market system" has produced various forms of school choice (Clotfelter & Ladd, 1996). The idea has been justified as a way to provide children with access to the schooling their parents want, rather than that which local civic elites and governments provide. The concept developed into a bargain. Individual schools are substantially deregulated; in return they are made subject to a combination of competition and binding contractual obligations. This trade is expected to promote entrepreneurialism and reduced performance gaps. Charter schools are deregulated in exchange for meeting contractual obligations, usually including student performance targets (Fuller, 2000). Voucher schools receive a direct subsidy for every student enrolled, and are less regulated than charter schools. They are expected to reorient leaders to parent satisfaction, a goal that may be sufficient to sustain schools judged more harshly by student performance and equity criteria (Schneider, Teske, & Marschall, 2000).

Evidence suggests that neither charters nor vouchers meet high student performance criteria for most students and that both charters and vouchers tend to exacerbate inequality (Witte, 2000). Although early evidence also suggests that markets impose hitherto unforeseen obligations on leaders and that leadership turnover is high (Henig, Holyoke, Lacireno-Paquet, & Moser, 2001), little systematic study clarifies whether and when the desired leadership behaviors occur. As important, we know little about how leaders in "regular" public schools experience market competition.

Professional Accountability

The external component of professional accountability comes from consensus among school leaders about what constitutes effective practice. This consensus is formally enforced through accreditation processes. But professional views of good practice are also subject to informal peer pressure and expectations internalized by individual leaders, perhaps as a result of their training or prior experience. School and district leaders demonstrate their professional commitments by the extent to which their actions coincide with current standards of expert knowledge.

Professional accountability also has deep roots. One response to the bureaucratization of schooling in the early 20th century was to propose that school and district leadership become distinct professions with specialized research-based knowledge and experience-honed judgment that could be applied to specific contexts by its practitioners. Educators created a required training regimen, certification requirements, and professional associations that gave guidance for nearly every problem an educational leader might encounter.

Even so, for much of the 20th century the shared identity among educational leaders depended as much on being farm-bred, Anglo-Saxon, Protestant males with the social standing to informally socialize with civic elites (Tyack & Hansot, 1982). It is no longer possible to assume that communal professional values will flow from shared life experiences: although underrepresented, women and ethnic and racial minorities have acquired leadership roles. The school leaders' professional associations (e.g., Interstate School Leaders Licensure Consortium, Education Leadership Constituent Council) are currently updating performance standards to respond to new leadership challenges, and to new assumptions about who becomes a leader. Yet the professional consensus remains weak.

The demands of instruction continue to spur disparate calls for improvements in leaders' professionalism. Some insist that school and district leaders should privilege teachers' knowledge and share leadership responsibilities by encouraging teachers' self-direction and promoting collaboration while recruiting those who fit the organizational culture (Johnson, 1990). These views of leadership professionalism draw by analogy on the importance of solidarity to teachers' professional practice (Darling-Hammond, 1996). A different approach argues for a "division of labor": school leaders relying on professional accountability to facilitate the improvement of instruction and district leaders identifying and monitoring problem areas as part of their outcomes-based bureaucratic responsibilities (O'Day, 2002).

We understand too little about how professional accountability currently works for school leaders—or its power over them at any level of the school system—to confidently propose any one version as a solution to the problems of low-performing and inequitable schooling.

Moral Accountability

Moral accountability assumes that leaders have internalized a socially encouraged value system that guides their practice. Personal integrity, adherence to personal and communal values, and empathy for others are expected to be the primary guides for behavior. Among the values that support moral accountability, we highlight social justice, which is central to American education, and supported by many external sources.

Moral accountability has its origin in the earliest days of American education. Nineteenth-century school leaders were quite moralistic about their passion for the public schools. The moral accountability school leaders inherited from this tradition allows them to determine which broadly shared touchstones (e.g., religious doctrine, vision of human nature) will draw their allegiance. But it does not imply that moral leadership is a matter of personal taste. Instead, moral accountability is proposed as an antidote to other forms when they fail to embrace fairness and justice.

Unlike other forms of accountability, moral leadership inspires internal compunctions (Sergiovanni, 1992). It has been called an act of resistance to "thoughtless banality, technical rationality, [and] carelessness" (Greene, 1995). These are felt obligations to protect values and social ideals in the face of rational opposition.

Reliance on moral accountability as a last resort assumes that better schooling outcomes (if not always higher test scores) will result from school leaders' and their followers' shared commitments. Some researchers see modern Catholic schools as exemplars of value-driven education, finding commitments to the common good in these institutions that are seldom replicated in public schooling (Bryk, Lee, & Holland, 1993). Trust (Bryk & Schneider, 2002) and caring (Noddings, 1992) have been identified as crucial to meeting others' expectations in public schools, but so too has social imagination developed in dialogue across differences by way of artistic narrative (Greene, 1995).

Social justice represents an enduring extension of American ideals for a common public education for all classes—"good enough for the richest, open to the poorest" (Reese, 2000). Today, education is sometimes called the modern religion, comprised of universalized "doctrines or rules providing meaningful linkages of humans . . . to this cosmos" (Meyer, 2000). Two key tenets of the American educational cosmology are that much information about the universe is ultimately knowable and that *all* individuals should be taught a complex common curriculum. The idea forms the ethical basis for the *No Child Left Behind* law and has adherents from both ends of the political spectrum. Moral accountability thus embraces its bureaucratic, market-based, professional, or political alternatives whenever they are useful to sustaining a widely held view of distributive justice.

In other social justice terms, schooling is expected to counteract the squalor amidst comfort that is identified by some as the global capitalist economy's dark side, as a natural condition of life by others. In this view, low-socioeconomic-status, disabled, rural, or inner-city children, and women in general, have a right to high quality education because it signals their readiness to transcend class, hold high-status jobs, or earn a decent living, and it gives them the tools to critique the social structure that places them at the bottom (Freire, 1983).

However, research in the tradition of social justice focuses less on leaders' moral accountabilities than on describing and explaining how disparities arise from economic circumstances exacerbated by unequal schooling. Our understanding of accountability could benefit from analysis that asks how moral accountability is manifest in schools deemed successful for different kinds of disadvantaged populations. (Chapter 8 in this volume provides a thorough conceptual analysis of moral leadership.)

This recitation of forms of accountability has identified many areas of weak research. Too little is known about how leaders experience, interpret, and respond to many forms of accountability. Accountability research rarely hones in on the improvement of teaching and learning or on equity. Another significant issue rarely addressed is how multiple accountabilities interact with one another in the context of schools and districts.

Conflicts Between Accountabilities

Leaders experience many accountability claims simultaneously, making the task of creating coherence out of mixed signals vastly more complex than it appears to most policymakers, advocates, or researchers. These obligations often conflict, pinning education leaders between constituents and superiors, professional standards and public expectations, market forces and regulators. A few examples should clarify.

Superintendents most often cite accountability conflicts between the political demands of their local communities and the attention required by state and federal bureaucratic mandates. For example, most state departments of education have asked superintendents to show regular increases in student achievement, anticipating that they will redirect fiscal resources and staff to that goal. This expectation ignores local political demands. Among the first to hire aspiring immigrants, African-Americans, and other minorities, public schools provide a well-documented pathway to social mobility for adults. Jobs and school contracts become rewards for unions, community groups, and local politicians. In response to these cross-pressures, superintendents may retain employees with dated qualifications instead of embracing new technologies they believe are needed to reach student performance goals, or they may press ahead, risking the loss of local support and the ability to sustain change (Fuller et al., 2003).

Professional accountability clashes with bureaucratic accountability when agency functionaries mistrust professional standards of good practice. For instance, at least 27 state departments currently threaten to sanction low-performing schools or students if they do not raise their test scores in short order. Until sanctions are administered, most schools leave local educators to figure out how to raise scores with existing resources. Yet current professional standards encourage leaders to build the instructional capacity of teachers and the self-confidence of low-achieving students, both of which take new resources and much time. The too frequent compromise includes both teaching to the test and educational triage, in which leaders show quick improvements by focusing limited resources on students whose tests scores are very near the mark and encourage poor performers to leave school, strategies that meet neither professional nor bureaucratic goals (O'Day, 2002).

Interacting market-based accountability and bureaucratic mandates can encourage other perverse consequences. Leaders of charter schools compete for families based on their school mission and its effectiveness. Good schools are expected to attract clients and support, while bad ones go out of business. District leaders or other agents also use their bureaucratic authority to regulate charter schooling, with the ultimate sanction of pulling a school's charter. But closing a charter school, even when it fails to meet its obligations for academic performance, conflicts with leaders' efforts to sustain a community of parents and teachers who are invested in an educational mission. The risk of disaffection among school customers is apparently not worth the bureaucratic benefit of maintaining high standards when the market does not. By 2001, nearly all charter schools were renewed, meaning most charter school principals never met a market test of accountability and district leaders lost the high ground of enforcing outcomes-based bureaucratic standards (Bulkley, 2001).

If these examples of conflicting accountabilities are not isolated incidents, and we suspect they are not, much more needs to be known about how they interact and where and when they are most likely to occur before we can hope to construct coherence in accountability systems that leaders face.

LOCAL RESPONSES
TO EXTERNAL ACCOUNTABILITIES

This section examines how leaders enact accountabilities. We focus on district leadership for two reasons. First, it receives less attention than school leadership. Second, there may be a misalignment between the design of accountability mechanisms and the way districts work. Much past work questions whether district leaders can influence teaching and learning, yet many external accountabilities are directed toward districts as if they do have such influence. In almost all states, local school districts are

- responsible through their school boards to voters,
- the first line of response to state and federal accountability demands, and
- the major conduit for expectations from the larger professional community.

Such accountabilities are misplaced if district leaders' influence over teaching and learning is in fact seriously limited.

After questioning district influence, we move to the central question: using an information processing perspective, we ask how educational institutions make sense of external accountabilities.

Can Districts Influence Teaching?

Past work provides a mixed picture of districts' potential for influencing teaching. The two arguments suggesting that district influence is limited focus on teacher isolation and the poor alignment of influence mechanisms. The first is that teachers can close their classroom doors and ignore efforts to persuade them to change practice. The original research supporting this perspective (Lortie, 1975) was carefully replicated (Cohn & Kottkamp, 1993). While this research highlights teachers' general imperviousness to influence, the research on principal leadership suggests that those closer to the teacher have some potential for overcoming teacher insularity (see chapter 2, this volume). Operating from farther away, district officials may have less influence.

The other argument against district influence is based on the confused pattern of numerous, poorly aligned influences on teaching, each of which is difficult for the district to control. This argument is like our argument that formal leaders face numerous, conflicting accountability pressures. A recent review lists over 20 "pathways" for influencing teaching that focus on such broad issues as supervising and training teachers, curriculum and assessment, organizing the system, and supporting students (Knapp et al., 2003). Pathways such as providing social support for students affect teaching very indirectly. With others, district influence is shared. For instance, the district may have some control over student assessment because it can mandate what tests are used, but it must share influence with states that require the use of their own tests and teachers who determine informal assessment. Such examples suggest that districts independently control few powerful means for influencing teaching and learning.

While past research offers a mixed view of district leaders' potential influence, a few recent studies of districts unusually successful in raising student achievement suggest more potential for district instructional leadership than pessimists thought. In these studies, districts influenced teaching through personal leadership and shared norms, as well as the orchestration of such policy pathways as textbooks, curriculum guides, and professional development. Normative influences include the creation of a district-level professional community with a strong culture emphasizing the primacy of student instruction for all units, including the financial office (Hightower, Knapp, Marsh, & McLaughlin, 2002).

Another part of the pattern is district leaders' effective coordination of many partially controlled pathways to influence instruction. These include hiring and firing principals and teachers; orchestrated, long-term professional development; curriculum alignment; and using student outcome data to guide decisionmaking (Hightower et al., 2002). District leaders use these pathways for several purposes: signaling what is important to the district culture, problem-solving, and building the capacity to meet the challenge set by the culture. These more successful districts have a distinct element of top-down leadership, but they also seem to encourage local initiative that supports the basic direction set for the district.

These case studies suggest that substantial, positive district influence over teaching is possible. However, studies vary in the persuasiveness of the link between district practices and instructional outcomes. A great deal must still be learned about how district influence is achieved under such varying conditions as district size, student composition, community wealth, and other contextual factors, and whether effective district influence can be routine or will continue to be, as these studies suggest, the exception.

How Do Districts Make Sense of Accountability Demands?

When districts influence teaching and learning, their leaders' interpretations of accountability demands become more consequential. Most past research assumed that external accountabilities drive internal decisionmaking, but some district leaders aggressively use external accountability pressures to justify internally initiated changes (Fuhrman, Clune, & Elmore, 1988). This active use suggests that environments are "enacted." Enactment implies choice in the aspects of the environment to which leaders attend. It also suggests interpretive processes through which leaders and others construct different environments in what appear to be the same circumstances (Huber, 1996). Debate about school leaders' leeway to enact environments, combined with limited empirical research, suggests the need for research on how accountability demands are interpreted.

To generate questions about how districts enact their environments, we borrow Huber's (1996) model of knowledge acquisition in organizations and apply it to the interpretation of accountabilities. This model highlights the problem of building a common interpretation when knowledge comes from many sources and is held by many people inside the organization.

The model's processes of knowledge acquisition, distribution, and interpretation appear more rational than turns out to be the case. Huber (1996) is careful to refer to them as processes, not stages. In fact, these processes often overlap in the messy manner suggested by Cohen, March, and Olsen's (1972) garbage can model. Moreover, the interpretation process provides considerable opportunity for the nonrational aspects of collective sense making to emerge.

Knowledge acquisition. Knowledge initially comes into a district through scanning the environment. The intensity of scanning can vary from high vigilance to modest sensitivity to anomalies. Scanning can be supplemented by a focused search to get information to solve specific problems. Environmental searching is carried out primarily by formal gatekeepers with ties to specific elements in the environment (Huber, 1996).

There has been little research on how broadly direct access to information about specific accountabilities is spread throughout schools and districts. Who learns first about what kinds of demands? Superintendents appear to be sensitive to demands from the school board and the community more generally. Principals may get the most information about parents served by their schools. Central office curriculum and content specialists learn first about state standards and assessments. Student group specialists—i.e., Title I or special education directors—know about policies related to those groups. Central office staff may also get the most information about professional accountability expectations in their areas.

Larger districts may have more central office roles with greater access to many sources of bureaucratic and professional information in their areas of expertise (Hannaway & Kimball, 2001). Yet in some small rural districts, teachers taking university courses or participating in a professional development program bring information about professional accountability issues to colleagues and superiors (Hightower et al., 2002). Such teachers are an important, but erratic, source of information. Consistent access to professional information probably depends on the presence of positions with time to develop networks to the local community, state agencies, and professional associations. These people probably also have the best contact with sources of information about state and federal accountability demands. They are often found in larger districts.

It is not clear who has the most information about relevant market conditions, but superintendents, financial officers, and board members are candidates. School board members and principals may also know about local political accountability, and their presence depends less on district size.

Certain kinds of information are also more broadly available than others. New professional expectations about good practice are probably less readily accessed than information coming from the public media. Once accountability demands become known to someone in a school or district, that information has to be distributed and interpreted.

Knowledge distribution. Few people in the district understand what the whole district knows because information is located in inaccessible or unexpected places. Knowledge appears to travel through some internal pathways better than others. Bureaucratic information travels down the hierarchy easily when leaders near the top want it to (Huber, 1996). So does some political information, but other information may spread broadly in spite of leaders' efforts to control it. Knowledge at the bottom of the hierarchy may also remain hidden. An elementary teacher's deep understanding about the National Council of Teachers of Mathematics standards and their implications for teaching in the primary grades may not be known to many district decisionmakers or even fellow teachers.

We need to know a great deal more about what characteristics affect the transmission of accountability information. Three characteristics seem pertinent. The first is the complexity of that knowledge. Information about the percentage of children who must score at a "proficient" level on a state test to avoid a state take-over seems easier to communicate than understandings about how to help children achieve "proficiency".

The second relevant characteristic is the urgency attached to the information. Urgency can be increased by the threat of credible bureaucratic sanctions—including high stakes directly linked to assessments—but also by more diffuse means, including fear of political repercussions from the community such as failure to pass a school budget. A mix of potential punishments, the strength of ties between state and district, and political culture all affect the attention that districts give to different external accountability demands.

A third crucial factor for sharing information is the density of networks within schools and districts. The few studies of school networks, informal links between teachers and principals within schools, suggest that denser networks with principals in central positions facilitate sharing information about effective practices (Friedkin & Slater, 1994). We know less about district networks, but they appear to be sparse, especially across central office departments (Spillane, 1998b). While denser networks should facilitate sharing accountability information, we know very little about how such networks develop, are organized, and changed.

Interpretation. Interpretation is the process through which information is given meaning and through which shared understanding and conceptual schemes are developed (Huber, 1996). At issue here is not just the meaning of various external accountability demands. Also important are how to weigh demands, relate them to each other, and strengthen or weaken links between those demands and leaders' views of purpose and means for achieving purposes. Interpretations influence ways of relating among adults and between adults and students.

Interpretation is much more complex and much less rational than most accountability theories would lead one to believe. Conflicting accountabilities and preexisting beliefs combine in an intricate calculus.

As an example of an interpretation of several accountability demands, one superintendent doubted that his district would be sanctioned by his state for low test scores. He did worry that low scores would undermine public confidence and impede budget passage. His understanding of the state standards and professional definitions of effective teaching in some areas was rather limited. To the extent that he understood state standards, he did not support them. Thus, he communicated to his staff the political importance of raising test scores without support for some of the innovations that standards advocates wanted to accompany the state's assessments. The central office staff communicated that interpretation to others throughout the district (Fairman & Firestone, 2001).

This example illustrates how the interpretation of conflicting professional bureaucratic and political accountability demands when filtered through personal beliefs can lead to interpretations that the designers of accountability systems may not support. As we traced the influence processes throughout the district, this case also reinforced our earlier conclusion that top district leadership can substantially influence interpretations of policy and, through those interpretations, practice.

A key question is how interpretations are distributed. The research on school effectiveness argues that uniformity of such beliefs as the primacy of student learning, high expectations for all students, and collaboration among staff in the service of those ends promotes student learning (Reynolds & Teddlie, 2000). An alternative view is that it is important to have a shared sense of purpose but also a wide variety of knowledge and beliefs that may help implement that vision. Some districts appear to have successfully raised student achievement by developing a culture that focuses on instructional improvement but by also using the diverse knowledge of available staff to learn how to improve teaching (Elmore, 1997).

Another important issue is how interpretations are influenced. Leadership is important here, but formal leadership is often contested. Moreover, leaders rarely provide a fully united front, as past research on district leaders' interpretations of accountability policies illustrates (Spillane, 1998b). Research that examines how shared interpretations develop can fruitfully draw on two broad theoretical approaches.

One is cultural. Norms about sharing and privacy may affect the spread of information. So may interpretations that suggest which accountability demands are important. Through these interpretations, moral accountability may influence the spread of information. The research on transformational leadership (Leithwood, Jantzi, & Steinbach, 1999) suggests that leaders can use a variety of more or less symbolic means to generate strong, shared norms and a sense of purpose. However, transformational leadership processes remain murky in schools, and even less is known about them at the district level. Moreover, most analyses of vision development through transformational leadership have not been linked to the interpretation of accountability demands, nor have many been done of districts.

District leaders who create a culture focusing on the continuous improvement of instruction appear to generate a demand for information from several sources, including test data and knowledge about teaching that comes from local inquiry, and encourage interpretation of external accountabilities to fit the culturally dominant view (Hightower et al., 2002). Where leaders focus more narrowly on getting scores up, inquiry about instruction may be less common and test data may be used differently.

The other approach, the micropolitical, focuses on power and negotiation (Blase, 1993). The cognitive approaches that are becoming more prominent in research on leadership (see chapters 3 and 4 in this volume) sometimes ignore the conflicts that develop within schools and districts about interpreting accountability demands and other issues. The micropolitical perspective explicitly addresses this critical dimension of the interpretive process. Formal authority confers on its incumbents considerable control over what information is shared and what is suppressed as well as the right to determine official interpretations. Yet teachers and others also have their own resources coming from such diverse sources as the power of unions, informal networks, and the capacity to close the door to one's classroom and proceed in many areas as one prefers. This power can successfully resist top leaders' interpretations.

Local interpretations determine the extent to which people acquiesce to specific accountability demands. Acquiescence is only one possible response. Others include compromise, avoidance, defiance, and manipulation (Oliver, 1991). The ways in which superintendents try to manipulate school boards representing local accountability demands have been extensively documented (Burlingame, 1988). The symbolic adoption of policies without following through on implementation is a form of avoidance. Even when the challenge to state policy comes not from opposition but misunderstanding, interpretations develop that represent degrees of integration of new practice with old (Coburn, 2004). The partial response to state standards where teachers adopt specific instructional procedures but accommodate them to their old modes of teaching is a common compromise in the face of new testing regimes (Firestone et al., 2004).

INTERNAL ACCOUNTABILITY, ACHIEVEMENT, AND EQUITY

The complexity of conflicting accountabilities and their openness to local interpretation leads to the primary hypothesis of this chapter. That is, educational leaders can contribute to greater and more equitable student learning by building a sense of *internal accountability* for such learning. External accountabilities contribute to student learning to the extent that leaders (formal and informal) use them to build interpretations that emphasize the importance of such learning. We offer this suggestion as a hypothesis for future research rather than a guideline for action. There has been little direct research on internal accountability, although related work suggests that the hypothesis has promise.

A small recent body of research suggests that internal accountability, a combination of shared norms—i.e., moral accountability—and peer-enforced professional accountability, may be more important than external accountabilities in moving schools toward positive student outcomes. Newmann, King, and Rigdon (1997) argue that internal accountability occurs where

> essential components of accountability [a]re generated largely within a school staff. Staff identify clear standards for student performance, collect . . . information to inform themselves about their levels of success, and exert . . . strong peer pressure within the faculty to meet the goals.

The idea of internal accountability is attractive because it makes professional and moral leadership explicit and defensible. Extant definitions emphasize a shared culture with strong professional norms governing expectations for students. They also suggest a well-developed capacity for teachers to collaborate around shared values. Thus this concept is congruent with the effective schools research (Purkey & Smith, 1983; Reynolds & Teddlie, 2000) and studies linking strong school professional communities with improved student performance (Newmann & Associates, 1996). It also fits with the research on transformational leadership, which suggests that leaders could promote this sense of internal accountability (Leithwood et al., 1999). However, at this point exploration of the concept consists of a couple of projects and a few cases (Carnoy, Elmore, & Siskin, 2003).

This line of work raises several important questions. One is whether internal accountability contributes to deeper and more equitable student learning. Few, if any, studies have attempted to operationalize the concept in ways that would link it to student outcomes. Some existing literature suggests that internal accountability is easier to develop in schools serving a higher socioeconomic student body.[1]

Moreover, internal accountability (like external accountability) may focus on different outcomes. It may be more feasible to promote a sense of accountability for order in a school than for high-quality student learning for all students. In fact, schools may develop internal accountability systems that promote low and inequitable expectations (Carnoy et al., 2003). It is critical to understand local definitions of accountability and how leadership contributes to internal accountability for high standards for all students, especially in the most challenging contexts.

So, how do external accountabilities promote or undermine internal accountability for student learning for all students? This question is especially important to ask about external accountabilities that are intended to promote student achievement by contributing to internal capacity. The evidence to date is that the theory behind state accountability systems is wrong. That theory was that external accountability—in the form of state standards, assessments, and sanctions—was necessary to build internal accountability. It now appears that schools do not respond effectively to external accountability unless they have the requisite capacity and sense of internal accountability. Moreover, sanctions that are too strong may work against the development of strong internal accountability that supports learning for all students (Carnoy et al., 2003; Newmann et al., 1997).

RESEARCH METHODS

This chapter asks two broad questions. First, how do accountabilities—separately and together—affect school and district leaders to create pressures for action? Second, how do leaders make sense of and act on accountability demands in ways that promote increased and more equitable student learning? Notwithstanding strong pressures from outside, internal, shared moral and professional accountability appear crucial to improving and equalizing student learning. While there is preliminary evidence, mapping the terrain may produce even more nuanced questions. How do leaders foster strong internal accountability? Is it so rare as to be unachievable in the complex accountability environments of most public schools?

These issues are best studied in natural settings; experimental methods and planned interventions are rarely appropriate. They may add to accountability pressures but will not clarify those that already exist or how accountabilities are interpreted.

Several methodologies may be especially helpful for clarifying how accountabilities are interpreted and enacted locally. Case studies can identify local interpretations and how they are constructed and distributed. Case studies also can explore how external actors (e.g., elected officials, parents, community organizations, bureaucrats, business executives) envision the responsibilities of school leaders and how leaders make sense of and act on the signals sent to them. For most settings we expect that such research would surface multiple and conflicting accountabilities—different arguments about what is needed and why. An institutional examination might surface shared interpretations that structure the understandings and actions considered legitimate by groups of school or district leaders. It might also explore how leaders negotiate their interpretations and communicate them to others. Longitudinal analysis can examine change or continuity in these interpretations and how leaders shape interpretations over time.

Some case studies should be conducted comparatively to assess how accountabilities and responses to them differ across contexts. For example, comparing accountabilities in suburban and urban districts subject to the same state and federal mandates may help explain why they often respond differently to similar mandates. How different state political cultures affect local political accountability norms or how variations in market structures shape accountability demands and local responses are other interesting comparisons. A mixture of interviews and records can create historical cases that permit comparison across policies and changing cultural contexts. Longitudinal studies that track changes in logics of action are one possible outcome.

Quantitative methods, including surveys of leaders and followers, can clarify the accountabilities that are perceived to be important across settings and where accountabilities are believed to reinforce or contradict each other. Surveys can explore the distribution of beliefs that shape the interpretation of accountabilities and can clarify the distribution of power and resources within and across schools and districts that influence who attends to which accountabilities.[2] Surveys can also reveal variations in sensitivity to accountabilities depending on the leader's position and policy context.

Cutting across the qualitative/quantitative distinction, network analysis can be used in both case study and survey research (Scott, 2000). It is especially useful for tracking information flows within and between districts and other external sources of accountability demands. The mathematical tools developed for network analysis provide precise analyses of whether the coupling within districts is loose or tight, and the ways in which information about accountabilities travels inside and outside of districts.

Other methods may also prove useful. Two crucial questions should guide the design of future research on educational accountabilities. First, does the design move beyond research that tracks individual accountability pressures and look at the interaction of accountabilities within schools and districts? Second, does the design take the next step to trace the relationship between leaders' interpretations of accountabilities and student learning? At that point the study of interpretations of accountabilities intersects with the broader study of how educational leaders contribute to increased student learning and educational equity.

NOTES

The authors wish to thank Larry Cuban and Karen Seashore Louis for their suggested improvements to an earlier version of this chapter. The remaining defects are the sole responsibility of the authors.

1. Carnoy and colleagues (2003) conducted a study of 15 schools in 4 states. A major purpose of the study was to explore how "better positioned schools"—i.e., those with stronger internal accountability—and "targeted schools"—i.e., those with weaker internal accountability—responded to state standards. They also examined achievement changes in those schools. Although they do not report on student composition of their schools directly, the case data available indicate that their better positioned schools generally had a higher-SES student body than their targeted schools. The relationship between student composition and the nature of internal accountability needs more exploration, but if strong internal accountability is linked to high student socioeconomic status, using this idea to promote equity may be an uphill battle.

2. Zehava Rosenblatt of Haifa University is currently developing scales to measure leaders' perceptions of the accountabilities they face.

CHAPTER 7

How Does Leadership Promote Successful Teaching and Learning for Diverse Students?

Pedro Reyes and Lonnie Wagstaff

Great variation exists among schools in the United States in terms of the quality and type of education they provide their students. This variation can best be understood in relationship to the multiple settings in which schools exist and function. These settings are as broad as geographical regions of the country or as specific as school districts within states or neighborhoods within school districts. In these settings, powerful contextual variables such as race, ethnicity, social class, teacher quality, and leadership skills strongly influence the kind and quality of education available to students.

The crux of our argument is that in such a wide range of schools, leadership is a most powerful intervening variable and can be the determining variable for whether schools are successful or not with their students, especially those from diverse backgrounds. Our argument is predicated on our own research and experience with schools (Reyes, Scribner, & Scribner, 1999); what we have observed and discussed with school leaders in various contexts (such as the Houston Annenberg Project) about high academic expectations, teacher performance, and student achievement; and our reading of the literature and research on the subject. Our stance is that student success is highly dependent on principal leadership. More specifically, we believe that the leadership ability and leadership values of the principal determine in large measure what transpires in a school, and what transpires in a school either promotes and nourishes or impedes and diminishes student academic success.

In this chapter, we examine the nexus between leadership and student achievement and raise salient questions about what the future portends for students from diverse backgrounds who attend public schools.

DIVERSITY

Diversity in schools refers to the ethnographic and demographic composition of the individuals and groups who matriculate or work there. Diversity is a complex, multidimensional concept that is usually freighted with real or imagined qualities that often intensify perceptions and evoke strong reactions. Diversity in American education is not a new phenomenon. American culture has always been heterogeneous even as it desired homogeneity. What is new is an approach to diversity that strives for an equitable pluralism that works to break down social barriers.

An example of this shift in our approach to diversity can be found in the discussion of diversity in higher education. A *New York Times* article (Rimer, 2002) titled "Colleges Find Diversity Is Not Just Numbers" helps in placing diversity in perspective and understanding its complexity. The article noted that in the 1980s, colleges had begun establishing diversity deans, ethnic studies courses, and ethnic and affinity houses to help minority students feel more at home on campus. However, today goals have changed and most discussions and programs now focus on breaking down the barriers between students of different backgrounds. Dartmouth College is among the leading institutions advocating this change in how colleges and universities approach diversity. This change emanates from an internal college report, which stated that over the years many minority students have actually felt damaged by the climate at Dartmouth. Specifically, the report stated, "To hear again so personally and repeatedly from students of color, women of all races, and gay, lesbian or bisexual students who felt hurt, unvalued and ultimately less important to the mission of the college than others was searing indeed" (Rimer, 2002). Moreover, Bowen and Bok (1998) cited data showing that graduates of colleges and universities attribute a great deal of their ability to get along and work efficiently with people of different racial and cultural backgrounds to their experiences in diverse settings in college. It has become clear that it is not enough just to place everyone on the same campus and thus denote the campus as "diverse." Higher education institutions continue to work to set up environments where diversity enriches the learning experience for all the students while at the same time providing nurturing environments for students who have historically been marginalized.

Most K–12 schools do not have the luxury of control that institutions of higher education can exert on their environments. This lack of control often leads to inaction when addressing the issue of diversity. Most school policies surrounding diversity have either taken the form of assimilation or basic tolerance (Spring, 2001). Several decades ago the concept of a "melting pot," which touted the blending of student differences, was a pervasive goal of K–12 schools. But skin color proved a more difficult, if not impossible, characteristic to blend. In response to this assimilation, many groups who were proud of their cultural heritage resisted efforts to be blended into forms of artificial sameness (Spring, 2001).

Over time, American K–12 schools have grudgingly reached a point where diversity is accepted in the makeup of the student population and professional staff. Court decisions and federal laws such as the two Supreme Court judgments in the *Brown vs. Board of Education* case and the Civil Rights Act of 1964 have pushed K–12 schools toward the acceptance of diversity. Schools were forced to accept many different students into their halls, but unfortunately they were not forced to create a supportive environment for all of their students.

While the national policy toward minority groups in America has shifted from segregation to benign neglect, the demographics of the nation have changed in important ways. According to the National Center for Educational Statistics, the population of minority groups as a percentage of the school population has been rising. In 1986 nationally, white students comprised 70.4% of the students enrolled in public schools while African-American, Hispanic, Asian-American, and American Indian students made up 16.1, 9.9, 2.8, and .09%, respectively. By 2000 white students only accounted for 61.2% of students enrolled in public schools nationally, while African-American, Hispanic, Asian-American, and American Indian students made up 17.2, 16.3, 4.1, and 1.2%, respectively. In 2000, school enrollment in Texas and California represented 22.3% of the national public K–12 enrollment, and white students accounted for fewer than half of these students (NCES Digest of Educational Statistics Tables and Figures, 2002). As diversity increases, the dangers of approaching diversity from the current assimilation model are becoming clear to all participants in the schools (Ladson-Billings, 1994).

We see diversity as a multidimensional concept that includes not only race, class, and gender, but also physical capability, language, sexual identity, age, and religion. As with the issues of race and ethnicity, schools were forced to serve students of varying physical abilities. Two court cases, *Pennsylvania Association for Retarded Children v. Commonwealth of Pennsylvania* in 1971 and *Mills v. Board of Education of the District of Columbia* the following year, assured that the schools must serve all children regardless of physical capability in accordance with the Fourteenth Amendment.

Another dimension of diversity in our schools is the issue of sexual identity. As Macgillivray (2001) noted, "The majority of openly identifying gay, lesbian, bisexual, transgender, and queer/questioning students experience significant levels of violence, harassment, and abuse in American schools" (p. 3). Schools have the responsibility to stop this violence and harassment and can be sued under Title IX for failure to protect a student from sexual harassment (Macgillivray, 2001).

Adding to the complexity is the fact that different people within the school have different visions of what diversity means and how it affects social boundaries. A fall 2002 survey conducted by the Southern Poverty Law Center (Carnes, 2003) asking teachers and students around the country to take a hard look at the social boundaries in their schools produced some interesting patterns:

1. Of the first 1,000 students, 53% described their schools as "quick to put people in categories."
2. Of the first 1,000 teachers, 56% rated their schools as "welcoming to all kinds of people."
3. According to the students, the top three factors that create group boundaries at school are style (60%), athletic achievement (53%), and appearance (52%); the students cited race and ethnicity at 25% and 18%, respectively.
4. From the teachers' perspective, academic achievement ranked as the top influence on boundaries among students (64%), followed by athletic achievement (59%); the teachers rated ethnicity at 50% and race at 42%.
5. When asked about crossing boundaries, students rated those of appearance (17%) and style (16%) as the most difficult to overcome.
6. On the same question, teachers cited race (20%) and income (19%) as the biggest social hurdles for students.
7. Regarding boundaries among their colleagues, teachers and staff pointed to beliefs as the strongest factor (52%), as well as the toughest boundary to cross (24%).
8. The two groups agreed on one count: students (68%) and teachers (77%) named the cafeteria as the school setting where social boundaries are most clearly drawn (Carnes, 2003).

Obviously there is a difference in how students and teachers perceive diversity in their schools. Students focused on style and appearance, while teachers focused on race and academic achievement.

Social boundaries are walls of separation and isolation that have developed in schools. It is interesting to note that students in the survey were aware that their schools were "quick to put people in categories," which is to say that efficiency practices, such as tracking, ability grouping, and degree plans, used in schools to deal with a diverse set of students tend to separate rather than integrate. Although teachers think of their schools as welcoming, they do notice the categorization and isolation that school practices have on students. In item 4 teachers note that the largest social barrier for students is academic achievement. In most schools tracking and ability grouping often foster these academic achievement barriers among students and tend to disproportionately divide students along racial lines (Scheurich & Skrla, 2003). Teachers recognize that although academic achievement is the largest social barrier, the most important hurdle for crossing that barrier is race, as shown in item 6. Lastly, it was agreed that the cafeteria was the place where these social barriers were most evident. This is important to note because it shows that in un-regulated environments, such as the cafeteria, the categorizations that schools use to more efficiently deal with diversity continue in the absence of the forced catego-rizations. Students are learning in our schools. One thing we are teaching them is how to categorize and isolate themselves and others.

To discuss diversity in schools invites a host of viewpoints, both positive and negative. Earlier we said that diversity often evokes strong reactions. This is be-cause diversity variables often describe the essence of who people are, and those variables have competing definitions. When deeply held beliefs contradict each other, conflict ensues. People often seek to avoid conflict, especially when it sur-rounds the sensitive subject of racism. People within schools implement many strate-gies, such as avoidance, disavowal, dismissal/patronizing, and recentering, to avoid addressing multicultural issues (Pewewardy, 2003). These strategies often silence the conversation around diversity. Unfortunately, if schools do not avoid the topic of diversity, they often approach it from a deficit model (Valencia, 1997). This deficit thinking has shaped the discussions of diversity at all levels of education. Skrla and Scheurich (2001) noted that

> Because of the insidiously pervasive deficit thinking in which superintendents, along with the vast majority of other educators including teachers and principals, have been more or less marinated throughout their careers, these superintendents tend to view the broad-scale underperformance of children of color and children from low-income homes in their schools as inevitable, something that is not within their power to change. (p. 237)

Powerlessness breeds inaction. If open conversations about diversity are not attempted, then racist attitudes continue and nothing changes. People become estranged from each other as well as the school. In schools where people are strangers to each other—within and across their respective groups—it is not reasonable to expect the high and intense levels of intellectual engagement required for good teaching and learning to take place. A prerequisite to high and intense intellectual engagement and learning is a climate that conveys the sense that everyone is valued.

Principals first and foremost must serve as the integrative force in schools. No one else has the authority and credibility to act in this role. As the integrative force, the principal leads in breaking down social boundaries and other walls of separation and isolation by building a culture of inclusiveness where all mem-bers of the school—teachers, staff, students, and parents—are valued and grow in getting to know each other. Weissglass (2001) spoke to this point when he wrote that we must "move beyond the celebration of diversity and declarations," that "all children will learn" in order to create "healing communities." Research has found that organizations, schools included, work best when relationships within them are viable (i.e., people know each other, respect each other, collaborate together on important issues, and seek to find common ground on which to base their decisions) (Scheurich & Skrla, 2003). Transforming a school from an organization into a community where all members are respected and embraced requires courageous leadership from the principal (Sergiovanni, 2001), leadership that approaches diversity in ways that do not categorize and isolate, but allow for the advance of equity and social justice.

Diversity has and continues to loom large in American schools. The future of many students depends upon the leadership provided by principals in determining what it means to be who they are in their schools. Being tolerant of student diversity is not a sufficient response or action for principals. Leadership in building an inclusive community where each student is valued will create the conditions for desirable results for all students.

WHAT DO WE KNOW ABOUT LEADERSHIP AND THE EDUCATION OF MINORITY STUDENTS?

The most critical challenge to educators today is to educate successfully student populations that are ethnically and linguistically diverse and those groups whose educational needs have not been met, who are typically located in urban and underfunded schools. Some educators have demonstrated commitment to the educational success of these students, and the students have achieved at high levels (Edmonds, 1979; Reyes, Scribner, & Scribner, 1999; Scheurich, 1998; Skrla, Scheurich, & Johnson, 2000). Not enough attention is being paid to the leadership of such schools or to the extant knowledge of the educators who are successful with these populations. These educators' leadership, whether it be administrative leadership (principals) or pedagogical leadership (classroom teachers), takes various forms, which foster organizational cultures that could result in better educational outcomes for students of diverse populations.

In addition to the concepts of leadership referenced earlier, Gooden's (2002) concept of the servant-leader attempts to address the unique challenges facing leaders of urban schools, who educate those who traditionally have been poorly served by the American educational system: students who are poor; children of color; English language learners; and immigrants from Spanish-speaking nations and East Asian countries such as Vietnam, Cambodia, Thailand, and the Philippines (Hallinger & Leithwood, 1996a, 1996b).

Gooden (2002) contended that the traditional leadership models, based on research studies of white male leaders, become problematic when applied to leadership in urban environments. Gooden described critical leadership as "that which questions existing practice, and sets new precedents where necessary for the sake of advancing organizational knowledge . . . making schools arenas . . . where students become critically reflective citizens." Gooden added that this critical preparation is made stronger by leaders' willingness to serve, despite the mismatch between the cultures of urban students and the dominant culture of society typically subscribed to by teachers and administrators. This also has been documented by Stoddart (1993) and Heath (1995).

Lomotey (1989), in his research on African-American principals of successful African-American school populations, found that these principals possessed several qualities found in the research on principal leadership, academic achievement, and other areas. Specifically, these principals developed goals, harnessed energies, facilitated communication, managed instruction, demonstrated commitment to the education of African-American children, showed compassion for and understanding of African-American children and their communities, and were confident in the educability of African-American children. Lomotey (1994) further developed his concept of leadership, calling leaders who combine these attributes "bureaucrat/administrators and ethno-humanists" who promote both "schooling" and "education" about students' culture, life, and where they fit into society and the world. Foster (1993) conducted interviews of 18 experienced, exemplary (as defined by local African-Americans) African-American teachers who were "educating for competence in community and culture" as well as academic achievement. J. E. King (1991) termed this type of approach "emancipatory pedagogy." Mitchell (1998), in a study of retired African-American secondary school educators, found that these teachers were willing to assume expanded roles of mediator, activist, and advocate to encourage students living in urban environments where many of their primary needs were unmet. The teachers sought to build on what the students brought and provide more effective support. The teachers themselves were influenced by their own upbringings in urban environments; their participation in efforts to improve the social condition of African-Americans, such as the civil rights movement; and their recognition of the relationship between race and the socioeconomic realities faced by their students.

Leaders of organizations that successfully educate children from diverse and oppressed backgrounds pay careful attention to the affective dimension of schooling. Fostering authentic, caring school climates that affirm culturally relevant, caring pedagogy can result in student academic success. Reyes, Scribner, and Scribner (1999) found that schools that were successful in educating Mexican-American students to high levels of achievement used (a) collaborative governance and leadership, including a clear vision shared by the school community; (b) collaborative, dedicated administrators; and (c) humanistic leadership philosophies. Without attending to distinctive contributions of culture, educational efforts with these students are likely to be unsuccessful (Garcia, 1995; Knapp & Woolverton, 1995; Ogbu, 1995; Reyes, Velez, & Pena, 1993).

Valenzuela (1999) suggested that "whenever the leadership is weak or ineffective . . . a culture of authentic caring is hard to create." Additionally, school environments that devalue or deny students' cultural identities and language, what she calls "subtractive schooling," alienate students and make them closed to learning, even in the face of obvious academic talent. She contended that these subtractive experiences plague the education of Mexican-American, Mexican immigrant, African-American, American Indian, and Puerto Rican students; however, the effects can be reversed through authentically caring pedagogy that builds on students' cultural strengths. Similarly, the "funds of knowledge" identified in research by Moll and González (1994) helped to affirm and build on the strengths of students.

Scheurich (1998) identified several core beliefs and organizational characteristics that school leaders consciously determined would be interwoven to shape the climate for schools that were successful with low-SES children of color. These variables included strong shared vision; loving, caring environments for both children and adults; collaboration; being innovative, experimental, and open to new ideas; being hard-working but not "burning out"; and an organizational culture that models appropriate conduct.

In another study of school culture and successful learning, Mitchell (1998) contended that minority educators are particularly adept at motivating minority students, bringing knowledge of student backgrounds to the classroom in ways that enhance students' educational experience. She suggested that what teachers do in the affective domain to establish or maintain student motivation and engagement is key to academic achievement. She cited the research of Ladson-Billings (1994) and others, which identified student motivation as a key factor of the resilience of at-risk students and the high achievement of students in academic and other settings. The work of other researchers has supported this position (Foster, 1993; Hunter-Boykin, 1992; King, 1993; Ladson-Billings, 1994, 1995). We believe that teachers create these learning environments within a culture that is encouraged by the school leadership.

These types of leadership need to be explored and encouraged by administrator preparation programs. Because schooling happens in a social context, higher education programs should prepare administrators by emphasizing the social context of schooling and education as it relates to students of diverse backgrounds. Such programs cannot claim to prepare educated leaders without providing sustained exposure to these areas of difference among groups and their impact on schooling (Parker & Shapiro, 1993).

The way principals lead in high-stakes accountability environments is critical to the success of student learning, particularly in urban schools. In her study of how principals in Chicago led in high-stakes accountability environments, DeMoss (2002) found that principals whose leadership goal was "leadership for privilege" or "leadership for professionalism and empowerment" had student test outcomes that steadily increased. These leadership styles were contrasted with principals who led programs that lacked focus and who led to avoid censure. By "leading for privilege" she referred to a system that excluded students who were behind grade level and removed teachers who did not want a focus of academic rigor. DeMoss notes that unfortunately this leadership style creates an "island of improvement rather than part of a whole continent of change ultimately making it an untenable policy model for systemic reform" (DeMoss, 2002, p. 127). A more viable model for leadership in a diverse school saddled with a high-stakes testing environment is "leadership for professionalism and empowerment." Leadership within this model is "committed to teachers' meaningful participation in instruction decisions" (DeMoss, 2002, p. 127).

THE ROLE OF THE PRINCIPAL

Leadership is always provided within a context; therefore, leadership needs to be context-specific. Context-specific leadership can be provided only by those who are deeply knowledgeable about the school, the community in which the school is located, the professional and nonprofessional staff of the school, the student population, and the relationship between the school and central administration.

Deep substantive knowledge in each of these five areas is the minimum requirement before context-specific leadership can be expected to be provided. Rorrer and Reyes (2000) illuminated what principals do to provide context-specific leadership. They found that the principals studied recognized that leadership is encompassed in a collective and is context-specific. The principals further understood that "because democracy is fundamentally process-oriented, each school must forge its own approach to democratic, empowering leadership" (Blase & Anderson, 1995, p. 130). Therefore, to achieve school and community integration for student success, many principals have adopted collaborative leadership approaches to school operations. These approaches invite teachers, parents, community members, and other constituents to support and advance the school in ways frequently counter to past strategies that promoted isolation, limited or unequal participation, and bureaucratic and authoritarian ideas.

Principals make boundaries more permeable and allow parents and community members to engage the school on their own terms (Beck, 1991). Principals serve as the arbitrator for accomplishing this task and ensuring that internal and external constituent roles in these processes are authentic. Anderson (1998) noted, "Authentic participation moves beyond concerns with legitimacy and public relations to shared control" (p. 595).

Principals demonstrate that "a sense of place matters" in leading schools. They negotiate among constituents to achieve horizontal networks of power. While a vertical network "links unequal agents in asymmetric relations of hierarchy and dependence," a horizontal network "brings together agents of relatively equivalent status and power" (Putnam, 1993, p. 173). By shifting the power distribution among constituents into a horizontal network, principals promote communities that are engaged in achieving success for all students by building public trust and cooperation.

Principals demonstrate a high degree of trust and respect for the teacher as a professional; thus they facilitate teacher growth. These principals frequently are more supportive of innovation and risk. Principals who work in schools where collaboration rules also invite teacher participation in decisions regarding the planning and delivery of professional development opportunities.

Early research indicates that principals must have mastered a body of knowledge to be effective leaders (Reyes, Scribner, & Scribner, 1999; Reyes, Scribner, & Wagstaff, 1999). We have identified that knowledge in Figure 7.1 under the headings of Leadership Ability and Leadership Values. The empirical research (Foster,

Figure 7.1. How Principals Function in Schools

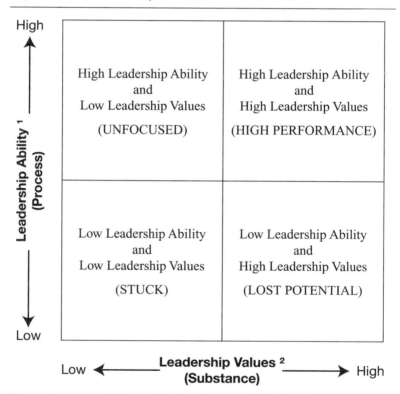

Notes: [1] Leadership Ability—skills necessary to make sense of the school and its context and to plan, organize, communicate, and take action for goal achievement.
[2] Leadership Values—perception of what is important for school to achieve and commitment to take action to achieve such.

1993; Mitchell, 1998; Parker & Shapiro, 1993) leads us to believe that principals should come from the ranks of successful teachers, thereby assuming that they have a solid grasp of teaching and learning and can work effectively with students and other teachers. Indeed, many of the principals with whom we have worked and who have been subjects of our studies have been highly competent and on the cutting edge of leadership as reflected in theory and best practice.

Illustrative of this was the principal who was determined to act as a transformative leader to facilitate the creation of a new school vision. The visioning process began each fall with a 2-day leadership symposium. During this time, teachers and administrators brainstormed what they wanted to see and where they wanted to be, as well as what they actually saw at the school. They compared the ideal and the real, and then identified ways to align more closely the real with the ideal. The result was a statement of vision, beliefs, and emphases for the school as a whole and for each major curriculum area. The draft document created then was discussed, refined, and eventually adopted by the entire faculty. A critical component of the visioning process was the participative nature of decisionmaking. A faculty member remarked, "Every single person knows the vision. . . . We all had a part, at some level, in creating it. . . . We talked about everything and made decisions together." The visioning process has become an example not only of exceptional principal leadership, but also of true teacher leadership.

In order to provide additional opportunities for teacher leadership and growth, the school day was restructured to provide daily opportunities for teacher collaboration and learning (c.f. Little, 1999). By reorganizing the school day, the teachers in the school secured time each morning to collaborate and gain new knowledge through study groups, focus groups, staff meetings, training, team planning, and guest experts. Teacher-directed study groups were designed to help teachers address the disparities between what they want to see in their classrooms and their present realities. Groups with similar professional development needs meet to study and discuss the latest literature on instructional techniques. Between meetings, teachers work to implement these techniques in their classrooms and to do further research on these topics with the intent of reporting their findings to the other members of their study group. Group members share their learning with the entire faculty through formal presentations. Focus groups are organized by subject matter and are composed of teachers in all grade levels to promote continuity of programs across grade levels. During the first year of the alternative schedule, the principal coordinated the entire program, but over time, the alternative schedule responsibilities have come to be shared among the faculty. The impact of daily opportunities for teacher leadership and learning is evident in decreased isolation and increased communication between teachers; staff cohesiveness; reduced stress; and professional norms of continual growth, collaboration, and reflection.

The effects of increased teacher leadership and teacher learning in this school-based reform school were not unproblematic. Several tensions emerged as the school engaged in innovative change successfully within a district that valued homogene-ity among schools and did not expect success from all student populations. Com-plications arose as the school became differentiated within the district, and power struggles emerged between confident, knowledgeable teachers and threatened dis-trict administrators. Although the school community may be comfortable and ex-cited about change, this does not mean that the central office administrators are ready to accept or support change.

PRINCIPALS, DIVERSE STUDENTS, AND SUCCESSFUL LEADERSHIP PRACTICES

Several new models of leadership will, we believe, enable leaders to serve diverse students well. For example, Sergiovanni (1992) proposed a new kind of leadership—leadership based on moral authority. Such leadership gives more credence to sense experience and intuition and views sacred authority and emotion as fully legiti-mate ways of knowing, equal in value to secular authority, science, and deductive logic. He asserted that this kind of leadership can transform schools into commu-nities and inspire the kind of commitment, devotion, and service that lead to suc-cess (p. 16). This kind of leadership begins with tapping into the human will of staff, students, and parents in a way that both motivates and inspires. This suggests what Senge (1990) called team learning. Team learning is highly dependent on dialogue. The purpose of dialogue, according to Senge, is "to go beyond any one individual's understanding." In dialogue, individuals gain insights that simply could not be achieved individually. Dialogue is a way of helping people to "see the rep-resentative and participatory nature of thought [and] . . . to become more sensi-tive to and make it safe to acknowledge the incoherence in our thought" (pp. 241–242).

Caine and Caine (1997) suggested that dialogue be used as a process to help participants in a group to begin gradually to shed masks, roles, and fixed ideas so that they can penetrate deeper meanings and come together in a genuine sense of communion. The skillful use of this tool or process can begin the establishment of the principal as moral authority of the school.

It is necessary to change the facts as well as the feelings that nurture and some-times divide the groups in a school. We conducted a study of migrant students (Reyes, Scribner, & Wagstaff, 1999) and found that principals of schools success-ful with their migrant students managed the meaning of what it meant to be a migrant student. Being a migrant student was not perceived as being negative; it was seen as an opportunity to travel, which served as a platform for learning. By managing the meaning of migrancy, the principals centered the conditions needed for migrant students to be an integral part of the school community and not a group standing apart. In fact, in several of these schools nonmigrant students wanted to be identified as migrant. Managing meaning neither denotes nor connotes dishonesty; it means examining all the data and information about a group and building a strong positive case for the group to be accepted and to be able to function as equals. Principals of these successful schools rejected deficit theories of learning associated with terms and concepts such as *culturally different, disadvantaged,* and *at risk.* Instead, they viewed migrant students as students who, like all other students, have needs that the school must get to know, understand, and address so that they can learn at the high levels expected of them. Knowing the students serves as the basis for the instructional practices used by teachers anchored in the belief that instructional practices must be adjusted individually and collectively according to the needs of the students.

Another potentially helpful perspective on leadership relates to the concept of social capital (Rorrer & Reyes, 2000). According to Pierre Bourdieu, social capital is "the aggregate of the actual or potential resources, which are linked to possession of a durable network of more or less institutionalized relationships of mutual acquaintance or recognition" (Bourdieu, 1997, p. 51). Social capital confers the ability of individuals and groups to develop resources by forming a multitude of social relationships, including those between children and adults and schools and their communities (Edwards & Foley, 1997; Rist, 1996).

Social capital is defined by its function. It is not a single entity but a variety of different entities, with two elements in common: They all consist of some aspect of social structure, and they facilitate certain actions of actors—whether persons or corporate actors—within the structure. Like other forms of capital, social capital is productive, making possible the achievement of certain ends that in its absence would not be possible (Coleman, 1988).

According to Norris (1996), social capital consists of "dense networks of norms and social trust, which enable participants to cooperate in the pursuit of shared objectives" (p. 474). Social capital includes the significant elements of social organizations, thus incorporating trust, norms, and networks horizontally and vertically in a manner that increases civic engagement (Coleman et al., 1966; Putnam, 1993). Consequently, it is entrenched in the structures and relations between individuals and groups.

Whereas larger social networks can expand employment and labor market opportunities for children later, a comprehensive social capital network can expand schools' financial and intangible resources as well as increase achievement outcomes. Principals who cultivate social capital realize its benefits because it "allows taking such resources and showing the way they can be combined with other resources to produce different system level behavior or, in other cases, different outcomes for individuals" (Coleman, 1988, p. 101). By changing the levels of collaboration and participation in schools by elaborating social capital networks, principals support generative conditions and innovative possibilities. "Through relationships with institutional agents, a segment of society gains the resources, privileges, and support necessary to advance and maintain their economic and political position in society" (Stanton-Salazar, 1997, p. 4). Access to social networks through educational experiences also contributes to a greater chance for an improved quality of life.

Civic commitment and trust are among the available moral resources that are "not fixed or limited as may be the case for other factors of production" (Hirschman, 1984, p. 93). Factors of production such as land and capital can be completely consumed in the production process, but moral resources regenerate as they are used. The presence and acceptance of such moral resources are important. As noted by Hirschman, these resources likely increase when used or engaged and may become "depleted and atrophy if *not* used" (p. 93). Driscoll and Kerchner (1999) referred to this as the "breeder" effect; resources are generated and regenerated as a result of social capital. In turn, these resources become beneficial to the larger community. In this case, civic engagement, internal and external constituent commitment levels, and the collective good grow as the principal encourages trust, collaboration, and participation. Collective goals and the collective good, which have become the most important end, replace self-interest.

Thus, it is essential that the principal develop and maintain the school as a community. Putnam (1993) noted, "Norms of generalized reciprocity and networks of civic engagement encourage social trust and cooperation because they reduce incentives to defect, reduce uncertainty, and provide models for future cooperation" (p. 177). By promoting an environment of collaboration and participation between internal and external school constituents, the principal weaves the community together.

Breaking down the walls of separation and isolation between and among the groups—teachers, staff, students, parents, and community—is the place for principals to start transforming their schools into productive learning communities. In addition to a welcoming climate, schools must have and function from norms and processes of inclusiveness. Etzioni (1993) noted that most schools, particularly comprehensive high schools in urban areas, are organized as if a powerful sociological engineer were intent on minimizing the bonds between teacher and students (p. 107). We have elsewhere (Reyes, Scribner, & Wagstaff, 1999) asserted that although the conditions described by Etzioni (1999, p. 105) are most commonly found in high schools, increasingly middle and even some elementary schools have become just as divided and depersonalized. It has been noted that a sense of place matters, so it is important that each individual in the school feels valued and knows how to function. School should feel like a safe harbor, where rights are understood and respected, where responsibilities are accepted and met, and where high-quality teaching and learning are the norm.

Caine and Caine (1997) stated that the direction education takes depends ultimately on the set of values and compelling beliefs that prevail in the school. Thus, the result depends as much on how much principals and teachers conceive and reconceive themselves as it does on what they ask others to do (pp. 257–258). They wrote further that the core of the belief system that prevails in too many schools is (a) only experts create knowledge, (b) teachers deliver knowledge in the form of information, and (c) children are graded on how much of the information they have stored (p. 258). This mechanical process of teaching and learning flies in the face of what is known about the dynamic quality of effective teaching and learning as embodied in constructivist perspectives and approaches.

Schools must create the conditions that promote the achievement of this possibility. Such conditions include the following: (a) an environment in which students—all students—feel safe to try, think, speculate, and make mistakes on their way to excellence; (b) teachers who understand that students' feelings and attitudes will be involved and will profoundly influence their learning; (c) teachers who respect students' ideas and their ability to conduct research and solve real problems; (d) teachers who recognize that the cognitive domain cannot be isolated from the affective domain, thus maintaining an appropriate emotional climate in the classroom and school; (e) teachers who reduce artificiality in instruction as much as possible by integrating real-world expectations; and (f) an environment with an underlying sense of coherence, borderlessness, and community.

Luis Moll and colleagues' (Moll & Diaz, 1987; Moll & Greenberg, 1990; Moll et al., 1992) studies about the "funds of knowledge" children bring to school have provided results that contrast sharply with prevailing and accepted perceptions of working-class families as somehow disorganized socially and deficient intellectually, perceptions that are well accepted and rarely challenged in education and schools. Teachers are the bridge between the students' world and the school, and their perceptions and attitudes about the students' world shape, in large measure, how they relate to them. Four important consequences were reported from one study, which include the following:

1. Teachers indicate that there is an abundance of knowledge in the household where their students live, challenging ideas about deprivation and dysfunctionality in such homes.
2. Teachers show how each household forms part of a broader social network that helps sustain its functioning, so that funds of knowledge and other resources can be accessed or provided (socially distributed) through the exchanges that their social networks facilitate.
3. Teachers document how the children have interests, abilities, and experiences beyond what is evident in the classroom, challenging the notion that these children are not motivated to learn.
4. Teachers establish qualitatively new social relationships with the families, based on conversations with them and on learning from their experiences, not on imagined characteristics.

SUMMARY

The leadership perspectives we are emphasizing challenge and disregard old sacred notions about organizational structure, authority and responsibility, line and staff, chain of command, and leader organizational member relationships. In the 1980s, the leadership and management literature began to eschew these old sacred notions, and today they have been almost totally discredited as "organizational rigor-mortis"-inducing notions that cause organizational failure. Yet we know that for some reason these notions persist in many schools where principals perceive themselves to be the boss and believe that all good ideas about how the school should function must emanate from them or a chosen few. We believe (reflected in the "stuck" quadrant of Figure 7.1) that principals who function from this belief system have low leadership ability and low leadership values, and their schools are stuck.

From our research, literature analysis, and direct observations of principals at work, we have concluded that a useful way to think about how principals function in schools can be conceptualized and presented as Figure 7.1. What we have deduced is that some principals are quite skillful in working with people, but quite inept at articulating and setting direction. On the other hand, some principals have a good sense of organizational direction and articulate it well, but lack the skills to mobilize staff, students, and community to achieve agreed-upon goals. Thus, principals fall into four distinct categories with varying leadership strength, which determine how they function.

Our position is that leadership for successful teaching and learning in schools with students from diverse backgrounds must be anchored in both substance and process. The principal must know what to do (substance) as well as how to do it (process). The substance of leadership is what we call Leadership Values in Figure 7.1. Substance is composed of what the principal perceives as important for the school to achieve, accompanied by the principal's commitment to take action to achieve such. In other words, substance is the "big picture" idea held by the principal about what the school needs to accomplish and a commitment to get it done. Substance cannot be externally imposed; it is internal to what the principal is capable of perceiving, making sense of, assigning value to, and motivating to achieve.

The process of leadership is what we term Leadership Ability in Figure 7.1. Process is composed of skills that are reflected in actions such as diagnosing, planning, organizing, deciding, comprehending, and initiating. We are not suggesting that principals are pure types according to the four quadrants, but that they have high and low capabilities in these directions, and that the most successful schools with students from diverse backgrounds have principals with high leadership ability and high leadership values. In other words, principals of schools successful with students from diverse backgrounds insightfully and skillfully integrate the interdependent parts of their schools—human resources, fiscal resources, physical resources—in such a way that each student becomes a valued member of the school community with opportunity for high-quality social and intellectual engagement according to need.

Commensurate with the aforementioned perspectives is that of leadership directed toward building leadership capacity in schools. Lambert (1998, pp. 16–17) described school leadership capacity-building as principal leadership that (a) allows broad-based, skillful participation of teachers in the work of leadership; (b) uses inquiry-based information to inform decisions and practice; (c) establishes roles and responsibilities that reflect broad involvement and collaboration; (d) uses reflective practice and innovation as the norm; and (e) focuses upon and generates high student achievement. To be sure, this is not an exhaustive listing of leadership perspectives and definitions—others exist and endure. But we select these to highlight because they are reflected in the empirical and conceptual studies we have examined and participated in, where a nexus between leadership and school or organization success was established.

Recommendations

Given the state of the literature in this area, we recommend the following areas for research.

1. We need to develop intensive and detailed case studies where students of diverse backgrounds are located. We need to evaluate principals' actions in accordance with leadership values and leadership ability, which have been conceptualized above (Figure 7.1). Evaluation of the leadership values will shed light on how principals use the ideas of inclusiveness, equitable pluralism, democracy, and critical questioning to lead in a diverse school. A study of the leadership process will help explore the technicalities of employing such an approach. We should be able to test different constructs of leadership and connect them to student academic achievement.
2. A growing body of research suggests that effective leaders develop leadership capacity within their schools. Researchers need to determine how leaders within diverse schools encourage teacher leadership and remove obstacles so that teachers can take on leadership roles in the school. We need to evaluate the extent to which such peer leaders embrace/change/improve the goals of the school. What are the types of structures these leaders create to develop leadership capacity in their schools? Who are those selected for leadership roles? How do they embrace their roles? What number of principals are actually hired out of school personnel? What is their relationship with other stakeholders?
3. How principals lead in high-stakes accountability environments is critical to the success of student learning, particularly in urban schools. We need to continue and expand the work of DeMoss (2002) to understand what

role leadership plays in approaching the challenges and the opportunities within accountability-oriented policy contexts. Research can determine how such challenges can be used to provide opportunities for student learning, particularly for economically disadvantaged children and children of color. This research should feed the discussion surrounding the effectiveness of the national policies that are designed to insure equity in outcomes. Does the high-stakes testing work, or does it just dissimulate the old systems of privilege?

4. As leaders go about building networks to sustain diverse students in highly successful teaching and learning environments, what types of relationships do leaders create with their communities to support student learning? In what ways can leaders expand social capital for diverse students? In what way do leaders use students' culture to develop their academic potential? How do they navigate racial bias and other divisive elements that prejudice people in diverse social contexts?

In short, research must focus on understanding the role of leadership in developing and sustaining academic success among students from diverse backgrounds. So far, case studies of successful schools only provide hints about how leaders connect with student learning. The field needs detailed scholarly work on the leadership role and academic success for students from diverse backgrounds.

CHAPTER 8

How Can Educational Leaders Promote and Support Social Justice and Democratic Community in Schools?

Gail C. Furman and Carolyn M. Shields

Social justice and democratic community have become urgent concerns for educational scholars and practitioners. This urgency is driven by many factors, including the growing pluralism of Western industrialized societies (Goldring & Greenfield, 2002); an ongoing awareness of gaps in both achievement and socioeconomic status between mainstream and minoritized children (Bowles & Gintis, 1976; Coleman, 1990; Valenzuela, 1999); the increasingly sophisticated analyses of social injustice in schools (Larson & Ovando, 2001; Macedo, 1995; McNeil, 2000; Rapp, 2002); and a sense of the need to prepare children to participate in democratic processes within an increasingly multicultural society (Apple & Beane, 1995; Goodlad, 2001).

While much of the literature related to social justice and democratic community has developed in the areas of curriculum theory and cultural studies, these themes are also increasingly present in the literature specific to educational leadership. In his 1999 monograph on the quest for a new "center" for the field, Murphy identified social justice and democratic community as two of the "powerful synthesizing paradigms" (p. 54) embedded in the "shifting landscape" of the field. Nevertheless, these concepts have been relatively neglected in mainstream research literature. For example, in the *Handbook of Research on Educational Administration*, edited by Boyan (1988a), social justice and democracy are each listed only once in the index. In the second edition of the *Handbook* (Murphy & Louis, 1999), these terms do not appear at all in the index.

Our purpose in this chapter is to address these relatively neglected areas by proposing a research agenda that focuses on the links between educational leadership practice and the normative concepts of social justice and democratic community in schools. In proposing this agenda, we recognize that social justice and democratic community are not the only legitimate "moral purposes" associated with schooling. We agree with Strike (1999b) and others that in a pluralistic society various moral goods play out in schools. However, we argue that embedding educational leadership in these concepts is foundational to the moral purpose of educational leadership in this century. Before proceeding with a proposal for a research agenda focusing on leadership for social justice and democratic community in schools,[1] we will argue first that the concepts of social justice and democratic community are integrally interconnected and that they must not be considered apart from concepts of student learning. We will also explore the links between these related concepts and various perspectives on leadership.

THE CONCEPT OF DEMOCRATIC COMMUNITY IN SCHOOLS

What is a "democratic community"? How do you know it when you see it? Can democratic community be created in schools, and if so, how? These are typical and understandable questions directed at advocates and researchers. Unfortunately, such questions cannot be answered to everyone's satisfaction, for several reasons. First, like many constructs used in education, democratic community can have many meanings. It is an example of a "shifting signifier" (Giroux, 1992), with meanings that vary according to the purposes of those who use the term. Second, further complicating its meaning, democratic community is a composite of two other constructs—community and democracy—which also shift in their meanings (Beck, 1999; Furman & Starratt, 2002; Maxcy, 1995). It is questionable whether research that reduces democratic community to a tidy definition or measurable variables would be particularly useful. Third, like the concept of social justice, democratic community is an ideal, a moral purpose toward which educators strive, one that is never fully realized; thus, democratic community is not a specific structure to be reified, defined, reduced, observed, and replicated. Rather, it may be understood more usefully as a process, a way of "ethical living" in a diverse society (Maxcy, 1995).

These are only some of the considerations that make democratic community a slippery subject for research. They suggest multiple challenges for advocates and researchers. To make headway on these challenges, we argue that researchers must acknowledge their point of entry and situate their discussions of democratic community in an explicit conceptual frame. Therefore, in the next section we will articulate the frames we use to propose a research agenda.

THE DEMOCRATIC COMMUNITY FRAME

Murphy (1999, 2002a) posits democratic community as one of the "new anchors for the profession" of educational leadership. However, though Murphy's analysis has been influential in legitimizing democratic community as a focus of research, it has not led to greater conceptual clarity. Furman and Starratt (2002) argue that to better understand the concept of democratic community, it is necessary to unpack the subsidiary concepts—democracy and community—and then to repackage the composite term; here we borrow elements of their argument as well as those of other writers.

In regard to democracy, a central issue is to distinguish between notions of democracy based on the values of classical liberalism and more contemporary notions of "deep" democracy that have continued to evolve from Dewey's (1916) seminal work. The understanding of democracy based on classical liberalism is strongly influenced by the ideology of individualism embedded in Western Enlightenment thinking (Bowers, 2001); in particular, this notion of democracy is concerned primarily with the right of the individual to pursue his or her self-interest (Barber, 1998; Maxcy, 1995). Strike (1999a) calls this "thin" democracy, in which individuals resolve their conflicts through "democratic" decisionmaking—typically, through one-person, one-vote elections in which the majority decides. Green (1999), Guinier (1994), Maxcy (1995), and many others have suggested the problems with this "purely formal" (Green, 1999) conception of democracy, in particular, that it is possible for the majority to "tyrannize" (Guinier, 1994; Shields, 2003) less powerful minorities by using "democratic" processes to serve their own interests. Democracy focused narrowly on the rights of individuals concerned with their own self-interest and with resolving conflicts through majority rule will not lead to the mutual understanding and sense of interdependence in working for the common good that is necessary in a multicultural, diverse society (see Green, 1999). Rather, the practice of thin democracy is likely to perpetuate and enhance misunderstandings and conflict between balkanized groups and leave power in the hands of ruling power elites.

In contrast, the concept of "deep" democracy offers ideas that are more promising and hopeful for an increasingly diverse society (Green, 1999; Gutman, 1987; Maxcy, 1995). Calling this "thick" democracy, Strike (1999a) states that it "attaches significant value to such goods as participation, civic friendship, inclusiveness, and solidarity. Thick democracy tolerates significant diversity in conceptions of the good as well . . ." (p. 60). Similarly, Green (1999) argues for a rendition of democracy that focuses more deeply on respect, participation, communication, and cross-cultural cooperation.

Starratt's (1991) suggestion that we treat others with "absolute regard" extends and clarifies Green's notion of respect. Maxcy (1995) supports the call for deep democracy in schools, arguing for a new postmodern liberalism built on three democratic values: "(a) the belief in the worth and dignity of individuals and the value of their expressions and participation; (b) the reverence for freedom, intelligence, and inquiry; and (c) the responsibility of individuals in concert to explore and choose collaborative and communal courses of practical action" (p. 58).

Drawing from these various analyses, we argue that the concept of democratic community that is most appropriate for increasingly diverse 21st-century schools is one that embraces the ideals, values, and processes of deep democracy, as this concept is being developed in literature specific to education.[2] These include:

> Respect and absolute regard for the worth and dignity of individuals and their cultural traditions.
> Reverence for, and the responsibility of individuals to participate in, free and open inquiry and critique.
> Recognition of interdependence and the importance of collective choices and action in working for the common good.

Even if deep democracy, as advocated by Green (1999) and others, is rarely or inconsistently practiced outside the school, in the local communities and larger society in which schools are embedded, "schools need to be as democratic as the civic ideals they wish to teach" (Barber, 1998, p. 231). Many analysts are concerned about growing threats to Western democratic processes, including those arising from economic globalization (Green, 1999; Guinier, 1994; Lasch, 1995). However, it is the hope of democratic school advocates, including us, that the experience of democracy in schools may help youth to eventually construct the democratic societies in which they wish to live.

It is clear, given the processual dimension of democratic community, that it must be practiced in schools rather than simply being taught didactically (Gutman, 1987). However, this is problematic. As Maxcy (1995) notes, democratic "minimalism" has dominated public schools historically, perhaps as a way of papering over deep divisions. Both within the school and in regard to local control or school governance, the scope of democratic decisionmaking and freedom of choice and expression has been extremely narrow. We argue that democratic community cannot exist in schools dominated by this minimalist approach to learning about democracy. Quite simply, democratic community must be practiced.

In sum, our concept of democratic community is that it is the practice of deep democracy in schools, involving participation in deep democratic processes by all members of the school community in the interest of the common good. While never fully achieved, the practice of deep democracy in schools is necessary to educate the citizenry for the practice of deep democracy in society (Green, 1999). While this stance may seem to be hopelessly utopian, there is case study evidence that many types of democratic practices can be implemented in typical public schools (Apple & Beane, 1995) and that even radical participatory democracy can be sustained in schools over long periods of time (Miller, 2002).

THE CONCEPT OF SOCIAL JUSTICE IN SCHOOLS

Many educators articulate what they mean by social justice by describing various ways in which it is manifested, such as avoiding negative consequences of high-stakes testing (Fashola & Slavin, 1998; Montecel, 2002), reducing the dropout rates of minority children (Hodgkinson, 1999), including students with disabilities (Sapon-Shevin & Zollers, 1999), guaranteeing equitable funding (Biddle & Berliner, 2002), welcoming the children of gay families into schools (Lamme & Lamme, 2001/2002), ensuring gender equity (Lundeberg, 1997), or responding appropriately to religious diversity (Kirmani & Laster, 1999). Others have attempted to bring more conceptual clarity to the term (e.g., Greenberg, 2001; MacKinnon, 2000).

Bogotch (2000) zeros in on what we believe to be a key component when he writes, "Social justice, like education, is a deliberate intervention that requires the moral use of power" (p. 2). The definition is beguilingly easy. What educators need to do is act deliberately and morally, yet there is little consensus over the processes of such intervention or the desirable outcomes. Shields (2002, 2003) argues the need for social justice to encompass education that is not only just, democratic, empathic, and optimistic, but also academically excellent.

These ideas help to define social justice as a deliberate intervention that challenges fundamental inequities that arise, in large part, due to the inappropriate use of power by one group over another. To supplant a hegemonic or neocolonial use of power with the power of agency and self-determination—not only for children, but also for parents and teachers—requires taking seriously the intrinsic worth and value of all individuals and the communities to which they belong. Educational leaders for social justice embed an explicitly moral practice in values that undergird an ethic of a deeply democratic community.

THE SOCIAL JUSTICE FRAME

Kincheloe and Steinberg (1995) use four terms that may act as guiding criteria to help us identify what type of schools we want to create. They suggest that education should be "just, optimistic, empathetic, and democratic" (p. 2). The four words each comprise multiple, contested meanings, yet they may provide guidance for action. Authors from what are sometimes termed "otherist" perspectives (Capper, 1992)—feminist, critical multicultural, antiracist, queer—all emphasize the need for any understanding of social justice to ensure that issues of race, gender, and ethnicity (among others) are attended to and that people are neither excluded nor marginalized on the basis of assumptions or practices that pathologize the lived experiences or abilities of specific groups (see, for example, the work of Dei, 1996; Kincheloe & Steinberg, 1997; Larson & Murtadha, 2002; May, 1994, 2000). Although there is a strong need for social justice to include the criterion of "fairness" (MacKinnon, 2000), there is also a recognition that fairness, like other criteria we propose, is a contested term. At times, if fairness is equated with sameness—treating everyone alike—it may become yet another argument in support of the status quo and be diametrically opposed to social justice. Farrell (1999) helps to clarify the concept of justice or fairness by emphasizing the notion of equality—again, not related to sameness, but associated with equality of access, sustainability, outputs, and outcomes. In sum, while terms such as justice, fairness, or equity may be generally acceptable, operationalizing them is still frequently problematic.

Education that is empathetic supports our contention that education has multiple moral purposes. Indeed, it suggests the need to include emotional, social, physical, and spiritual goals, for only by attending to students as whole people can we achieve education that is truly empathetic (see Shields, 2002, 2003). Optimistic education challenges and transforms inequities that may occur in the status quo, the distribution of power, and other resources in order to provide all children with doors of opportunity and windows of understanding. Optimistic education ensures that all children achieve outcomes (including GPAs and test scores) that permit equitable access to future educational opportunities. And education that is democratic, as we discussed earlier, encourages participation by all members of the school community in shaping a just, empathetic, and optimistic education.

Our understanding of social justice is robust and dynamic—one that is not based on a single attribute, but on a broad and holistic conception of learning. To the four terms of Kincheloe and Steinberg (1995), we might add, as Freire (1983) does, an explicit acknowledgment of the need for critique, achieved through what Maxine Greene (1978) calls "wide-awakeness."

Diverse meanings of social justice are constructed by the members of any given community, drawing from their understandings of the historical context, their present circumstances, and the moral purposes of their organizational contexts. While we do not believe it is possible (or healthy) to attempt to prescribe what these meanings look like or how they play out in a given organization, we would maintain the need to come to some agreement about which key components are included in our understandings of social justice. Otherwise, as Greenberg (2001) writes, "Our studies are likely to suffer from operational circularity: Justice is whatever justice scholars measure or manipulate" (p. 212).

Leaders of educationally just organizations must acknowledge and redress fundamental inequities where they exist in the status quo. Such inequities may be material, such as differential funding, instructional materials, facilities, and resources (Rothstein, 2000); they may also be attitudinal—expectations that certain groups (e.g., the poor, those whose home language is other than English, the minoritized) are intrinsically less able to succeed in the academic program of a school, exercise leadership, or make viable democratic decisions. Regardless of how and where inequities are found, to redress wrongs involves a recognition of how power has been achieved and is used and of the differentiation between the undeserved or unearned privilege of specific groups and hard-earned individual accolades. Educators must recognize that some groups may represent a numerical majority but still have been minoritized and excluded in certain contexts—an issue often ignored in discussions of social justice.

Another core, but rarely addressed, aspect of education for social justice is its relation to pedagogical practice. Too often we focus on the fundamentally relational aspects of democratic community or social justice, but ignore the need to address the underlying pedagogical implications. Yet what is taught and how it is taught are critical influences on the nature of "justice" in schools. Freire's (1983) argument of the necessity of reading both the word and the world is crucial here. Although we often refer to social justice in discussions related to providing more equitable access to education or more balanced demographic representation, Connell (1993) describes these concerns as issues of "distributive justice" and asserts the underlying weakness of an appeal to social justice that "is indifferent to the nature of education itself" (p. 3). Focusing on the nature of the curriculum that is taught and the instructional practices used to address it explicitly recognizes the importance of the core work of schools in working for social justice (Apple & Beane, 1995).

Drawing from these various analyses, we argue that the concept of social justice that is appropriate for increasingly diverse 21st-century schools is one that focuses on multiple aspects of equity. These include:

robust and dynamic understanding of social justice;
acknowledgment of injustices related to power and privilege
    (including inputs and outcomes, behaviors and attitudes);
recognition of individual prejudice as well as collective inequities; and
a concern for pedagogical implications of social justice.

Justice is present on a daily basis when educators examine both the formal, prescribed curriculum and the informal and hidden curricula (English, 1992) to eliminate barriers they may present to student learning. Justice occurs when there is space created into which students may bring their lived experiences, their whole selves, inquisitive about the world and the words, when no voices are silenced or experience devalued. Leadership for social justice requires a careful examination of one's own beliefs and practices and those of the institution within which one works, for injustice is played out in both individual relationships and systemically, in policies that assume that any single approach to curriculum, programming, resource allocations, or accountability is appropriate for all children.

DYNAMIC INTERPLAY: DEMOCRATIC COMMUNITY AND SOCIAL JUSTICE

Our conception of social justice is not possible without deep democracy; neither is deep democracy possible without social justice. Each holds within itself the notion of both individual rights and the good of the community. While justice is often related to individual rights, it is tempered by the term "social"; while democracy is often related to the protection of individual rights, community reminds us that individual rights are bounded by concerns about ways in which we must live together in society.

   Democratic processes permit dialogue that helps us to develop shared understandings of social justice. Yet, sometimes these understandings become fixed and reified and, over time, lead to new injustices. When the demographic, social, cultural, or economic makeup of a community changes, so too must its practices and understandings of social justice and democracy. Thus, social justice and democratic community are interdependent concepts. Each relies on the other to inform it, for its construction of meaning, and for its continued vitality in a given context. Neither social justice nor democratic community can ever be completed or finally realized; rather, they require processual striving and constant reexamination.

DEMOCRATIC COMMUNITY AND SOCIAL JUSTICE: ENSURING A PEDAGOGICAL FOCUS

We began this chapter by explicitly acknowledging that both social justice and democratic community constitute moral purposes of schooling. In this section, we argue that these foci are integral to the construction of understandings of learning that acknowledge the whole person. Moreover, we argue the centrality of learning within this moral landscape. Creating socially just and democratic communities and emphasizing academics and intellectual development are not necessarily oppositional goals. Indeed, our goal is to develop a model that will help educational leaders to create the conditions under which all children can learn well, within a socially just and democratic context.

   Too often educators wanting to emphasize social justice seem to ignore academics in a misguided belief that it is more important to develop self-esteem, cultural awareness, or social skills. The dichotomy is unfortunate and inappropriate; if public education abrogates its responsibility to provide intellectual stimulation, who will take it up? While we advance the claim that learning is the fundamental purpose of schooling, we are painfully aware that learning is too often equated with narrow definitions of intellectual development, separating it from basic emotional, social, physical, and spiritual development. Moreover, narrow conceptions taken to the extreme are often tied exclusively to test scores thought to represent achievement and learning.[3]

Replacing transmissive approaches to instruction with more recent constructivist pedagogies is not only more effective pedagogically, but also enhances the possibility of a socially just education. Freire and Macedo (1998) argue that any pedagogy that reduces the student to the role of passive learner is an "empty shell" (p. 8). Macedo (1995) notes that because at present curriculum is generally developed from the perspective of the dominant majority, it is implicitly designed "primarily to reproduce the inequality of social classes, while it mostly benefits the interests of the dominant class" (p. 54).

When a narrow conception of learning legitimizes certain images of success, privileging certain social and cultural groups and marginalizing others, or when broader conceptions that might take into account the needs and abilities of all children are ignored, education cannot be considered either socially just or deeply democratic. Learning in and for democratic communities is based on multiple meanings that are socially constructed, meanings that must take into account multiple perspectives and the moral purposes of education.

Because learning is based on constructed, multiple meanings, it also requires multiple and dynamic measures for its assessment. The challenge is to ensure that views of excellence in academic achievement are constructed, not in technicist and rational ways that assume objective measures and measurable outcomes, but in holistic ways that take into account the health and well-being of individuals and society as a whole.

Grumet (1995) emphasizes that our "relationships to the world are rooted in our relationships to the people who care for us" (p. 19). She claims that "curriculum is never the text, or the topic, never the method or the syllabus"; but curriculum is "the conversation that makes sense of . . . things. . . . It is the process of making sense with a group of people of the systems that shape and organize the world we can think about together" (p. 19). This understanding of relationships as the basis for pedagogy, as the root of curriculum, is fundamental, we believe, to the creation of all learning environments. Moreover, because living in relationship to others, deep democracy, and social justice are so intertwined, we submit that all true learning is inherently about democracy and justice.

Deep democracy allows alternative meanings to surface and be legitimated so that social justice in its deepest sense may be enhanced. Learning (another socially constructed and contested concept) is central to notions of social justice and democratic community. Figure 8.1 demonstrates the integral and mutually dependent relationships among the three concepts.

One cannot have social justice without socially just learning, constructed through the processes and ethics of democratic community. Maxine Greene (1988) captures this optimistic and holistic view of pedagogy grounded in social justice and democratic community when she concludes that being a citizen of the free world is "having the capacity to choose, the power to act to attain one's purposes, and the ability to help transform a world lived in common with others" (cited in Banks, 1991, p. 32). Educational leadership for learning in the contexts of democratic community and social justice takes these goals seriously.

SOCIAL JUSTICE AND DEMOCRATIC COMMUNITY: IMPLICATIONS FOR LEADERSHIP

Our interactive model of social justice, democratic community, and learning has implications for how one thinks about leadership in schools. Our model suggests that leadership grounded in the moral purposes of democratic community and social

Figure 8.1. Learning in the Contexts of Democratic Community and Social Justice

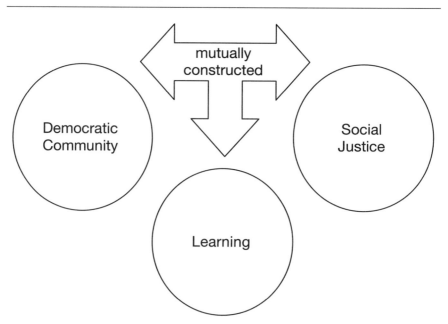

justice is, first and foremost, about pedagogy—a socially just pedagogy that is both created and sustained in the context of the processes of deep democracy. Thus, one of the overarching considerations for thinking about and researching leadership is how leadership impacts the environment for pedagogy and learning.

Other considerations for thinking about and researching leadership can be gleaned from the core dimensions of our interactive frame. We summarize these core dimensions below and identify some implications for thinking about leadership.

1. The ethical and moral dimensions. Social justice offers a construction of moral purposes that provides the compass for democratic community. In turn, engaging in and facilitating the processes of democratic community requires an ethical stance: absolute regard for individuals, their communities, and their cultural traditions and for the processes of open dialogue and critique. For leaders, this suggests having an explicitly moral sense of purpose as well as embracing the ethical practice of democracy. Moral leadership theory is relevant here. As represented in the works of Greenfield (1991), Hodgkinson (1991), Sergiovanni (1992), and Starratt (1994), moral leadership theory focuses on the idea that values are a central part of all leadership practice and that leadership should be concerned with right and wrong, not simply with attitudes, styles, or behaviors. The moral and ethical dimension of our frame interfaces with moral leadership theory to suggest that leadership studies should focus on how the values and ethics of leaders themselves are evident in their leadership practice.

2. The communal and contextual dimensions. Deep democracy is essentially communal. The processes of open inquiry and critique suggest a broad scope of participation across members of a community in working for the common moral good of social justice. The nature of this inquiry and the scope of participation suggest that meanings of social justice as well as decisions on collective actions are context-based—they are constructed by the members of the community in the midst of their unique local context. Two leadership theories are relevant here. First, constructivist leadership theory (Lambert et al., 1995) suggests that leadership aims at the construction of meaning and purpose by members of a community through their communicative relationships. Second, distributive leadership theory suggests that leadership within a school is distributed among many actors, that is, leadership is not the purview of administrators only, but is exercised by people in many positions (Smylie, Conley, & Marks, 2002). There are many different models of distributive leadership, but taken together, they suggest that not only is leadership distributed throughout the school, but that leadership "multiplies" through the type of interactions described in constructivist theory.

The communal/contextual dimension of our frame, along with constructivist and distributive leadership theories, suggests that leaders should focus on the facilitation of these communal processes and relationships and should allow "meaning" and "purpose" to emerge. Further, these frames suggest that the study of leadership should explore how moral leadership becomes constructed and "distributed" across a school community.

3. The processual dimension. Our frame suggests a "processual striving" toward social justice in schools. The processes of deep democracy—open inquiry, communication, and collaboration, combined with sensitivity, respect, and absolute regard—are key. It is these processes that create, sustain, and renew democratic community and allow for the emergence of meanings associated with social justice. As with the communal dimension, constructivist leadership theory is relevant in its emphasis on the processes of communication and "dialogic conversation" (Lambert et al., 1995, p. 87), which allow meanings to emerge. The processual dimension suggests that both leaders and leadership need to focus on facilitation of collaboration, open inquiry, and dialogue (see Shields & Edwards, 2005), and that leaders need the skills to both engage in and facilitate these processes.

4. The transformative dimension. Embedded in our frame is the notion that the processual striving for social justice necessarily involves critique and transformation. Injustices need to be identified and examined before they can be addressed through the processes of deep democracy. Thus, leaders for social justice and democratic community need to engage in the "ethic of critique" (Starratt, 1994) and encourage others to do so. As Goldfarb and Grinberg (2002) state:

> Leaders interested in fostering and forwarding social justice ought to problematize existing practices and reform proposals with the purpose of not just becoming more efficient at doing more of the same, but with the purpose of imagining and constructing new institutional possibilities. (p. 162)

Transformative leadership (for example, as represented by Foster, 1989, and Shields, 2003) holds that leadership should be oriented toward social change; it starts with altering consciousness and leads to the transformation of social conditions and relations. The transformative dimension suggests that research should consider the role of leadership in overcoming barriers to change and facilitating these "new institutional possibilities."

5. The pedagogical dimension. Finally, our discussion of leadership for social justice and democratic community has explicitly recognized the need for a pedagogical focus. It is not enough to teach about these concepts; rather, educators must both orient and organize instruction in such a way as to practice social justice and democratic community. This dimension acknowledges the role of the educational leader in rethinking the nature of curriculum around the values of social justice and democratic community. Similarly, it acknowledges the role of the educational leader in helping others to confront their own behaviors, to "examine unconscious, often deeply held assumptions; to acknowledge their own privilege or resentments; and to recognize how their own values, priorities, and attitudes, and those of other different ethnic or cultural groups, are expressed in community life and in school" (Parks, 1999, p. 14). It requires educational leaders to understand that, as Madeleine Grumet (1995) states, curriculum is "the conversation that makes sense of [these] things" (p. 19). The pedagogical dimension suggests that leadership studies consider the links between leadership for social justice and democratic community and the core work of schools.

Considering these dimensions and implications for leadership, we summarize our conceptual frame for leadership for democratic community and social justice in schools. (Figure 8.2 constitutes a graphic representation of this summary.) Leadership permeates and facilitates democratic community, social justice, and learning. Leadership is not simply the purview of those in formal positions, but results from the deliberate and thoughtful intervention of all members of a community dedicated to the moral purposes of education. Leadership requires commitment to and internalization of the moral purposes of social justice and the ethic

Figure 8.2. Leading for Learning in the Contexts of Democratic Community and Social Justice

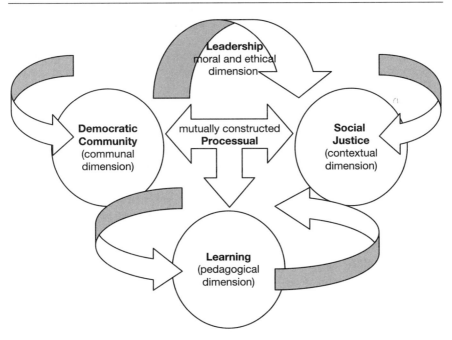

of deeply democratic community; it both arises from the community and facilitates communal participation; it is relational and dialogic; it nurtures the communicative processes that are foundational to participation; it challenges policies, practices, and structures that impede community participation and create injustices; and it focuses communal activity and problem-solving on socially just pedagogy and learning as the common good of schools.

A RESEARCH AGENDA: HOW CAN EDUCATIONAL LEADERS PROMOTE AND SUPPORT SOCIAL JUSTICE AND DEMOCRATIC COMMUNITY IN SCHOOLS?

To this point in the chapter, we have developed a model that integrates dynamic concepts of leadership for learning in socially just and deeply democratic school communities. Without apology, we have presented these as normative concepts. We have also considered various leadership concepts that may be productive frames for studying leadership in the service of social justice and democratic community.

Taking a dynamic, integrated, and normative approach has significant implications for research, in terms of both the methodology and the questions that might be appropriate. We suggest that research in this domain will be fundamentally interventionist and advocacy-oriented. We are not aspiring to the development of "grand theory" with its implications of prescription and exclusivity; nor are we advocating scientific approaches to research that, in the past at least, have led to technical solutions, predictability, and control. Leadership research focused on understanding how one advances the cause of education as a moral endeavor is complex and must be, in and of itself, just and deeply democratic. For that reason, the methods we outline here take account of the context and participants in socially just and deeply democratic ways.

Griffiths (1998) advances an understanding that educational research should attend to that which may enhance positive outcomes for individuals and society. This in no way implies that we should distort our findings or ignore perspectives that differ from our own, simply that as educational researchers, our goal is not an objective one. The questions we choose to ask are deeply moral; hence the ways in which we select questions, conduct research, develop meanings, and discuss our interpretations must be sensitive to, and consistent with, these moral purposes.

The questions that we select to guide inquiry are fundamentally connected to questions of meaning, relationships, agency, and power. Educational research conducted by, with, or for people is therefore essentially different from research designed to identify trends or make projections. This is not to deny the possibility of finding strategies to "improve" schools, strategies that might well require an examination and critique of extant practices or approaches that seem particularly "successful" with some students. The key, however, is to understand that each strategy or approach, each word or action is embedded in a set of signifiers relevant to a specific context and to acknowledge that the findings cannot be exported to other contexts without careful consideration of the unique situations of each school.

Bishop and Glynn (1999) argue from a New Zealand context that if researchers are to ensure that issues are not examined purely from within the framework of the "dominant discourse," we must address and redress neocolonial assumptions and practices. Similarly, Griffiths (1998) critiques research about racism in which the researcher "made the decision to give more weight to the expressed views of the powerful" (p. 53), that is, the teachers, and tended to ignore the perspectives of African-Caribbean pupils. Research for and about social justice must begin with careful consideration by researchers of whose perspectives they are seeking and whose voices are being heard, and with reflection on how to ensure that the powerful are not having undue influence either on the processes and conduct of the research or the meanings and interpretations that result. Reflexivity on the part of researchers about their own positions and interests, values and assumptions is essential and is an ongoing struggle for all, including ourselves, who claim the status of researcher in education.

Several recently developed research approaches are consistent with these principles.[4] For example, Thompson and Gitlin (1995) develop the idea of "conversation as method." They note that sometimes educators working from a critical theory perspective call for change yet reproduce existing power relations. Thompson and Gitlin advocate for the development of "we" relationships in inquiry, that is, inquiry is not just about knowledge production but is also about the relationship itself. Furthermore, conversation as method "refers to a process rather than a procedure" (p. 17); instead of conducting inquiry according to assumptions about accepted practices, conversation allows for "experimental shifts" in the relationship, shifts that can lead to creative directions for growth. In these ways, conversation as method can lead to what Thompson and Gitlin call reconstructed knowledge, a form of knowledge that "looks to create spaces in which relationships among the [research] participants are realigned, shifting the balance and authority and thereby challenging the ways in which institutional relations and local actions construct what is important in these relationships" (p. 7). They acknowledge the important contributions of standpoint theory in reminding us that we always "stand" somewhere and that our location influences how we think, see, and respond. As Thompson and Gitlin (1995) say, "knowledge is always referenced to some standpoint, and that such standpoints may represent significant political investments in the claims and characterizations offered," and in the recognition of the links between the personal and the public (p. 13). They go beyond feminist postmodernism and feminist standpoint theory to call for a method that does not focus so much on hearing from oppressed or marginalized groups, but emphasizes "relations with members of groups other than one's own" (p. 15).

Conversation as method seems to us to offer considerable promise for conducting research on leadership for social justice and democratic community. It calls for the researcher to acknowledge his or her standpoint. It recognizes that roles (e.g., researcher, principal, teacher, student) are institutional and embodied, but can be reconstructed (Thompson & Gitlin, 1995). Moreover, although the standing forms of power remain in place, "a space is created in which the roles and relationships involved may be problematized so as to effect new possibilities" (p. 21). In other words, conversation as method is a relational process through which both researchers and researched can be transformed in certain ways and engage in action toward new possibilities.

Rusch's (1995) research models many aspects of conversation as method. Concerned about the dissonance in many restructuring efforts and the apparent difficulties experienced by schools wanting to align their beliefs with democratic practices, she studied six network schools that were working with the Northwest Regional Laboratory's Onward to Excellence Program. Drawing on her own feminist and standpoint perspectives, she designed a research process consistent with democratic practice. Like Thompson and Gitlin (1995), Rusch focused on relationships and reciprocity, on people learning "with each other rather than from each other" (p. 9). Her findings illustrate the potential for this approach in surfacing the values that support democratic practices as espoused and enacted by the principals she studied.

We therefore posit that research that helps us to better understand leadership for socially just and deeply democratic communities will be fundamentally relational and contextual, learning with those in schools who share our interest in this question. Believing that deeply democratic processes focus on how people live, work, and interact, how they develop relationships and learn together in these relationships, we would want to better understand the nature of the relationships in a given school, how they were developed, how they change, and how people learn together. Taking seriously the idea that democratic community can occur within current institutions and structures, we would also want to investigate the ways in which power is understood, shared, and exercised, as well as the ways in which relationships are shaped by political interests. We would seek to identify those who are included or excluded, privileged or marginalized, listened to or silenced; we would ask who benefits and who is disadvantaged by any given decision, practice, resource allocation, or curricular representation. Most important, we would understand leadership not only as the effect of people in roles, but also as the effect of people with ideas acting communally to accomplish their goals. While the agenda for such research cannot be totally predetermined, we suggest it may be guided by some preliminary questions drawn from the concepts we have developed in this chapter.

DIRECTIONS FOR INQUIRY

The foregoing conceptual framework and discussion of methodology suggest a direction for inquiry related to leadership for social justice and democratic community in schools. We propose the five dimensions of leadership we identified earlier as an organizing framework for such a research agenda: ethical and moral, communal and contextual, processual, transformative, and pedagogical. In addition, we propose conversation as method as a general methodological stance from which to conduct such research in specific school sites.

To illustrate the application of these proposals, we imagine ourselves invited to work within a specific school setting to help identify issues of social justice and democratic community and consider the possibilities for leadership. Working with the school community members, we explore the opportunities for in-depth conversation around these issues. Realizing that our agenda cannot be fully predetermined, we nevertheless begin with a series of tentative questions to be explored, organized around the five dimensions of leadership in our framework. Table 8.1 illustrates some possible initial questions. Note that the aim of these questions is primarily to stimulate conversation aimed at "reconstructed knowledge" (Thompson & Gitlin, 1995) within a specific context, thereby leading to new directions for leadership action. Thus, while the initial questions inevitably reflect our own standpoint as researchers concerned with the conjunction of leadership, social justice, and democratic community, conversation as method is intended to negate the privilege of this standpoint, allowing others to surface with equal influence. The outcomes of such a study cannot be anticipated as "answers" to specific questions. Indeed, since the direction of a conversational/interventionist study cannot be predicted, the outcomes are co-created by researchers and participants as the study progresses. The hope for such outcomes is twofold: First, that they are valuable to and benefit the participants at the particular school site as well as the researchers (Griffiths, 1998); and, second, that they generate useful understandings regarding the dynamic relationships among leadership, social justice, and democratic community that can be effectively disseminated to the field.

MOVING FORWARD

We have advanced a normative concept of schools as socially just and deeply democratic communities and of educational leaders as taking a stand for education based on explicitly moral purposes. We believe that leading and learning are fundamentally moral activities whose ethical and ideological bases are constructed in and by the community that comes together in each school. Each is dynamic, constantly being reexamined, challenged, and reconstructed, taking into account changes in

Table 8.1. Dimensions of Leadership and Related Initial
Research Questions

Dimension of Leadership	Key Issues/Questions
Ethical and Moral	What are the stated values of the school community? The formal "leaders"? Whose values are included and whose excluded by these conceptualizations? What congruity and what dissonance are noted? How can leaders help the community negotiate its divergent values so that inclusion is fostered and exclusion is reduced? What values are reflected in the policies and practices of the school community? What changes should be made in these to better reflect inclusive values?
Communal and Contextual	What is the sociocultural/economic community of the school? What cultural traditions are evident in the community and how are they incorporated/validated? What are the patterns of interaction of various groups (e.g., teachers, teachers and students, different ethnic or social groups?) What are the activities in which the community engages together? Who is included and who excluded by these practices? What changes can be made to create practices that are more inclusive and deeply democratic? How are the understandings and practice of "leadership" influenced by these communal processes?
Processual	What are the opportunities for inquiry, critique, and dialogue? Who initiates them? Who is included, privileged, or marginalized in decisionmaking and dialogue? How are the outcomes of decisionmaking and dialogue assessed in regard to social justice and deep democratic community? (i.e., Who benefits? Who is disadvantaged?) How can leaders use dialogue to foster social justice and democratic community?
Transformative	What changes have been introduced in either school cultures or structures and for what reasons? Who initiates these changes? What changes have been identified as desirable in beliefs or practices and how are these being addressed? What changes are needed to enhance social justice and democratic community? What are the barriers to change and what can leaders do about them?
Pedagogical	*Curriculum:* What formal curriculum is in place and what perspectives does it represent? Who selected it? On what basis? *Informal curriculum:* What are the assumed norms, beliefs, or values taught throughout the school? How are these communicated? Who is represented and who excluded by this conception of curriculum? *Assessment:* What are the dominant images of success and how are they assessed and legitimated? How can school leaders influence the conceptions of curriculum and pedagogy to promote dialogue about and understanding of social justice and deep democracy?

the social, cultural, economic, and political context within which schooling occurs at a given time and place. Research aimed at understanding leadership for social justice and democratic community cannot be neutral. It requires an acknowledgment of the multiple, sometimes conflicting, sometimes consensual perspectives that coexist in a deeply democratic community and of the moral basis for choosing among them. To engage in the type of transformative leadership required to achieve schools that are constantly constructing deeply democratic and socially just communities requires the type of dialogue described by Delpit (1990), dialogue that requires "a very special kind of listening, listening that requires not only open eyes and ears, but open hearts and minds" (p. 101).

Engaging in research that leads to a better understanding of the links between educational leadership practice and the normative concepts of social justice and democratic community requires that researchers, too, approach the task, listening and questioning—not only with our eyes and ears, but with our hearts—seeking to put our beliefs on hold in order to understand how to start the dialogue that may result in better understanding and in purposeful action. The research agenda we have proposed in this chapter is a step toward initiating this type of research.

NOTES

1. The extent to which this discussion applies fully to private as well as public schools may depend on their national context. For example, in some parts of Canada, private schools are heavily supported by public funds and hence have more representative populations than schools elsewhere that are not supported by public funds.

2. We acknowledge that the deep democracy concept is still being developed in education; further scholarship is needed to develop this concept and to link it to conceptual developments in other disciplines.

3. We are not arguing against testing or accountability per se; indeed, we are cognizant of the arguments that suggest that in some cases, accountability measures may help to promote social justice (see, for example, Skrla et al., 2001). We are arguing against the widespread tendency toward excessive or exclusive reliance on standardized test scores as proxy measures of learning and as indications of the type of knowledge and learning that is mot valued in society.

4. See, for example, Tillman's (2002) work on culturally sensitive research approaches, Smith's (1999) argument for "decolonising methodologies," Kaomea's (2003) writing on "defamiliarizing interpretive methods," and Griffiths's (1998) framework for research for social justice.

CHAPTER 9

What Do We Know About Developing School Leaders? A Look at Existing Research and Next Steps for New Study

Mark A. Smylie and Albert Bennett
with Pamela Konkol and Carol R. Fendt

School leader development is getting a lot of attention these days. The subject arises in a number of ways. First, it has become increasingly clear how important leadership is to school improvement and effectiveness (see Chapter 2, this volume). And it is expected that issues facing schools will grow in complexity and intensity in the years ahead, making school leaders' work more difficult and demanding but perhaps all the more important (Lugg, Bulkley, Firestone, & Garner, 2002). Second, most observers expect that demand for new school leaders will grow rapidly as the average age of that workforce increases, rates of retirement rise, and growing job demands take their toll (Papa, Lankford, & Wyckoff, 2002). Demand may be greatest in local markets with high concentrations of underresourced and low-performing schools (Roza, 2003). While there is some debate about whether shortages of school leaders now exist, there is increasing concern about whether there will be sufficient numbers of *well-qualified* school leaders to meet demand in the years to come (Educational Research Service, 1998). Then, there is growing skepticism about the ability of conventional means of school leader development to cultivate effective school leadership, and there is a growing imperative for change (Hess, 2003; Tucker & Codding, 2002). According to Hale and Moorman (2003), "Today, school leadership—more specifically, the principalship—is a front burner issue in every state" (p. 1). Conventional assumptions and practices of school leader development are being contested not only in the policy arena but also in the real world of schools.

With this matter squarely before us for the foreseeable future, there is a need to take stock of what we know and what we need to know about how to promote school leader development effectively. The purpose of this chapter is to assess the existing research on school leader development and to propose areas of new study. Our discussion is organized around three broad questions: (a) What should we know about school leader development to promote it effectively? (b) What do we know about these things now? (c) What among these things do we need to know more about? Our general conclusion is that the existing research tells us little about these things and that we face the problem of school leader development with remarkably weak evidence to guide us.

Before we begin, it is important to frame our work. We defined school leader development somewhat narrowly, as a problem of building individual school leaders' capacities through initial or preservice preparation, socialization and induction, and opportunities for in-service professional learning and development. We considered but, because of its extensive scope, did not adopt a broader human resource management or workforce development perspective. Such a perspective would bring into focus a larger set of issues, including supply and demand; recruitment, selection, and retention; supervision and evaluation; compensation and rewards; "management" of school leaders as an organizational resource (i.e., entry and exit, mobility, "allocation" across tasks and worksites, etc.); and the promotion of effective performance through incentives, accountability, and supportive work environments. It would treat school leader development not simply as a problem of developing individual school leaders but as a more comprehensive and complex problem of developing and managing a system of school leadership. There is a small but growing literature that begins to address these issues; however, it has not been synthesized or linked to the literature on individual leader development.

Also, the vast majority of the literature on school leader development focuses on the principal. There is relatively little research on the development of assistant principals, teacher and parent leaders, superintendents, midlevel system administrators, union leaders, or school board members, not to mention municipal, state, or federal policymakers and education officials. This is a serious shortcoming. The importance of these leaders to the improvement and effectiveness of schools and school systems is becoming increasingly apparent, but since so little attention has been paid to their development, we focus on principals.

Finally, our discussion of existing research is not meant to be comprehensive. We searched the major academic educational leadership and administration journals and ERIC and EBSCO databases to map the terrain. We gave preference to reports of original research and research that focused on outcomes of school leader development rather than essays and advocacy literature. Because of space limitations, we draw on a fraction of the literature we reviewed. Our objective was to paint a representative picture of the available evidence to lay a foundation for new study.

WHAT WE SHOULD KNOW

In order to promote school leader development effectively, we believe we should know a good deal about at least three related subjects. These subjects derive from the literature on human resource management (e.g., Wright, Dunford, & Snell, 2001) and from literature on leadership development in noneducation settings (e.g., Bass, 1990; McCauley & Van Veslor, 2004). They are also suggested by the literature on teacher professional learning and development (e.g., Sikula, 1996; Smylie & Miretzky, 2004).

First, we should know what capacities—knowledge, skills, and dispositions—are required of school leaders to perform their jobs well now and in the future. We should know about differences in capacity required for school leadership in different school, community, and system contexts. And we should know about differences in capacity required for school leaders to achieve different objectives, including school improvement and student achievement, development of democratic community, and promotion of social justice (Marshall, 2004; Murphy, 2002b). Such knowledge provides goals and content for school leader development as well as criteria to assess its effectiveness. Without the direction that such knowledge provides, school leader development is aimless. Without understanding which capacities are most conducive to effective leadership performance, it is pointless.

Second, we should know about the social, psychological, and cognitive processes by which capacity for leadership develops. Knowledge of these processes—*how* school leaders learn and *how* they develop skills and dispositions at different stages of their careers—provides the conceptual and theoretical foundation for assessing the efficacy of known development strategies and for choosing among them. It provides a basis for developing new, potentially more effective strategies.

Third, we should understand the function and relative effectiveness of different sources, strategies, and resources to promote school leader development. By *sources* we mean settings and providers. By *strategies* we mean practices and experiences intended to promote learning and development. By *resources* we mean money, time, curricula, instructional supplies, and other tangible materials. Such knowledge, with theoretical knowledge of development processes, provides understanding about how and why school leader development practices might work (or why they don't). It also provides evidence for planning and decisionmaking. It is also important to understand factors that support or constrain school leader development activity. Such knowledge can reveal contexts most conducive to school leader development and to the efficient and effective use of resources for that purpose.

WHAT WE KNOW (AND DON'T KNOW) NOW

We now turn our attention to what the literature tells us about each of these subjects. In our discussion, we assess the state of the existing research, noting its strengths and weaknesses. We find that overall we know very little, and what we think we know rests on shaky empirical ground.

Capacities for Effective School Leadership

Efforts to identify the knowledge, skills, and dispositions associated with effective leadership have a long history (Bass, 1990; Yukl, 2002). In education, we have approached the matter in several different ways. We have surveyed school leaders and teachers for their views about what school leaders need to know and be able to do. We have observed how schools are changing and have argued about how schools ought to be changed, and then we have pointed to particular capacities that leaders need to be effective in light of these changes. Primarily, we have looked to research on leadership practices associated with student achievement and school improvement and inferred the knowledge, skills, and dispositions that might be needed to enact those practices. We contend that knowledge of effective leadership practices is not the same thing as knowledge of the capacities required for enactment. Our understanding of effective school leadership practice has grown tremendously in recent years, and much of that understanding is presented in chapters of this book. However, our understanding of the knowledge, skills, and dispositions required for school leaders to be effective is much less well developed.

Three recent projects to articulate a base of knowledge and skills for effective school leadership illustrate this point. These include the efforts of the National Commission for the Principalship and the National Policy Board for Educational Administration to establish a national certification process for school principals and standards to improve the quality of school leader preparation programs (Thomson, 1993); the University Council for Educational Administration's (UCEA) study to identify relevant knowledge for leadership practice and inquiry in educational administration (Hoy, 1994); and the work of the Interstate School Leaders Licensure Consortium to develop standards for school leader preparation, licensure, and practice (ISLLC, 1996).

Each of these projects identified similar areas of knowledge, skills, dispositions, and behaviors. The UCEA project identified seven domains of knowledge deemed "essential" for educational leaders: (a) societal and cultural influences in schooling; (b) teaching and learning processes; (c) organizational studies; (d) leadership and management processes; (e) policy and political studies; (f) legal and ethical dimensions of schooling; and (g) economic and financial dimensions of schooling. The ISLLC (1996) project identified six areas associated with effective school leadership: (a) "facilitating the development, articulation, implementation, and stewardship of a vision of learning that is shared and supported by the school community" (p. 10); (b) "advocating, nurturing, and sustaining a school culture and instructional program conducive to student learning and staff professional growth" (p. 12); (c) "ensuring management of the organization, operations, and resources for a safe, efficient, and effective learning environment" (p. 14); (d) "collaborating with families and community members, responding to diverse community interests and needs, and mobilizing community resources" (p. 16); (e) "acting with integrity, fairness, and in an ethical manner" (p. 18); and (f) "understanding, responding to, and influencing the larger political, social, economic, legal, and cultural context" (p. 20). The National Policy Board identified similar domains and in 2002 released a revised set of standards that mirrored ISLLC's six areas. Because of these similarities, we focus on the UCEA and ISLLC projects.

Although they have been subject to debate, these projects represent the most comprehensive efforts to date to articulate a knowledge base of capacity for effective school leadership. The question most relevant to this discussion is not, "How do we know what school leaders need to do to be effective?" Rather, it is, "How do we know what capacities school leaders need to develop to be effective in their practice?" One way to address this question is to look at how the UCEA and ISLLC projects were conducted and at the "evidence" on which their conclusions rest.

The UCEA project convened study teams of academic researchers, one for each area of knowledge. These teams were asked to identify "the essential content and processes of their domain" and to consider empirical evidence, interpretive perspectives, "wisdom of practice," and "knowledge of scholarship" (Hoy, 1994, p. 179). Each team was to incorporate multicultural, emergent, feminist, and traditional perspectives. The ISLLC standards were drafted by representatives of 24 state education agencies in affiliation with 11 professional education organizations (ISLLC, 1996). They were derived from research on academically effective schools, instructional leadership, and school improvement; expert professional and scholarly opinion; and predictions about new demands that school leaders will face from anticipated changes in school and society. What is important is that these projects used multiple sources of "evidence," but most of the empirical research they relied upon focused on school leader behavior. Their "findings" concerning knowledge, skills, and dispositions needed for effective leadership were informed but largely inferential (Murphy, personal communication, September 24, 2004).

Indeed, there is remarkably little empirical evidence on school leader knowledge, skills, and dispositions and their relationship to leadership practice. In the early 1990s, several studies were conducted that found positive relationships between principals' problem-framing and problem-solving skills and their orientation toward instructional leadership and ability to solve problems (Hallinger, Leithwood, & Murphy, 1993). More recently, evidence has begun to emerge about the importance of "leadership content knowledge," that is, principals' knowledge of academic subject matter, what it takes for students to learn that subject matter, and what it takes for teachers to teach it (Stein & Nelson, 2003; also chapters 3 and 4, this volume).

There are other matters concerning our knowledge about capacity for effective school leadership that deserve attention. First, as reflected in the focus of the ISLLC standards on a common core of capacities, we have not gone very far in articulating the range of knowledge, skills, and dispositions that may be associated with effective role-specific leadership (e.g., assistant principal, superintendent) or leadership in different school and community contexts and reform environments (e.g., underresourced and low-performing schools, decentralized school governance, and centralized high stakes accountability). Nor have we identified specific capacities that may be required to deal with some of our most perplexing educational problems (e.g., the minority achievement gap).

Second, the literature on teacher learning and development emphasizes the importance of how outcomes are conceptualized (e.g., Mumby, Russell, & Martin, 2001). Present thinking focuses on *what* school leaders should know and *what* dispositions they should hold. We have not thought much about different ways of knowing and believing. Learning theorists distinguish among learning outcomes that are more and less conducive to intellectually, socially, and ethically demanding work. For instance, Merriam and Caffarella (1991) contrast task-specific, instrumental learning with conceptual, reflective, self-empowering learning. Argyris and Schön (1978) distinguish proactive, creative, critical, reflective learning from passive, reactive, unreflective learning. And Van Maanen and Schein (1979) contend that learning can lead to conformity or to innovation. Those who study the development of professional knowledge generally and teacher professional knowledge in particular (e.g., Cochran-Smith & Lytle, 1999; Eraut, 1994; Wilson & Berne, 1999) distinguish between declarative and procedural or technical knowledge and conditional or craft knowledge that involves knowing when, how, and why to apply technical knowledge in particular practice situations. And they distinguish between "novice" and "expert" ways of knowing (National Research Council, 2000).

This literature concludes that while technical knowledge is important, it is insufficient for effective practice if not accompanied by well-developed craft knowledge. If school leadership is a "complex and multi-faceted task" (ISLLC, 1996, p. 5); if, in order to be effective, school leaders must act as moral stewards, community builders, and change agents (Murphy, 2002b); and if school leadership is highly intellectual ethical work, then it is important to understand a great deal more than we do now about the ways in which school leaders know and think that may be associated with effective leadership.

Processes of School Leader Learning and Development

The literature is largely silent on the social, psychological, and cognitive processes by which school leaders learn and develop (Vandenberghe, 2003). The one area in which learning and development processes have been explored somewhat systematically is role and organizational socialization. In his 1988 review of literature, Miklos examined the socialization that occurs prior to job appointment; the influences of sponsors, mentors, and role models; and the formal and informal socialization that occurs after job appointment. He pointed to the importance of social (gender) and work role structures and the prior learning, experiences, and characteristics of individuals who are the means and subjects of socialization. He also pointed to the importance of organizational context as a mediator and source of socialization.

Miklos (1988) did not explore very deeply the social and psychological processes by which socialization and induction occur. That work was taken up later. In her analysis of leader succession, Hart (1993) drew on various theories from psychology, sociology, and social psychology to explore socialization as a learning and influence process. She examined the motivation to interact and the nature and function of different interaction processes. She applied different process theories of social interaction (e.g., cultural structuring, symbolic interactionism, dramaturgy and interaction rituals) to show how utility, exchange, individual self-concept, and information interpretation, among other things, shape the individual and organizational outcomes of new leader socialization.

Beyond these analyses, little attention has been paid to the characteristics of school leaders, to the contexts in which they work, and to how they may relate to school leader learning and development. Little is known about how processes of learning and development may vary for school leaders in different stages of life or in different phases of their careers (see Weindling, 2000). McGough's (2003) recent research on career paths of experienced principals is one of very few studies that examines the biographic sources of principals' perspectives on leadership. While there has been growing attention in recent years to diversity in the school leader workforce (e.g., Pounder, 1994; Shakeshaft, 1999), little has been said about the development of women and racial and ethnic minority school leaders or the ways in which their development might be promoted (Rusch, 2004). Some attention has been paid to factors affecting the career decisionmaking and the socialization of women and minority school leaders (e.g., Brunner, 1999; Young & McLeod, 2001), but larger questions concerning their learning and development remain unasked and unexplored. Also, while some attention has been paid to the development of urban school leaders (e.g., Neufeld, 1997; Portin, 2000) and to the development demands of different educational reforms (e.g., Ricciardi, 1999), there is little research on the role of different workplace and policy contexts as sources and mediators of school leader development.

Effectiveness of Means of School Leader Development

There has been a great deal written about the preservice preparation, induction, and on-the-job professional development of school leaders. The research on outcomes is remarkably weak (see also Murphy & Vriesenga, 2004). In general, this work is conceptually ambiguous and atheoretical. Most studies are poorly constructed and rely on self-report data. The literature is dominated by descriptive, anecdotal, and promotional reports of local programs and practices, often written by those who develop or implement them.

Several other observations can be made about this literature. The existing research provides little understanding of "best practice." There are no critical masses of studies on similar development strategies from which to draw generalizations (Tschannen-Moran et al., 2000). Scant attention has been paid to the goals or content of school leader development. There is virtually no consideration that different strategies might be more or less conducive to promoting different development objectives. The research tends to focus on gross design characteristics of programs and practices with little sense of the outcomes they seek to achieve. In addition, there is little research examining different sources of and resources for school leader development. As noted below, there are a few surveys of school leader preferences regarding sources and logistics of professional development, but no studies attempt to tie these preferences to outcomes. We found no research examining the costs of school leader development or the cost effectiveness of different development sources and strategies.

The effectiveness of different means of school leader development cannot be fully understood without examining the outcomes they seek to achieve. Nor can their effectiveness be understood without examining the interactions among or the cumulative effects of those different means. The literature comes up short in this regard. Typically, individual studies examine one means of development apart from others. The research fails to examine different means of school leader development as they operate across school leaders' careers. For that matter, there are virtually no studies that provide empirical evidence concerning relationships among school leader development opportunities, recruitment and retention, and other workforce issues. As a result, it is difficult to see how different means of development may function as a "system" of influences across school leaders' careers.

A small related body of research concerns school leaders' "opportunities to learn." These studies usually proceed from a logic that if school leaders are not provided adequate opportunities to learn particular things, they will lack capacity for these things in practice. Two examples of such analyses are Marshall's (2004) assessment of school leaders' opportunities to develop "social justice value stances and skills" (p. 6) and Rusch's (2004) study of university educational leadership faculty members and students' opportunities to learn about issues of gender and race in school leadership. Analyses such as these draw on earlier surveys of university faculty or curriculum reviews of university-based preparation programs, or present original data to argue that school leaders have few opportunities to learn about issues of educational inequality and cultural diversity. Similar analyses have been made of opportunities for school leaders to learn about teaching and student learning (e.g., McCarthy, 1999; Stein & Nelson, 2003).

Preservice preparation. The literature on the preservice preparation of principals is quite large. It includes general surveys describing program designs and curricula and descriptions of local programs, most considered promising or exemplary, but only a few of which have been evaluated. The literature also contains descriptions of and arguments for particular pedagogical strategies, again, only a few of which have been evaluated. There are essays presenting frameworks and recommendations for improving preservice preparation, mostly without theoretical or empirical support; and studies describing external influences on preservice preparation programs and practices, such as state and national policy, professional organizations, national boards, and foundation-supported initiatives. There are also a growing number of surveys and social justice critiques of the curriculum and pedagogy of preservice preparation programs that point to inadequate opportunities for the study of social justice issues.

The few reviews that have been conducted of research on principal preparation are indicative of the state of the literature. Miklos's 1983 review was "more a description and analysis of evolving beliefs about preparation than . . . about actual preparation programs" (p. 154). Sixteen years later, McCarthy's (1999) review examined external influences on and changes in college and university departments of education leadership and administrator preparation programs. McCarthy observed then, as do we now, that there is a good bit of descriptive literature on administrator preparation programs, but there is little evidence on the outcomes of these programs or efforts to improve them. More recent reviews by Murphy (in press; Murphy & Vriesenga, 2004) focus primarily on the history and critique of leader programs and also note the dearth and poor quality of research on program outcomes.

We found that most studies of program outcomes are based on noncomparative survey designs. Typically these studies rely on graduates' reports of satisfaction with or perceived usefulness of their programs. Or they rely on central office administrators' or school staff members' perceptions of graduates' general effectiveness. It is almost impossible to find studies that use direct measures of preservice leaders' knowledge, skills, dispositions, or behaviors before or after completion. Most evaluative studies fail to explore how local context may affect the outcomes they document. We found no studies comparing outcomes of different preparation programs and practices. There are a number of reports *describing* different strategies used in principal preparation programs, including problem-based learning, simulations, mentoring and internships, cohort models, and portfolio- and performance-based assessments. However, evidence on the outcomes of such strategies is quite limited. Most of it comes from a handful of small-scale studies conducted as part of local programs, often by investigators who are associated with them.

Of the two published evaluations we found of problem-based learning, one found a positive relationship between preservice leaders' problem-framing ability and their differential exposure to problem-based learning (Copland, 2000). The other, a study of university-based programs participating in the Danforth Foundation's Program for the Preparation of School Principals, found that graduates considered seminars and opportunities for problem-based learning among the most valuable aspects of their preparation, and teachers and colleagues working with them generally perceived them to be effective leaders (Leithwood, Jantzi, & Coffin, 1995).

The half-dozen studies we found assessing the outcomes of cohort models provide rather weak and indirect evidence of their effectiveness. These studies do little to distinguish the effects of cohort organization from other factors, such as curriculum and instructional quality. One study that surveyed university faculty members found that those working in cohort programs perceived organizational efficiencies and immediate learner benefits, whereas those who did not raised concerns about program rigidity and personal costs for students (Barnett, Basom, Yerkes, & Norris, 2000). Another study that surveyed students and faculty at another university identified several outcomes of a cohort program there—strong student support, opportunities for exchange among students and faculty, and potential for student influence on program planning and decision (Teitel, 1997). This study also identified a downside to cohort models—fears of being "trapped" in long-term conflictive relationships. Yet another study found that teachers perceived principals prepared in cohort programs to be more effective than principals prepared in other programs (Leithwood et al., 1995).

Several recent reviews claim a number of positive outcomes of mentoring (Daresh, 2004; Ehrich, Hansford, & Tennet, 2004). For beginning principals these outcomes include support, empathy, and encouragement; help developing job-related knowledge and skills and solving professional problems; and positive reinforcement and feedback on performance. They also include support for adjusting to new work settings and developing new role conceptions (Browne-Ferrigno & Muth, 2004). For mentors, benefits include opportunities for professional development and networking, and personal and professional reward. It is difficult to tell how much evidence there is to support these claims (Grogan & Crow, 2004). For instance, Ehrich and her colleagues (2004) draw on "research-based" literature, but it is unclear what this means.[1] Like the literature on other means of school leader development, much of the literature on mentoring is descriptive, anecdotal, and relies on participant self-reports rather than more objective measures of outcomes. Most studies focus on *anticipated* benefits of mentoring rather than *actual* outcomes.

A few studies have examined factors that affect the development and function of mentoring relationships (see Ehrich et al., 2004). Among those factors are skills and attitudes that protégés bring to their mentoring relationships, the preparation of mentors, and competing demands on protégés' time and attention. Overall, this research suggests that the benefits of mentoring are likely to be greater when mentors and protégés are prepared for their work together and there are fewer competing demands on protégés. In addition, this work suggests that mentoring may be more effective as part of preservice preparation than during induction because once they are on the job school leaders may be exposed to competing sources of influence.

Socialization and induction. Miklos's 1988 review provides a good portrait of the literature on school leader socialization and induction through the mid-1980s. Much of that literature derived from concerns about the underrepresentation of women and minorities in educational administration. Miklos cited research on gender role conflicts that women may experience entering male-oriented administrative work. He discussed studies of the importance of role models and mentors to women school leaders. Noting that the "administrative culture" is often transmitted through informal interaction with established administrator groups, Miklos pointed to research showing that women and minority school leaders are not likely to have the same access as male and white school leaders, thus putting them at a competitive disadvantage for leadership positions. Socialization experiences of men and women were reported to vary considerably because of differential access to informal networks. Miklos noted that while mentors' role models were frequently mentioned in this early literature, little attention was paid to the processes of leader socialization or its outcomes.

Studies of school leader induction and socialization conducted since the mid-1980s fall into four general categories. The largest consists of descriptive reports of local programs that do little more than discuss program objectives, design characteristics, and activities. A second category consists of needs assessments of induction support. A third category consists of studies of induction and socialization experiences that often include self-reports of what aspects of those experiences beginning principals consider most useful. A fourth category includes studies of induction and socialization influence. This research is typically more theoretical than the rest and goes beyond self-reports to document and analyze socialization influence directly. We focus on the last two categories of studies.

In general, the research suggests that beginning principals find most value in personal, intensive, and collaborative induction experiences with veteran school leaders (Elsberry & Bishop, 1993; Ricciardi & Petrosko, 2000). Formal training programs, university coursework, involvement in professional organizations, books and journals, and technology programs hold less value. Several studies suggest that induction experiences vary considerably and that perceived benefits are related to the principals' personal characteristics and the characteristics of the school in which they work (e.g., Norton, 1994). Teachers and supervisors have been found to be strong sources of socialization influence, the former being particularly influential in shaping beginning principals' sense of control over instructional and personnel issues. Yet another study identified social trust, mutual appreciation, job stress, and personal efficacy as important factors in new principal induction (Vandenberghe, 2003).[2]

The literature on leader succession provides additional insight into principal learning and development through socialization. Hart (1993) has described socialization as an ongoing, interactive, mutually influential process between the principal and the school organization and argued that the most influential sources of socialization are informal. She pointed to several studies that support this conclusion. In one, Leithwood, Steinbach, and Begley (1992) found that among the myriad of socialization experiences of Canadian principals and vice principals those that seemed most valuable were informal and embedded in the social contexts of their schools. In another, Cosgrove (1986) found that existing school social groups, particularly teacher groups, had stronger influence than mentors in the socialization of new principals, especially in the area of instruction. Similar findings have been reported in subsequent studies (e.g., Weindling & Earley, 1987).

In-service professional development. Much like the literature on preservice preparation and induction and socialization, the literature on in-service professional development of principals is largely descriptive and anecdotal. There are very few systematic evaluations. The literature contains a number of surveys of principals' professional development needs and preferred professional development experiences, but there are virtually no studies of outcomes.

Different surveys of principals report different professional development preferences. In one survey, principals preferred in-house training to other forms of school-based professional development and believed that they learned best from activities they helped plan and that addressed problems they confronted in their work (Brown, Anfara, Hartman, Mahar, & Mills, 2002). In another survey, principals preferred a cohort approach to professional development, stating that this approach provided opportunities to collaborate with colleagues, observe others' practice, and develop self-analytic skills (Neufeld, 1997). Perhaps the most comprehensive findings come from Walker, Mitchel, and Turner's survey (1999). For principals in that study, effective professional development would proceed from an agenda developed with their input. It would take place after school and would involve teachers as well as principals' immediate supervisors. Topics would address different needs of beginning and experienced principals and be related to specific problems and contexts. Continuity and follow-up would be priorities.

While these findings are consistent with general principles of effective principal professional development (e.g., Evans & Mohr, 1999), there is little empirical evidence that the learning experiences principals prefer or consider effective promote capacity for school leadership or improve leadership practice. Most studies that purport to measure outcomes are based on participant self-reports of how easy or difficult it is to implement strategies presented in professional development programs. There are virtually no studies that follow principals into their schools to see if professional development programs actually affect their behavior. We found no studies of the comparative effectiveness of different models of professional development.

WHAT WE NEED TO KNOW MORE ABOUT: NEXT STEPS FOR NEW STUDY

We began this chapter with an argument that in order to promote school leader development effectively we should know about three related subjects. The first is the capacities—the knowledge, skills, and dispositions—required of school leaders to perform their jobs well now and in the future. The second is the social, psychological, and cognitive processes of school leader learning and development. And the third is the function and effectiveness of different sources, strategies, and resources that could be used to promote school leader development. We argued that understanding these subjects would provide a theoretical and empirical foundation for determining what learning and development should be promoted and how that learning and development might be promoted effectively. Our assessment of existing research led us to conclude that we know very little about these subjects and that we face the problem of school leader development with remarkably little empirical evidence to guide us. Our suggestions for new study follow from this argument.

We begin by laying out some overarching needs. Then we turn to more specific recommendations for inquiry. We conclude with a discussion of how different areas of research interrelate and implications for conducting this work. The rationale for our recommendations is largely practical, guided by a sense of what new knowledge would be helpful to guide efforts to design and implement more effective policies and practices for school leader development. Our recommendations are not exhaustive, but represent a series of "next steps." Where appropriate, we mention methodology, but we do not discuss this subject in much depth. We believe that advancing knowledge about school leader development will require a variety of research designs and analytic strategies.

Overarching Needs

There is a general need for systematic reviews and syntheses of existing literature. Notably, the rather large descriptive literature on local programs and practices should be mined for the lessons it provides. We might also learn a great deal by looking to the literature on teacher professional learning and development, adult learning and career development theory, and learning and development in other professions (e.g., Daresh & Playko, 1995; Ehrich et al., 2004). And much might be gained from relevant theoretical literature from noneducation fields and disciplines (e.g., chapters 3 and 4, this volume).

We found remarkably little research on the development of underrepresented groups of school leaders, notably women and racial and ethnic minorities. We could learn much more about the experiences of women and minority school leaders in programs of preservice preparation and in-service professional development. We could examine more systematically the learning and development needs of these school leaders as they confront issues of race and gender in their work, especially as these needs relate to job retention and performance. In addition, as alternative preparation programs and routes to licensure develop in the years to come, growing numbers of nontraditional candidates will assume school leader positions. Their learning and development needs and the means to address them are other important areas of investigation.

We remarked at the beginning of this chapter that almost all of the literature on school leader development focuses on the principal. We strongly encourage research on the development of other school leaders, including assistant principals, teacher and parent leaders, superintendents, midlevel system administrators, union leaders, and school board members. And as we learn more about leadership as an organizational or distributive property of schools and about the importance of relationships among building, district, and state levels of school organization, we should also examine ways to develop more comprehensive systems of leadership within and across roles and levels.

Finally, recall that for this chapter we defined school leader development rather narrowly, as a matter of building individual school leaders' capacity for leadership. We noted the potential benefits of adopting a broader human resource management perspective that would frame the problem as one of individual *and* collective capacity development and management. We indicated that a more comprehensive perspective might help us understand the relationship of the development of school leader knowledge, skills, and dispositions to a larger system of issues including but not limited to supply and demand; recruitment, selection, and retention; entry, exit, and mobility; and effective job performance. We have not developed good conceptual and theoretical frameworks for studying such a system. But inasmuch as the practical problem of developing an effective school leader workforce requires attention to all these matters, such a perspective would be extremely useful.

Next Steps

Our review of the literature opens the door to a wide range of studies on many different topics. We suggest three areas on which to focus first.

First, while great progress has been made to develop knowledge about effective leadership practices, there is a need to better understand the knowledge, skills, and dispositions associated with those practices. It is from such understanding that all else follows. We should continue to investigate the common knowledge, skills, and dispositions associated with leadership practices that can promote school improvement, student achievement, and social justice outcomes. This inquiry should make problematic and test the inferences about school leader capacity contained in current school leader standards, in reports of expert opinion, and in value-based arguments. We might learn a great deal from studies that examine whether school leaders who develop these capacities over time actually become more effective in their practice. In addition, we should explore variation in the capacities associated with the effective performance of different leadership roles and with effective leadership in different school, community, and reform contexts.

Our review also suggests that we would benefit from knowing more about *how* (and why) different ways of knowing and believing may be more or less conducive to effective leadership practice. We distinguished between declarative, procedural knowledge and conditional or craft knowledge. We also identified differences between learning associated with reflection, creativity, and innovation and learning associated with task-specific, routine, instrumental knowledge. We should deepen our understanding of different forms of professional knowing, thinking, and believing that make for more or less effective "doing." Differences between novice understanding and veteran expertise should also be explored more thoroughly.

The other two areas we suggest as next steps are related—the quality and effectiveness of different ways to prepare school leaders and to support their induction and transition to practice. As noted earlier, most observers predict a growing shortage of school leaders in the near future and a concurrent need to prepare a substantial number of new leaders to meet future demand. By demand we refer not only to numbers of new school leaders who may be needed to fill vacant positions, but also the need to address effectively new demands placed on school leaders from changes in school and society. In relation, there is substantial attention now being paid to improving school leader preparation. Conventional approaches are being subjected to increased scrutiny. Experimental and alternative programs are proliferating. There are unprecedented opportunities to engage in comparative studies of conventional and alternative approaches. There are also growing opportunities to conduct design experiments of newly developed programs and strategies. New research on these two aspects of school leader development may inform the debate about the most effective ways to prepare future school leaders. It may also provide guidance for program and policy development.

Our review has suggested a number of areas of school leader preparation and induction that are important to study. Among them are organizational and program design features, curriculum and subject matter content, the quality of pedagogy, and the role of field experiences and internships. Future research on these and other areas of school leader preparation and induction support should be grounded in consideration of goals and content. We should develop our understanding of different means of school leader development not as generic, unintentional activities but as purposive ones that seek to achieve valued and defensible outcomes. If we are interested in learning more about effective means of school leader development, we should understand their effectiveness in terms of achieving important objectives.

A need exists to focus more systematically on outcomes. Existing research on the effectiveness of different means of school leader development suffers tremendously from problems of defining and measuring outcomes. Future research must move past self-reports and secondhand perceptual data to more direct measures of school leader capacity, measures that are associated theoretically and empirically with effective leadership practice. It should also explore ways to establish evidence of relationships between learning and development and subsequent changes in practice. Future research on school leader preparation and induction should examine the impact of different strategies for achieving particular objectives with different groups of leaders. Future research might also explore whether particular strategies vary in their effectiveness with regard to different leadership roles, organizational contexts, and policy environments. We encourage study of how initial preparation and induction might interact and function as a coherent system of learning and development. The proliferation of new programs and strategies provides numerous opportunities for comparative studies of "natural experiments."

To accompany this closer look at outcomes, we suggest a related line of implementation research. It will be difficult to draw meaningful conclusions about the effectiveness of different programs and strategies without knowledge about what it takes to enact them. Once greater understanding is gained of effective development strategies, it will be very important to know more about individual, organizational, and environmental factors that promote or impede their implementation and outcomes. In addition, it will be important to learn more about the efficacy of different sources and delivery systems of school leader preparation and induction support. The literature provides little evidence about the relative ability of major institutional providers, such as colleges and universities, professional associations and networks, school systems, educational agencies, and commercial enterprises, to prepare and support school leaders effectively and efficiently. We have little understanding about which sources are best suited to "supply" what aspects of school leader learning and development across the career span.

And finally, there is the issue of cost. The literature contains no systematic accounting of the financial, material, or human resources that are spent on school leader preparation and induction support. There is no evidence of the relative costs of different programs and strategies. Nor are there estimates of cost-effectiveness as measured against outcomes. We believe that while we need to develop our understanding of effective strategies for school leader preparation and induction support, it is also very important to know more about the resources that are required for them to be successful.

CONCLUDING THOUGHTS

Looking across these suggestions for new study, we see a number of important interconnections. For instance, our understanding of effective means of school leader development is tied to our knowledge of capacities associated with effective leadership practice. And our understanding of the function and outcomes of different means of school leader development is related to our theoretical and empirical knowledge of the processes by which school leaders learn and develop. These and other connections point to a programmatic quality of future inquiry and to coherence not found across existing research. This implies long-term commitment, coordination, and levels of resources often difficult for individual or small groups of researchers to secure and sustain. This also suggests a need for patience and persistence to engage in the in-depth and longitudinal work required to develop critical masses of cumulative knowledge for the long haul, a stance that runs counter to pressures for quick answers and action.

It is difficult to think about getting very far without collaboration among researchers, school systems, and providers of school leader development, and without leadership to guide and support the work. The American Educational Research Association and the University Council for Educational Administration, with national professional associations of school leaders, have the capacity to convene these parties to set priorities and craft specific agendas and programs of new research. Once under way, these organizations can be instrumental in coordinating and promoting cross-pollination among separate studies and the accumulation of new knowledge and understanding. Moreover, these organizations have the capacity to work with foundations, government agencies, and other sources of funding to support and sustain this work over time.

Of course, the challenges facing schools and school leaders will not wait until everything gets figured out. There is a sense of urgency to do something now, however well or poorly informed. Thoughtful experimentation with new approaches to school leader development can be a good thing if accompanied by theoretically sound and politically disinterested inquiry. The challenge will be to avoid overstating knowledge claims, to be constructively skeptical in the absence of credible evidence, and to subject to scrutiny and inquiry new efforts to promote school leader development. The objective should not simply be to act, but to act with the intention to promote new knowledge and understanding and, it is hoped, more effective policy and practice in the future.

NOTES

1. Ehrich et al. (2004) refer to two earlier papers that are said to contain additional details about the literature contained in their review. Because their review was published just as this chapter went to press, there was no opportunity to obtain these earlier papers.

2. In general, the literature is largely silent on the possibility that close, collaborative induction and socialization experiences can serve to reinforce undesirable attitudes and outcomes, for instance reinforcing negative stereotypes of low-achieving students and low-income and minority students. Grogan and Crow (2004) raise this issue in terms of the role of mentoring in perpetuating "business as usual."

CHAPTER 10

What Research Methods Should Be Used to Study Educational Leadership?

Carolyn Riehl and William A. Firestone

In this volume, authors have raised questions to be addressed through new research and have suggested how that research might be pursued. Here, we explore further the appropriate methodologies for significant new research on educational leadership.

We first acknowledge multiple sources of knowledge for leadership practice and policy, to situate empirical research within a broader ecology of leadership knowledge. We then turn to the special case of systematic inquiry, the focus of this volume. We discuss some current, relevant critiques of educational research. Then we summarize promising research methods, referring to the suggestions for research presented in preceding chapters of this volume. We conclude by briefly describing some implications of these ideas.

SOURCES OF KNOWLEDGE FOR LEADERSHIP

A cursory look at debates about educational research might suggest that the only valuable knowledge is that developed by using rigorous research methods to study empirical phenomena. But in any field of practice, authoritative guidance typically comes from several sources, each with different kinds of knowledge claims and different warrants for those claims.

For example, sources of normative knowledge about core ideals and values for a field of practice may come from scholarship in the humanities, ethical and philosophical analyses, cultural studies, and even religious beliefs. Such sources of knowledge draw out conceptual, logical, and moral insights and provide ideas and principles to undergird practice. Normative scholarship in educational leadership has a long history. A century ago, educational leaders often spoke and acted like philosophers of education. After the rise of scientific management, professional expertise came to be associated less with normative knowledge about schooling than with operational knowledge, particularly knowledge derived from formal inquiry. Currently, even the most avid promoters of scientific inquiry in education acknowledge that normative knowledge should inform the profession (e.g., National Research Council [NRC], 2002b).

Reflective practice is a second source of insight. Practitioners learn by thinking carefully about what they do (Schön, 1983). Practical wisdom about organizational leadership has been written down to be shared at least since 1938, when Chester Barnard published his reflections on corporate management. Unfortunately, knowledge derived from reflective practice sometimes has been treated as similar to research-based knowledge and criticized for having thin methodological grounds. This undercuts the valid epistemological basis for the wisdom of practice. Reflective practice need not ignore or contradict research-based knowledge. In fact, research can provide concepts that frame how practitioners think about their work. This point has been made for teaching by Shulman (1987), who sees the wisdom of practice as a valid source of knowledge, and Richardson (1994), who suggests that formal research can help structure practitioners' reasoning.

A somewhat more disciplined third source of knowledge is often termed practical inquiry or action research. Such inquiry is explicitly intended to add to knowledge in local contexts (Riehl, Larson, Short, & Reitzug, 2000). It may use formal methods for gathering information and drawing conclusions, but methodological choices are made to maximize the ability to inform local policy or practice quickly. Action research usually does not aspire to generalization or wide dissemination. It is often conducted by practitioners and by those who work closely with practitioners. In education, increased respect for local inquiries stems from an emphasis on schools as learning organizations (Senge, 1990) or places where inquiry is essential for continual improvement. Ideally, practical inquiry leads to conclusions consistent with those derived from more systematic inquiries. The risk that this may not happen is borne because the benefit of contextualized knowledge that is quickly available (and quickly revisable) overrides the risk.

We term the fourth source of knowledge systematic research (though we do not mean to suggest that practical research is not systematic, nor that systematic research cannot be practical). This enterprise generates knowledge through well-established means of gathering and interpreting empirical evidence and through the process of reporting evidence, validating it through peer review, and making it broadly available. Such research aims for knowledge that contributes to the conceptual understandings that usefully inform practice beyond specific contexts. Rather than entering into debates about what constitutes scientifically based research, we ask a more pressing question: What kinds of research can produce well-warranted knowledge that can help improve practice and policy? This volume argues that systematic research that produces such knowledge can take many forms, from descriptive research to interpretive research to hypothesis-testing research. It can rest on a variety of philosophical positions and can use diverse strategies for gathering evidence and producing conclusions, from case studies to experiments to critical ethnographies to surveys to design research.

These four sources of knowledge have fluid relationships and fuzzy boundaries. Each can look to the others for insight (NRC, 2002b; Riehl et al., 2000). Without reifying artificial boundaries separating knowledge domains, we want to focus attention. The concern of this volume is with systematic research that informs leadership policy and practice.

EDUCATIONAL RESEARCH QUALITY

Many analysts find much of merit in educational research and acknowledge the inherent difficulties of producing authoritative and durable knowledge in the field (e.g., Labaree, 1998). Still, educational research has been criticized for, paradoxically, being both too theoretical and abstract and too close to practice. It has been maligned for being dispersed and unfocused, inconclusive, and easily disputed (Kaestle, 1993; Lagemann & Shulman, 1999).

Research on educational leadership has received similar criticisms. Methodological shortcomings include inadequate samples, incomplete theoretical models, and simplistic measurement and analysis techniques (c.f. Hallinger & Heck, 1996a). Studies within problem areas do not accumulate and grow in sophistication. Studies are sporadic in coverage of important topics in the field, and they have not linked leadership to student learning. Some have criticized research on educational leadership as being too technical and positivistic (e.g., Evers & Lakomski, 1991; Scheurich, 1997).

The Experimental Question

Three general themes pervade many criticisms of educational research. The first is a more specific version of the concern that research has not used the most effective designs or methods. Following the current interest in "scientific" research, this critique assumes that research should help answer the question, "What works?" in the most authoritative way possible (Slavin, 2004). The preferred method for doing so is thought to be experiments that test the outcomes produced by particular interventions, with subjects randomly assigned to treatment groups in order to eliminate possible selection biases. In some experiments, theoretical understandings might be tested instead of specific interventions. This approach assumes that well-crafted experimental research does not simply present a "one-size-fits-all" solution, but instead specifies conditions under which alternative treatments work better or worse (Slavin, 2004). This deflects the criticism that the experimental approach ignores local conditions and aspires too much toward context-free generalizations.

Experimental research usually requires that an intervention be implemented uniformly across settings. But extensive research has documented that virtually any intervention undergoes substantial local adaptations (e.g., Berman & McLaughlin, 1978). In addition, the experimental approach overlooks research that serves other functions, including descriptive research that details current conditions or process research that explores the mechanisms through which interventions that work do work. In many areas, knowledge is simply not developed enough to test specific interventions. Arguably, the most productive educational research over the last few decades has not been experimental research, but instead research that has looked closely at the cognitive processes of learners, teachers, administrators, and even policymakers (e.g., Hallinger, Leithwood, & Murphy, 1993; Palincsar & Brown, 1984).

The Foundational Question

The second critique focuses on the philosophical foundations of research methods. Experimentalists (and many others) assume that research can generate objective, accurate—but never perfect—portrayals of a generally stable world. In the wake of Kuhn's (1962) account of scientific paradigm shifts, others assert that researchers' conclusions about reality are colored by theories and values. In still other views, reality is understood to be at least partly socially constructed—a product of experience and perceptions and a combination of material and subjective conditions. Then the researcher's role is less to describe reality than to elicit actors' accounts of how they make sense of the world and act on their understandings. The most radical position is that a researcher's interpretations are so heavily dependent on one's own beliefs that they cannot be verified or challenged by others. This postmodernist perspective makes the prospect of sharable knowledge too dim to reconcile with aspirations for systematic research.

Views of causality are a source of foundational critiques as well. The more realist position is to search for antecedent conditions that cause other things to happen with regularity. Others believe that causality is not so mechanistic but is instead responsive to local variation and human volition. Their goal is to search for connections among thoughts, actions, and events to produce a convincing interpretation of how one thing led to another. In this way, processes are exposed as meaningful, but not determinate.

Proponents of each perspective tend to find research conducted within other frameworks less than informative and sometimes even delusional for building knowledge and improving practice. These debates are concentrated in academic circles, but they affect others as well. Since most end-users of research look for technical solutions to problems of policy and practice, they tend to gravitate toward research that presents the world as more objective and knowable. They discount other forms of research, especially those presented in "insider" language that is hard to grasp. This denies them the opportunity to encounter interesting and potentially helpful insights.

The Critical Question

Rather than assuming that better data and more rigorous methods will yield better-warranted results intended for the general good, the critical critique is that researchers hold values that privilege the status quo and currently dominant interests. Advocates of this view see finding an unbiased truth as less significant than challenging established relationships of power and privilege. An important function of research is to uncover and document what is happening from the perspective of those being ill served to publicize inequities in the existing system and advocate for the victims of the system.

Taken together, the experimental, foundational, and critical themes challenge fundamental epistemological concerns, the core intentions of research, and the potential for different research approaches to generate findings that will lead to authoritative knowledge that can inform practice.

FEDERAL POLICY AND THE NATIONAL RESEARCH COUNCIL

These three themes converge in the discussion generated by recent federal education policy in the United States and by an important report on research from the National Research Council (NRC). The federal government's approach to research can be gleaned from research review and policy initiatives such as the National Reading Panel (National Institute of Child Health and Development, 2000), the What Works Clearinghouse (2004), and the *No Child Left Behind* legislation (U.S. Congress, 2001). These initiatives share a vision that research should facilitate the selection of the most efficient and effective way of achieving educational outcomes. This vision rests on assumptions that educational problems are straightforward, solutions can be identified, and educators will simply accept and implement "proven" practices. Through these initiatives, the government has prioritized "scientifically based research," preferably experimental or quasi-experimental designs with random assignment. All of these efforts have been criticized for being ideologically driven and for ignoring much high-quality research (e.g., Allington, 2002).

In 2000, the NRC established a task force to consider ways to define and conduct scientific research in education. Concerned with how the political controversies might affect researchers (Eisenhart & Towne, 2003), the task force set out to delineate what would count as high-quality scientific research in education, under the assumption that scientific research is necessary for the growth of knowledge about education. The task force report (NRC, 2002) has been the catalyst for an extended conversation about research, especially among researchers themselves.

The report asserts that scientific inquiry in education is no different from scientific inquiry in other fields. It is "a continual process of rigorous reasoning supported by a dynamic interplay among methods, theories, and findings" (NRC, 2002, p. 2). Moreover, the report also seems to eschew determinative models of causality in human life:

> Today, it is recognized that many phenomena of interest across the domains of the social sciences and education research result from voluntary action (or from the unintended or aggregate consequences of such actions) even though direct measurement of such phenomena is typically not possible. Thus, research on human action must take into account individuals' understanding, intentions, and values as well as their observable behavior. (NRC, 2002, pp. 15–16)

Many respondents find much to admire in this report, although some challenge the philosophical underpinnings it assumes and the methodological options it includes under the umbrella of scientific research. For example, the report suggests that knowledge can be created and shared objectively and is potentially generalizable, which seems to contradict the more interpretive stance reflected in the quotation above. Maxwell (2004) suggests that the report adopts a "variance-oriented" approach to research, in which associations between two or more constructs are studied in isolation from the contexts in which they co-occur, in contrast to a "process-oriented" approach, which seeks to describe actions and processes as they are actually lived out or experienced. Erickson and Gutierrez (2002) caution that researchers who attempt to isolate such cause-and-effect associations should, at the least, "cultivate skepticism and humility" because their results will probably amount to little more than rough guesswork or approximations (p. 23).

Although the federal government's approach and the NRC stance have occasionally been conflated, they present important contrasts. For example, the NRC report directly questions the "translation" of research into prescriptions for practice (2002, pp. 153–154) and suggests that the best understandings of education will emerge from "the integration of scientific knowledge with insights from the humanities and other scholarly pursuits" (p. 131). The NRC report also acknowledges that research is theory-laden (p. 62) and that knowledge typically influences practice in very indirect ways (p. 154). This view was articulated some time ago by Carol Weiss (1980), who challenged the usual definition of "use" as the direct application of research-based suggestions. Instead, Weiss argued, practitioners who already have considerable knowledge and have embedded it in ideas, programs, and institutions are not likely to apply research findings quickly. But research can "enlighten" them "by challenging ideas currently in vogue and providing alternative cognitive maps" (p. 98).

That perspective is reflected in the present volume, with its view that research can develop knowledge that is useful for practice by addressing a variety of complex problems using diverse research designs, and by recognizing educators' practical knowledge. Our view assumes that leadership practice is complex and that leaders have many reasons for doing things, including normative justifications and the wisdom of experience. Not all research, therefore, need be concerned with installing best practices (although evaluation of alternatives is certainly one outcome of research). Instead, some research can provide enlightening information, perspectives, and frameworks for leaders and help them to think differently about the value choices, sociopolitical realities, and complex technical decisions they face. This view of research use extends far beyond the adoption of new "evidence-based" strategies.

This view acknowledges a wide array of research questions and methodological approaches. To begin, it permits multiple approaches to the foundational question. The chapters in this volume uphold a productive tension between seeing the world as an objective, material reality versus something that is constructed and experienced more subjectively. Concrete conditions affecting schools and leaders are taken into account. Leadership is understood as a social influence process in which leaders construct their own interpretations of the world and then seek to influence the thoughts and subsequent actions of others (see chapter 2). The meanings that actors assign to things, and what they say and do because of those meanings, must be factored into any comprehensive account of leadership for learning.

In our view researchers can uncover strong patterns of meaning and action that suggest regularly occurring patterns and sequences. These do not become law-like statements or generalizations, but they can generate probabilistic accounts that may be relevant to many different contexts. Other inquiries illuminate the multiple, contingent pathways from one action to another, so that generalization is more difficult. Rather than seeking mechanistic models of causality, good research uses interpretive methods that are open to scrutiny and that seek to eliminate alternative explanations in order to present the most reasonable accounts of what happens (Miles & Huberman, 1994).

We also assume that theoretical orientations, conceptual frameworks, and methodological tools provide lenses that highlight some aspects of the world but filter out others. Some authors in this book argue that researchers have personal positionalities that influence their research and should be disclosed. Research conducted from particular standpoints provides accounts that are "partial, positioned, and perspectival" (Hall, 1999), but that is neither surprising nor disheartening. Most researchers would agree that there is rarely one correct interpretation of phenomena. As the NRC report acknowledges, all research is partial, which makes it critically important that research be subject to confirmation from the community. The challenge for systematic research is to identify the strategies that permit others to have confidence in the validity of one's research.

With regard to the experimental critique of educational research, the chapters in this volume do not call for much experimental research. A few authors avoid experimental research on foundational grounds. They see leadership as too complex a phenomenon to lend itself to experimental research. In their view, the challenge of leadership requires mediating between a multifaceted environment and an intricate teaching process. Leadership challenges are so multidimensional and situational that it is hard to imagine codifying what is knowable as an intervention that can be uniformly applied across contexts. These authors assume a relatively knowable but highly complex world where the research challenge is to use the best tools of social and behavioral science to inform the practical knowledge of educators.

Finally, this volume also responds to the critical question. The authors of several chapters suggest that certain moral goods are essential to improve education; among these are equitable learning for all students and the deliberate pursuit of social justice and democracy. Researchers can properly be committed to such moral goods as they study how schools can achieve these ends. This is a departure from most accounts of scientific research in that our authors propose to examine phenomena with explicit value orientations. (We suspect that most researchers study outcomes they care about.) We avoid a radical relativistic view, however. Rather, we agree with Carspecken (1996), who suggests that deeply held moral values need not contaminate research. In these cases, researchers must determine how to conduct the research that will earn the confidence of all who receive it, not just advocates of the valued end.

PROMISING STRATEGIES FOR NEW RESEARCH ON EDUCATIONAL LEADERSHIP

We now turn to suggestions for specific research strategies that can be used in a new research agenda. This chapter cannot describe in detail all of the methodological possibilities open to leadership researchers. Instead, we focus on ideas that extend in new ways what have been common practices in the field.

Comprehensive Case Studies

Many of the chapters in this volume suggest the need for case study research that is more comprehensive than many typical studies in educational leadership. As the focus of inquiry expands to include the thinking and actions of multiple actors, and as context becomes a more important object of study, it becomes necessary to capture a more complex slice of reality. For example, Coburn (2003) argues that to understand "deep and consequential" changes in classroom practice, researchers may need to collect extensive data through in-depth interviews and classroom observations, systematic collection of student work samples, and teacher activity logs. The research requirements would be multiplied to study leaders' thinking and the impact of school-based leadership on teaching practice, and multiplied even more in order to understand the impact of district leadership, community context, and higher-level policy directives. To understand the spread and sustainability of an educational innovation, through different levels of an educational system and into different areas of the instructional program, researchers will need yet more opportunities to examine the interplay of thoughts, actions, structures, strategies, and effects.

One important focus for case study research would be leaders' cognitive processes—how leaders construct meanings and act on them to influence others and to impact teaching and learning. Research on expert practitioners (e.g., Leithwood & Hallinger, 1993) suggests the use of methods such as "think-aloud protocols" to access leaders' thinking. In chapter 3 of this volume, Stein and Spillane posit that the "cognitive mediational" paradigm that has revolutionized the study of teaching and learning can be adapted to examine how school leaders influence teacher thinking. Similarly, in chapter 4 Prestine and Nelson claim that it may be helpful to study "leadership content knowledge" to tap into leaders' understandings of what they need to know in order to help teachers. In chapter 6, Firestone and Shipps focus on leaders' understandings of accountability, and Driscoll and Goldring in chapter 5 suggest that leaders' constructions of learning influence how they think about learning, community development, and school–community linkages. Firestone and Shipps argue for extended case studies to understand how accountability sources impinge on schools, create pressures for action, and ultimately influence instruction through leadership. Such studies must be wider to encompass broader contexts than many typical case studies, and also deeper in order to accommodate the cognitive/constructivist aspects of leadership that these authors emphasize. For the most part, such studies would probably focus on issues that arise in natural settings. Nonetheless, as we discuss below, similar questions can sometimes be studied more efficiently when interventions are explicitly designed.

Driscoll and Goldring also advocate case study research for studying schools and communities as contexts for learning. They highlight the need for more careful definition and measurement of constructs such as "learning," "instructional leadership," and "community." This admonition is applicable to many realms of leadership research, if for no other reason than that a more careful specification of constructs would facilitate efforts to compare and combine findings across studies. Additionally, Driscoll and Goldring highlight the need for case studies to capture dynamic processes and reciprocal effects through longitudinal designs that balance describing the uniqueness of specific contexts and identifying commonalities that permit generalization.

Furman and Shields's (chapter 8) research agenda on leadership for socially just and democratic school communities is explicitly "dynamic, holistic, integrated, and normative." They characterize their approach to case study research as relational, because researchers work side by side with practitioners seeking to establish just and democratic conditions and processes in schools. This is a fundamentally different way of influencing practice than the process of developing predictions, installing interventions, and searching for control over technical solutions. Consistent with the critical question described above, this form of research monitors whose perspectives and voices are heard so that all parties can have influence over both the conduct of the research and the interpretations that emerge. These authors say their research agenda is "interventionist and advocacy-oriented" and stress that because it explicitly seeks to understand a normative aspect of schooling (the pursuit of the moral goods of justice and democracy), it differs from much scientific research. However, the approach they espouse allows them to carefully scrutinize the relationships, processes, and outcomes they study. As the authors explain, their goal is to "better understand the nature of the relationships" in schools and to "investigate the ways in which power is understood, shared, and exercised."

Reyes and Wagstaff in chapter 7 suggest intensive case studies of contexts in which students of diverse backgrounds are educated. While they affirm the need for studies of successful "outlier" schools consistent with Edmonds's (1979) research on effective schooling, their approach departs from earlier work in two regards. First, like Furman and Shields, they acknowledge the normative aspect of leadership that works for equitable learning for all children; thus, their research is to promote a valued end. Second, they broaden their focus to extend from the macro level, as reflected in the effects of accountability systems on diverse schools, to the micro level, reflected in the leader's influence on student learning.

Design Research

Design research has been relatively unfamiliar to leadership researchers. It is a process in which theories are developed, tested, and refined in real contexts. It attends to the linkage between research and practice by simultaneously developing both theories and useful tools (Brown, 1992). Design research strives for wide applicability because the theories, tools, and products it generates should be applicable beyond the context in which they were developed (Edelson, 2002). Design research iterates through cycles of design, enactment, analysis, and redesign as it seeks to understand how outcomes are the "joint product of the designed intervention and the context" (Design-Based Research Collective, 2003, p. 7). Design-based research aspires to objectivity, reliability, and validity through techniques such as thick description of the cycles of design, testing, and redesign; carefully defined measures and systematic analysis of data; replication; and consensus-building around interpretations of data. It differs from most case study research because researchers intervene in situations and document the outcomes rather than minimizing their impact on what is studied.

Experimentally oriented skeptics question whether design research can generate valid warrants for its conclusions with so many uncontrolled factors (Shavelson, Phillips, Towne, & Feuer, 2003). Others have more confidence in the model. Cobb et al. (2003) assert that "design experiments create the conditions for developing theories yet must place these theories in harm's way" (p. 10), thus emphasizing that design research tests alternative conjectures and does not just confirm hoped-for relationships.

This model holds some promise for the study of educational leadership. However, it is important to clarify the theories that are well enough developed to benefit from development through design methodology; the leadership interventions that can be designed; the contexts, inputs, and processes to be studied; and the outcomes to be assessed.

Consider for a moment the question of what would be designed. In teaching research, these are usually instructional tools or technologies, such as the reciprocal teaching technique for fostering student reading comprehension. What are the technologies and tools of leadership? Some scholars have claimed that the most important tool for leaders is language (Gronn, 1983); so, for example, a "designed" tool for leadership might be a particular kind of discourse pattern intended to support teacher learning, much like the discourse strategies that are thought to be effective in mathematics classrooms or the discussion formats that can strengthen reading comprehension.

In chapter 9 of this volume, Smylie, Bennett, Konkol, and Fendt suggest that leader preparation programs could be designed and studied. Prestine and Nelson claim that design research enables one to observe the nested actions of individuals, groups, and institutions or cultures within layers of context. They offer as one example the design and study of schoolwide communities of practice. The best example of design research for leadership now extant is a program to help principals and supervisors understand the complexity of teaching mathematics using a constructivist approach (Nelson & Sassi, 2000).

Driscoll and Goldring also suggest that design research can help explain the evolution of contexts over time, a condition that is essential to the study of dynamic school–community relationships. These authors offer a caveat, however: in the study of instructional designs, classrooms are bounded and thus provide a potentially manageable context to study, but communities outside the school represent almost boundless contexts and studying them could be very difficult.

Furman and Shields's emphasis on research for social justice and democracy in schools could also be considered a form of design research, because they expect that more sophisticated theories of justice and democracy can be forged in the process of trying to establish these conditions in schools.

Quantitative Research

The paucity of recent quantitative research on educational leadership seems to suggest that this methodology is not well matched to most current research questions. This reflects a dramatic change over the past 20 years, as researchers have adopted a more catholic approach to epistemology and methodology and as the nature of research questions has changed (Heck & Hallinger, 1999). This view is reflected in this volume as well, as none of the authors have emphasized survey research, quantifiable data, or statistical analyses as optimal methodological tools for studying the questions they pose. Instead, most propose research that looks closely at phenomena that were not well understood, or even identified, some time ago. New lines of research often begin with close descriptions and process studies that are best conducted using qualitative designs.

This does not preclude the use of quantitative methods at some point, however. Many questions can be addressed quite appropriately through survey research and other quantitative, quasi-experimental methods, especially when they seek to identify trends across widely dispersed populations and when measurement tools are sophisticated. Desimone and Le Floch (2004) argue that survey research will be more useful to researchers when data reliability and validity are improved. They suggest approaching survey development through cognitive interviews with respondents, asking participants to think aloud and talk through their reasoning as they answer the survey. In this way, researchers can close the gap between how they frame issues and how respondents frame them, so that survey questions can tap participants' understandings more accurately. Such an approach could help develop quantitative studies around issues such as teachers' perceptions of instructional leadership efforts, leaders' responses to multiple accountabilities, or trends in school–community partnerships.

Some researchers have attempted to measure the effects of leadership on student learning using quantitative methods (c.f. Hallinger & Heck, 1996a; Scheerens & Bosker, 1997), but this effort is still in need of much development. Rowan, Correnti, and Miller's (2002) assertion that "the magnitude of teacher effects on student achievement depends to a considerable extent on the methods used to estimate these effects and on how the findings are interpreted" (p. 1536) is equally applicable to the measurement of leader effects on student achievement. The problems range from careful development of construct measures to appropriate modeling of causal patterns, because in complex processes extending over long periods of time and many actors, the measurement of outcomes and assignment of variance can be quite complicated (Scheerens, 1997).

Experimental Research

Finally, we address the possibility of using experimental research in leadership studies. Experiments are most useful when the question is whether a clearly defined causal agent (such as a particular instructional strategy) influences a clearly defined outcome (such as student performance on an achievement test) and whether that association is stronger than other competing alternatives. Randomized experiments are especially effective in eliminating "noise" that might cause a misspecification of the relationship between intervention and outcome. But we have already noted the serious epistemological issues that argue against pursuing experimental research all the time, especially the argument that experiments assume a model of causality that simply might not be informative for much educational phenomena. Other logistical problems arise as well, including the difficulty of recruiting experimental subjects (whether individuals or whole schools), the challenge of keeping the test conditions pure, and the concern that the research effort might not be matched by equal effort to utilize findings (Cook, 2002).

The new research advocated in this volume does not include much experimental research. Reasons for this are suggested by the relatively stronger preference for design research. Experimental research usually assumes the presence of a clear theoretical chain of reasoning, a well-developed intervention and specific targeted outcome, and enough capacity to control for context so that the intervention's effects can be isolated. Design research, on the other hand, can be useful when theories are strong but need further development, when causal processes are assumed to be complex and to involve intricate contextual variation, and when the goal is to develop and refine an intervention that leads to desirable outcomes. This approach describes the current moment in educational leadership more accurately than the experimental approach.

In our view, the field is not quite ready for experiments, and it is still unclear whether experiments will ever be the preferred methodology for understanding leadership. This parallels the situation in the highly touted health sciences. Though there is good evidence that randomized trials present an appealing option for testing the effects of particular medical treatments or procedures on health outcomes, most systematic research on leadership in health care is not experimental but instead relies on qualitative case study methodologies (Riehl, 2004).

IMPLICATIONS AND CONCLUSION

Many research efforts proposed in this volume will be broader, deeper, more comprehensive, and more complex than much current research on educational leadership. Among other things, this argues for more programmatic research, in which research topics are investigated through interrelated sets of studies that progress from identifying problems to describing current situations, explicating processes, developing novel interventions, and assessing those interventions in many different contexts. These tasks cannot all be accomplished in single studies.

Systematic, coordinated, and cumulative programs of research do not spring forth in a vacuum. This is not to suggest that research on educational leadership should be heavily managed or centrally monitored, but instead points to the need to attend to factors that will make research improvement more likely.

The NRC report asserts that high-quality research needs three enabling conditions: time, fiscal resources, and public support for sustained scientific study (NRC, 2002). In a recent paper about research in mathematics education, the RAND Mathematics Study Panel emphasized the need to build "a community of multidisciplinary professionals who have experience and expertise," and to involve disciplinary experts, researchers, developers, and funders in the enterprise (RAND Mathematics Study Panel, 2003). The panel stated two broad criteria by which to assess the quality of a research and development program: first, whether it frames, designs, and conducts significant research on pressing problems in appropriate ways; and second, whether it builds structures for communication, information-sharing, and critique, in effect creating an engaged community of practice around mathematics education research. The panel envisioned that funding agencies (including government and private foundations) could play a central coordinating role, provided they work closely with others. A second important element is a system for rigorous peer review, a strategy likely to enhance the participation of high-quality researchers and galvanize the attention of the entire community of interested persons.

Parallel claims could be made for educational leadership research. Our field could benefit from more time, fiscal resources, and public support for our research, but we must ensure that our work deserves these supports. To earn such trust, we must first provide appropriate preparation for researchers. Researchers need better training in the philosophical foundations of inquiry (Paul & Marfo, 2001), so that they make appropriate choices for situating their work and so they can communicate with others whose paradigms are not their own. Researchers need opportunities to develop sophisticated methodological expertise and should be held to high standards for the design and conduct of research (Riehl et al., 2000). The more that knowledge about educational leadership overlaps with knowledge about both teaching and learning and the larger institutional system, the more that researchers will need to be well-versed in these related domains and to find avenues for collaborating on research with experts in these other areas.

Both the quality of research and public support for it will increase as researchers in educational leadership develop a lively scholarly discourse and also find ways to communicate effectively with practitioners, policymakers, research funders, and the general public. Rather than presenting small, independent studies in a cacophony of voices, each making its own claim to novelty, researchers should seek ways to communicate across studies to demonstrate areas of theoretical and empirical convergence and build a core set of reliable results that are accepted both by the research community and the public. The strategic use of research syntheses, meta-analyses, and interpretive reviews of research can be helpful, along with more use of consensus panels, a strategy that has helped strengthen confidence in knowledge in other fields (Slavin, 2002). Research knowledge should be subject to the oversight of the scholarly community (NRC, 2002), and researchers can welcome the scrutiny that serves both as a corrective and as affirmation. Finally, researchers should reach out to professionals and the public to identify ways in which research can be communicated with these audiences.

In its defense, Berliner (2002) calls educational research one of the hard-to-do sciences, given factors that limit opportunities for theory-building and generalization, the confounding power of context, the rarity of simplistic causal relationships, and the problem of "decade by findings" interactions that render educational knowledge moot in relatively short time spans. The methodological challenges facing researchers in educational leadership are formidable, but they are not insurmountable.

CHAPTER 11

Conclusion

William A. Firestone and Carolyn Riehl

We introduced this book by asserting the need for more robust and better warranted research on how educational leadership can contribute to improved and more
equitable student learning. In the chapters that followed, scholars from a variety of
ideological, methodological, and disciplinary viewpoints have fleshed out research
questions that establish a broad yet coherent program of research. This program
has considerable promise for informing leadership practice. The preceding chapter drew out methodological implications from this work. Here we summarize the
main substantive implications of these chapters and draw them together as an interrelated set of research questions within a unified framework. Figure 11.1 provides a graphic representation of the framework. It highlights five broad themes:
the diversity of student outcomes, the complexity of teaching, the importance of
community, the problem of policy, and the unknown of leader preparation.

THE DIVERSITY OF OUTCOMES

Collectively, the authors of the chapters in this text adopt rich and demanding ideas
about what America's schoolchildren should learn. Two chapters (Stein & Spillane,
chapter 3, and Prestine & Nelson, chapter 4) draw very heavily on the cognitive
revolution in research on teaching and learning to guide the development of questions about leadership. This revolution suggests that learning specific facts is necessary for children, but not sufficient. Students should also understand the bodies

Figure 11.1. A Model of How Leadership Influences Student Outcomes

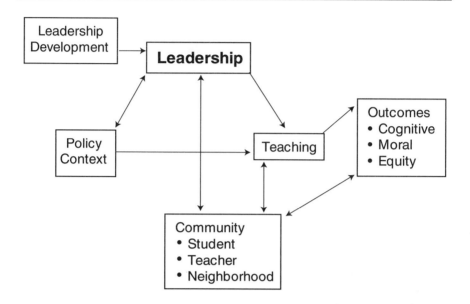

of knowledge that make up the curriculum. Drawing on studies of expert knowledge and knowledge application, researchers have developed a refined sense of what understanding entails. It includes both the connections among different elements of knowledge and some sense of how to apply knowledge developed in one context to another context. A considerable body of work suggests that helping children learn to *understand* bodies of knowledge like chemistry or history is much more difficult than getting them to memorize a table of elements or list of dates (Bransford, Brown, & Cocking, 2000; Hiebert & Carpenter, 1992).

Although concerned about application to the real world, the cognitive revolution focused largely on teaching and learning the subjects making up the curriculum. It has not focused on the development of moral reasoning. Yet a major focus for American education from its earliest days and a continuing concern today is the moral development of children (Kaestle, 1984; Wilson, 1993). This concern is especially apparent in Furman and Shields's chapter 8 on how leaders might promote social justice and democratic community. While it explicitly argues on moral grounds for a set of school conditions, it implicitly suggests a set of learning outcomes. As described in their discussion of democratic community, these include absolute regard for the worth and dignity of individuals and their cultural traditions, the responsibility to participate and support free and open inquiry and critique, and recognition of the importance of collective choices and action in working for the common good. Similarly, Reyes and Wagstaff in chapter 7 point to the importance of developing school norms that avoid the exclusion of individuals on any of the dimensions of diversity (including ethnicity, gender, language, sexual preference, or disability) that are so widespread in this society. The recommendations of these authors reflect efforts from a broad range of sociological and political science research to identify the cognitive, evaluative, and affective orientations necessary to support a democratic society. A review of a great deal of this research suggests—as Furman and Shields point out—that schools should do more to challenge the rampant individualism in American society (Slater & Boyd, 1999).

Finally, the chapters in this book all adopt a view of equity that requires reducing the achievement gaps among groups of students differentiated by race/ethnicity, social class, gender, or other characteristics. Thus, Reyes and Wagstaff argue that "the most critical challenge to educators today is to educate successfully student populations that are ethnically and linguistically diverse and those groups whose educational needs have not been met, who are typically located in urban and underfunded schools" (p. 106) Similarly, Furman and Shields maintain that justice requires that educators and policymakers reject deficit thinking that implies that certain class, cultural, or ethnic groups are unable to learn in school and furthermore that educators are obligated to remove curricular (and other) barriers to student learning. Thus, the outcomes of schooling have become more diverse, and increasingly they are expected to be distributed more equally across different groups of students.

THE COMPLEXITY OF TEACHING AND LEARNING

The same cognitive revolution that gives us a richer conception of what students need to learn has also thrown new light on processes of learning and teaching. To begin with, as Stein and Spillane point out in chapter 3, learning is not a passive process of receiving information. It comes through active mental processes, and those processes mediate teachers' work. Moreover, according to Prestine and Nelson in chapter 4, this learning process begins from students' preconceptions about the subjects taught (Bransford et al., 2000). Teaching is most likely to succeed if it takes those preconceptions into account. The importance of children's preconceptions and the conceptions they develop while learning a subject area prompted intensive analyses of how students make sense of specific subjects and topic areas. Researchers have gone further to explore the instructional moves that are most likely to help students overcome misconceptions and develop more accurate understandings.

Identifying appropriate instructional processes requires extensive, complex problem-solving by teachers. Intensive studies of teacher thinking that parallel the work done on students has clarified the centrality of teachers' pedagogical content knowledge to those thought processes (Shulman, 1987). What teachers need to know about mathematics differs from what mathematicians need to know because the issues in teaching are different from the issues in advancing mathematical knowledge.

In addition, as both Prestine and Nelson and Stein and Spillane point out, learning for understanding is not just a dyadic process between teacher and student. It also includes conversations among students. An important part of teaching, then, is creating communities of practice (Wenger, 1998) among students, both by providing tasks that require complex, collective problem-solving and by encouraging suitable norms for what constitutes useful conversations among students. The picture of teaching as "not telling" that comes out of this body of research is foreign to most teachers, and extremely complex (Cuban, 1993).

Research on instructional leadership is just beginning to take advantage of this new view of teaching. In fact, the study of instructional leadership is only a little over 20 years old, having been triggered by the effective schools movement. A great deal has been learned, but this knowledge primarily concerns how leaders in formal positions—most notably principals—can create contexts that are conducive to the improvement of teaching. As Leithwood and Riehl describe such knowledge in their review in chapter 2, that work fits very well with the general literature on leadership. However, it says very little about the specific challenges of improving teaching, much less the varied problems of improving the teaching of different subject areas. These issues are raised by cognitive research on teaching and learning.

The chapters in this book suggest that cognitively oriented research on teaching raises five important questions. First, *what leadership practices contribute to improved teaching and learning?* More specifically, how can principals help teachers learn what they need to know to be better teachers? The introduction of a more learning-oriented paradigm is an important shift in researcher attention. In chapter 3, Stein and Spillane suggest two ways to address this issue. Researchers might work outward from studying teachers, just as teacher researchers worked outward from the study of students. While substantial attention has been paid to how teachers interpret several policies, there is less research asking how teachers make sense of the work of principals. What meaning do teachers give to such principal actions as inviting certain people to participate in committees, giving some teachers discretionary funds for specific purposes, or using staff meetings in particular ways? By clarifying teachers' interpretations of actions that appear to support instructional improvement, researchers may offer guidance on how formal leaders can contribute to that end.

Another possibility is to draw on the growing work on teacher learning. Researchers could ask about the extent to which school or district leaders engage in the activities shown to contribute to teacher learning, the reasons that leaders give for taking actions that might affect teacher learning, and the conditions under which different actions are taken. In fact, a first question is the extent to which principals attend to teacher learning at all and then what kinds of learning principals and other formal leaders view as important. Stein and Spillane suggest that one reason there has been so little research on principals as facilitators of learning is that such facilitation has not been a major part of principals' work. Like Prestine and Nelson in chapter 4 on other issues, they suggest that intentional efforts to create situations where principals have more responsibility for teacher development will be necessary to carry out such research.

The second question is, *what do leaders need to know to support improved teaching and learning?* This question applies the cognitive perspective directly to the study of administrators. While some research on administrator problem-solving has been undertaken (Hallinger, Leithwood, & Murphy, 1993), both Prestine and Nelson and Stein and Spillane suggest a new tack. The research on teacher thinking became much more fruitful when it focused on teacher thinking *about the subjects taught*—for example, pedagogical content knowledge. Stein and Nelson (2003) argue that the administrative equivalent of pedagogical content knowledge is "leadership content knowledge"—that is, what leaders know about how to help teachers improve their teaching of specific subjects. Their own work is preliminary and has done more to suggest hypotheses than to produce strong support for them. Still, in mathematics, their work suggests that what principals need to know may be different from what assistant superintendents for curriculum need to know. More generally, the knowledge to support in-class supervision is somewhat different from the knowledge needed to design and carry out professional development. A great deal could be learned by pursuing these and related hypotheses across different subject areas, administrative roles, and settings for improving teaching.

The third question is, *who are the leaders for improving teaching and learning?* This question raises the issue of distributed leadership, discussed extensively by Prestine and Nelson. The idea behind distributed leadership is that the tasks of leadership may be stretched over a variety of individuals, including those in formal positions of authority and those who are not. The leaders in practice may not be the formal leaders, or formal and informal leaders may work together in ways that are not always apparent (Spillane, Halverson, & Diamond, 2001). While the idea of distributed leadership has become quite "hot" (Archer, 2004), many questions remain about how leadership is shared and with what consequences.

A major issue concerns the distribution of leadership. How are leadership tasks shared across roles? Do patterns differ by subject area, by grade level, in rich or poor schools, or according to the predilections of those in formal leadership positions? How do intentional efforts to create teacher leader positions affect the distribution of leadership work? It should also be noted that much of the focus on distributed leadership has been at the school level and has examined the interaction of principals and teachers. Yet leadership can be distributed across whole districts. District offices also play a critical role in efforts to influence teaching. How leadership is distributed among teachers, principals, district content specialists, and other district officials is an important issue (Cobb, McClain, Lamberg, & Dean, 2003; Firestone, Schorr, & Monfils, 2004), but more needs to be known about how leadership tasks are distributed across all these levels.

While distributed leadership has considerable popularity and apparent conceptual power, in chapter 2 Leithwood and Riehl point out that there is still little evidence about how it contributes to student learning. In fact, the question is not so much whether distributed leadership facilitates improved teaching and learning. To some extent, leadership is always distributed (Archer, 2004). A fourth question, then, is, *what patterns of leadership distribution contribute to improved teaching and learning?* Moreover, as Prestine and Nelson point out in chapter 4, distributed leadership can also contribute to conflict in and around schools, which may or may not be productive. Thus, it is important to identify productive and counterproductive patterns of distributed leadership.

Fifth, *how much does the idea of distributed leadership overlap with two other ideas: "professional community," which comes out of the sociology of school improvement (Louis & Kruse, 1995), and "communities of practice," which comes out of cognitive psychology (Wenger, 1998)?* Some work is required to identify the similarities and differences between these ideas. Otherwise, related research communities will continue to communicate past each other in ways that undermine the common search for a better understanding of how to improve student learning, specifically, how leaders can improve student learning indirectly by contributing to the improvement of teaching.

THE IMPORTANCE OF COMMUNITY

Another theme apparent in these chapters is the importance of community for effective learning. The collective nature of student learning as identified through cognitive psychology and related disciplines just begins to hint at the importance of community for learning because at least three communities are relevant: the student community, the professional community, and the community surrounding the school.

The Student Community

The cognitive revolution has not yet connected well to an earlier literature that asks what motivates students to succeed in school, though there are efforts to do so (Turner & Patrick, 2004). Yet the active learning required by the instructional approaches based on cognitive science requires more student engagement than approaches where teachers take more responsibility for moving the classroom action forward (Lee, Bryk, & Smith, 1993). Given this importance of student motivation, three observations from earlier research need to be highlighted. First, students form a community of their own within the school. This observation, which goes back to Waller (1932), is implied in the discussion of student social capital by both Driscoll and Goldring in chapter 5 and Reyes and Wagstaff in chapter 7 and is quite manifest in an earlier literature on how ties among students affect their achievement (Braddock & McPartland, 1993). Second, there is a strong mutual dependence between teachers and students. The alienation of each contributes to the alienation of the other (Lee et al., 1993). Teachers are more likely to work to improve their craft if they get a positive response from students, and students will try harder to succeed in school with encouragement from teachers. Finally, poor and minority students are less likely to partake of this cycle of mutual reinforcement than white middle-class and upper-middle-class children or even to have personal ties to teachers (Braddock & McPartland, 1993; Crosnoe, Johnson, & Elder, 2004). This last observation lies behind Furman and Shields's assertion in chapter 8 of a moral obligation for school leaders to redress the inequities of schooling, and Reyes and Wagstaff's call in chapter 7 for learning climates that convey the sense that everyone is valued.

These observations raise the fundamental question: *How do leaders contribute to a community where all students feel included in the school and accepted into the educational enterprise?* There appear to be at least two ways for leaders to help students feel more included in a school. One strategy is to create a culture supportive of teacher learning, since teachers are the major influences over so many factors that affect student engagement, such as creating opportunities for student success and making assignments more relevant to students (Braddock & McPartland, 1993). In fact, it has been argued that the active approaches to student learning derived from cognitive science may be more engaging for students than approaches that require students to passively listen to teachers. Yet some research suggests that working through teachers is a fairly weak path for promoting student engagement (Silins, Mulford, & Zarins, 2002).

Another strategy is to address student culture. This can be done by using more formal approaches such as enforcing discipline rules in a way that promotes student safety but is not seen to discriminate against any group of students (Lee et al., 1993). A complementary approach is more dramaturgical, relying on rituals, collective events, and interactions with individual children to create a climate that values all students. Reyes and Wagstaff provide case studies in chapter 7 describing how leaders manage the meaning of being in a marginalized group to turn liabilities into assets and help students who are normally classified as especially problematic to be seen by themselves and others as having special, positive attributes. It will be important to clarify the relative power of leadership approaches that focus on students and teachers and also on how the two can be combined to build a more inclusive community.

The Professional Community

A strong community of professionals also appears to support improved student learning. This conclusion is supported by research on school improvement that illustrates the benefits of strong professional communities among adults for learning new instructional approaches (Louis & Kruse, 1995). It can also be argued by analogy from the work on communities of practice among students. If such communities promote learning among students, they should do so among teachers as well, according to Prestine and Nelson in chapter 4. More detailed research using the communities of practice metaphor helps to clarify what communities should form around to improve teaching. Here again, according to Stein and Spillane in chapter 3, subject matter is crucial. Not only do teachers form different social patterns for learning about reading and math, but communities that form around the problem of teaching specific content areas may be especially useful for supporting the improvement of practice.

Another potential benefit of strong teacher communities that is not highlighted by the cognitive research is its motivational value. Such communities can build strong teacher commitment (Rosenholtz, 1989).

The literature on teacher communities suggests two important questions for further studies. First, *how does the organization of teacher communities (and teacher interaction) affect teacher learning?* There is evidence already that less isolated teachers learn more. The challenge now is to develop a more fine-grained understanding to help clarify how different patterns of interaction lead to different kinds of learning, and how interaction patterns are affected by such formal elements of the school organization as the existence of departments or other groups that focus on different subject areas.

Second, *how do leaders contribute to the organization of teacher communities, and what leaders matter for what purposes?* Research using both the professional community and distributed leadership paradigms suggest that principals can substantially influence the social organization of teaching (Louis & Kruse, 1995; Smylie, Conley, & Marks, 2002). Yet sometimes teachers organize themselves rather well without strong principal leadership (Heller & Firestone, 1995). Considerable work is still needed to clarify how principals contribute to the social organization of teachers, what other factors matter, and how these factors condition each other.

Distributed leadership suggests that leadership tasks can be shared by individuals with and without formal leadership positions. One conclusion that might be drawn from the earlier research on instructional leadership is that principals create a context for teacher learning but do not directly facilitate that learning process. That task may fall to either teachers or district staff. Yet a great effort is now being made to help principals develop the knowledge they need to become effective coaches in specific subject areas (Nelson & Sassi, 2000). A finer-grained analysis of how leadership tasks are spread across roles should help determine whether the goal of principal as instructional expert and lead facilitator is realistic or necessary. More generally, both Prestine and Nelson (chapter 4) and Stein and Spillane (chapter 3) conclude that a better understanding of how the leadership tasks related to instructional improvement are distributed will be a powerful tool for developing more effective strategies for achieving the outcomes that all the authors of this volume prize.

The Neighborhood Community

The community surrounding the school can support or undermine the achievement of desirable educational outcomes. In chapter 5, Driscoll and Goldring identify several ways that the community may influence learning. First, communities are contexts for learning, the source of many student preconceptions about the academic curriculum. Some communities may provide experiences that are better aligned with that curriculum than others. Moreover, the community may become a site for planned learning events that support deeper understanding and wider ability to apply knowledge to a variety of settings. Second, communities are sources of social capital, the webs of interpersonal relationships that support individuals in a variety of ways. Social capital is important because students in appropriate networks are likely to achieve at higher levels and to stay in school longer. Reyes and Wagstaff suggest in chapter 7 that the absence of appropriate social capital disadvantages some minority groups when they go to school. Third, social capital may affect schools' ability to make desired changes. When schools propose to make certain kinds of changes in their instructional programs, including those shown to help children achieve more challenging and equitable academic goals, communities with extensive social capital and objections to those programs may most effectively stop their implementation.

Driscoll and Goldring's treatment of the neighborhood community suggests two master questions. The first is, *how do leaders build constructive linkages to the neighborhood community?* These authors have substantially expanded the range of constructive linkages from what most researchers imagined previously. The issues of maximizing learning opportunities outside the school walls, helping students build the social capital that will help them in schools (and valuing the social capital that students bring with them, an issue raised by both Reyes and Wagstaff and— less directly—Furman and Shields in chapter 8), integrating instructional and social services, and building external support for changes in curriculum and instruction may all require different kinds of leadership. For instance, linkages to social service agencies may depend on formal relationships, while ties to sources of less formal learning opportunities may require operating very differently.

While Driscoll and Goldring believe that much can be gained through tighter linkages to the community, they wisely reserve judgment on the ultimate benefits of such linkages. Thus, they raise a second question: *What are the opportunity costs of investing heavily in building linkages to the community?* They recognize that people in formal leadership positions have only so much time. Typically, time spent on building relationships to the community cannot be devoted to improving teaching. Thus, they point out—and their warning is appropriate for other prescriptions for effective leadership as well—that trade-offs are inevitable. The existence of such trade-offs creates a challenge for researchers. It is not enough to offer evidence for the value of one approach to improving student outcomes. The benefits of one strategy must be weighed against other ones.

Cutting across all these areas is the question, *what do leaders need to know and be able to do to develop and support an effective school community?* Just as the concept of leadership content knowledge suggests that leaders need to know certain things about the subjects taught in their schools, it seems likely that leaders need to know certain things about how communities form, how to diagnose the conditions of communities, and the kinds of things they can do to promote such communities.

THE PROBLEM OF POLICY

The policy environment in which schools and districts operate has become increasingly complex. Some changes in policy at least give greater attention to academic outcomes. Formal state testing policies that hold people accountable for educational outcomes ensure that attention is paid to those outcomes, although there is considerable debate about whether they help or hinder efforts to achieve them (Firestone et al., 2004). As Firestone and Shipps point out in chapter 6, other sources of policy may prioritize objectives that are either unrelated to or contradict achieving positive outcomes for all students. These include reducing taxes, obtaining jobs, and advancing the careers of individual politicians. Moreover, according to Firestone and Shipps, the variety of accountability pressures coming from different policy sources creates confusion and cross-pressures that may impair efforts to focus on improving learning for all students.

This turbulent policy environment raises two questions for educational leadership. The first is, *how do leaders interpret these potentially competing accountability demands?* The problem is compounded, Firestone and Shipps argue, because information about different accountability demands comes into different parts of the organization. This is especially true when one examines a whole school district, which may have specialists for dealing with different parts of the environment. Yet while accountability demands are known differentially, common action is often required with regard to such issues as curriculum and instructional improvement. More needs to be known about how people in different positions do or do not pool information and how they weigh and interpret the variety of demands that are made. Ultimately, it is important to understand how this interpretation process affects the conditions that facilitate or undermine student learning.

A related pair of questions is, *can educational leaders be proactive in this complex accountability environment* and *what kinds of proactivity contribute to student learning?* Furman and Shields argue in chapter 8 that leaders should be proactive on moral grounds. The concepts of democratic community and social justice demand that leaders create certain conditions in their schools regardless of external accountability demands. Recognizing that educators often feel a moral accountability that may be at odds with external accountabilities, Firestone and Shipps ask how moral accountability, such as internalized concerns like those raised by Furman and Shields, interacts with external accountability.

Firestone and Shipps point to work on "internal accountability"—that is, situations where a school or district takes responsibility for acting morally and enforces expectations on peers. Such internal accountability is another form of a strong teacher community, although it would seem to be more all-encompassing, including administrators as well. While there has been a fair amount of research on teacher communities in general, there has been very little on internal accountability. What has been done suggests that external accountability demands may undermine the development of a strong professional community that promotes internal accountability. Moreover, internal accountability does not always develop around the social justice that Furman and Shields advocate.

We need to know a great deal more about what forms internal accountability takes, the conditions that promote more constructive forms, and, in particular, the contribution of leadership to promoting just and democratic internal accountability.

THE UNKNOWN OF LEADERSHIP PREPARATION

Leadership preparation, according to Smylie, Bennett, and colleagues in chapter 9, is a field where there has been a great deal of writing but relatively little research, even compared to other areas addressed here. Some existing literature suggests that informal processes of selection and socialization are extremely important for leadership training—probably more important than formal preparation. Much the same is true with teacher preparation. The existing research tends to ask what students and recent graduates of programs find satisfying without looking for more theoretically grounded and empirically validated outcomes of training. There are hints that the current mix of formal and informal training helps to reduce the anxieties of new incumbents of leadership positions, but it may also reinforce conservative leadership practice that is insufficient to promote the learning and equity outcomes that schools need to achieve.

Two sources of intellectual guidance appear especially useful in formulating and executing an agenda for research on the preparation of school leaders. The first, which has been mentioned in several chapters of this book, is the research on teacher learning. There are a number of parallels between the development of leaders and teachers, and the methods and conceptualizations used in teacher research can be very useful in this regard. This is a point on which Smylie and colleagues and Stein and Spillane in particular agree. The second is the out-of-education literature on workforce development. This literature suggests an extremely complex agenda that includes not only preparation but the cost-effectiveness of specific preparation strategies. Smylie, Bennett, and colleagues suggest that while the workforce development framework is helpful, it is too broad to address comprehensively given our current state of knowledge.

Smylie, Bennett, and colleagues suggest a more parsimonious approach that focuses on four broad questions. First, *what are the knowledge, skills, and commitments of effective principals?* This question synthesizes most of the research proposed above. Effective principals, in our view, are those who can build communities to support teaching that promotes learning, not just of cognitive abilities, but also normative orientations that support justice and community, and that promote such learning for all children. Second, *what is the distribution of this set of knowledge, skills, and commitments in the current leader workforce?* Answering this question requires synthesizing the work that has been done, but it also demands the development of new instruments to measure leaders' knowledge. While at one level it is easy to measure knowledge with paper-and-pencil instruments, there is a risk of getting socially acceptable responses. Thus attitude measures may need to be triangulated with direct observation. It is not at all clear that conventional paper-and-pencil tests will capture the full range of what principals need to know and be able to do. This is especially likely because much leadership knowledge is nondeclarative and "tacit." Many important leader characteristics are commitments or values, not knowledge. Even the development of paper-and-pencil instruments will require extensive effort, time, and funding.

Third, *what are the processes by which leaders learn these knowledge, skills, and commitments?* This question requires attention to the ways in which learning happens, the particular interactions among learners, peers, and teachers. Here again, the research on teacher learning can be particularly helpful. Finally, *how effective are specific means for preparing leaders?* This requires examining the outcomes of formal programs for preservice leader preparation, leader induction, and in-service. However, studies must be much more fine grained to compare the effects of different leader programs—i.e., those with or without cohorts, with or without certain curricular elements, with or without internships—and then to examine the interaction of preservice, induction, and in-service over time.

We have framed these questions about leaders in general. Smylie, Bennett, and colleagues point out that most work is about the preparation of school principals, and most of the demand seems to be for greater knowledge about preparing people for that role. However, both the organization of school districts and the new interest in distributed leadership suggest that a wider focus is needed. Research should address the challenges of preparing teacher leaders, incumbents of key central office roles, and superintendents as well as people in out-of-district leadership roles relevant for the improvement of education.

Smylie, Bennet and colleagues also raise an equity concern. There has been some research on the preparation of women and minorities for educational leadership roles. Given the informal nature of most socialization for leadership and its apparent focus on the preparation of white males, it is important to understand how the challenges of preparing leaders differ by gender and ethnicity, to the extent that they do.

IMPLEMENTING THE AGENDA

The separate chapters focus closely on their own topics; in this conclusion, we have tried to show how they link and relate through an overarching framework on leadership. As research proceeds in each area, it is important to ask how it dovetails with research in related domains.

The agenda proposed here is extremely ambitious. Addressing it rigorously and in a way that shares what we learn broadly should go a fair way to supporting the frequent calls for improving education by improving leadership. However, doing so will require reaching out in at least two directions. The first is to our colleagues in related disciplines. While much of the intellectual capital for advancing this research agenda can be found among those already studying educational leadership, new ideas are needed. Historically, educational leadership has looked first to general theories of leadership from outside education for intellectual guidance. While this work still has something to offer, it is now important to turn to research from the elements of psychology and cognitive science (in its more individualist and social variations) that developed through the study of students and teachers.

The second direction is toward those outside the research community who provide the resources for large-scale inquiry. The agendas proposed here will require work of a scope that has not been common in past research on educational leadership. Getting support for such work will be challenging. While many people call for reforming educational leadership, those setting the agenda for educational research—the federal government and the foundations—seem to have other priorities. Moreover, our reputation among research funders is not generally high. The recent criticisms of educational research have been leveled at other fields that have a stronger base than the work on leadership. This is not to say that the situation is impossible. Selected foundations and the National Science Foundation are funding extremely interesting research on educational leadership that does address important parts of this agenda. Important work is also being done in other countries that those in the United States often ignore.

Nevertheless, more is needed. It will be necessary both to work together and to recruit colleagues from related fields. It may also be important for professional associations to play a role. These include the associations for researchers on educational leadership. As mentioned before, this volume is the report of the second task force to improve the quality of research in the field of educational leadership initiated by Division A of the American Educational Research Association. The Division and organizations like the University Council for Educational Administration will need to continue actively working to improve the quality of research in the field for this agenda to be realized. Moreover, it will be important to build bridges to the professional associations for leaders—principals, superintendents, and others—and get their support to move the agenda forward.

We conclude by noting that this agenda may miss questions that are or will soon become important to the improvement of leadership. A vigorous research agenda should engender new questions if it successfully helps a research community to coalesce and focus. Our hope is that the overarching framework presented here provides a durable, flexible structure within which new questions can be posed and useful guidance offered to educational leaders.

References

Allington, R. (2002). *Big brother and the national reading curriculum: How ideology trumped evidence*. Portsmouth, NH: Heinemann.

Anderson, G. (1998). Toward authentic participation: Deconstructing the discourses of participatory reforms in education. *American Educational Research Journal, 35*(4), 571–603.

Anderson, L. (1984). The environment of instruction: The function of seatwork in commercially developed curriculum. In G. Duffy, L. Roehler, & J. Mason (Eds.), *Comprehension instruction: Perspectives and suggestions* (pp. 93–103). New York: Longman.

Apple, M. W., & Beane, J. A. (Eds.) (1995). *Democratic schools*. Alexandria, VA: Association for Supervision and Curriculum Development.

Archer, J. (2004, March 17). Weaving webs. *Education Week*, pp. 50–54.

Argyris, C., & Schön, D. A. (1978). *Organizational learning: A theory of action perspective*. Reading, MA: Addison-Wesley.

Ball, D. L. (2000). Bridging practices: Intertwining content and pedagogy in teaching and learning to teach. *Journal of Teacher Education, 51*(3), 241–247.

Banks, J. A. (1991). Multicultural education: For freedom's sake. *Educational Leadership, 49*(4), 32–36.

Banner, D. K., & Gagné, T. E. (1995). *Designing effective organizations: Traditional and transformational views*. Thousand Oaks, CA: Sage.

Barber, B. R. (1998). *A passion for democracy: American essays*. Princeton, NJ: Princeton University Press.

Barnard, C. I. (1981). Cooperation. In O. Grusky & G. A. Miller (Eds.), *The sociology of organizations* (2nd ed., pp. 84–97). New York: Free Press.

Barnett, B. G., Basom, M. R., Yerkes, D. M., & Norris, C. J. (2000). Cohorts in educational leadership programs: Benefits, difficulties, and the potential for developing school leaders. *Educational Administration Quarterly, 36*, 255–282.

Barr, R., & Dreeben, R. (1983). *How schools work*. Chicago: University of Chicago Press.

Bascia, N. (1997). Invisible leadership: Teachers' union activity in schools. *Alberta Journal of Educational Research, 43*(2–3), 69–85.

Bass, B. M. (1990). *Bass and Stogdill's handbook of leadership: Theory, research, and managerial applications* (3rd ed.). New York: Free Press.

Becher, T. (1989). *Academic tribes and territories: Intellectual enquiry and the cultures of disciplines*. Bristol, PA: Open University Press.

Beck, L. G. (1994). *Reclaiming educational administration as a caring profession*. New York: Teachers College Press.

Beck, L. G. (1999). Metaphors of educational community: An analysis of the images that reflect and influence scholarship and practice. *Educational Administration Quarterly*, *35*, 13–45.

Beck, L., & Foster, W. (1999). Administration and community: Considering challenges, exploring possibilities. In J. Murphy & K. S. Louis (Eds.), *Handbook of research on educational administration* (pp. 337–358). San Francisco: Jossey-Bass.

Beck, M. S. (1991, Spring). Increasing school completion: Strategies that work. *Monographs in Education*, *13*, 394.

Bennis, W. (1984). Transformative power and leadership. In T. J. Sergiovanni & J. E. Corbally (Eds.), *Leadership and organizational culture: New perspectives on administrative theory and practice* (pp. 64–71). Urbana: University of Illinois Press.

Bennis, W., & Nanus, B. (1985). *Leaders: The strategies for taking charge*. New York: Harper & Row.

Berliner, D. (2002). Educational research: The hardest science of all. *Educational Researcher*, *31*(8), 18–20.

Berliner, D., & Biddle, B. (1995). *The manufactured crisis: Myths, fraud, and the attack on America's public schools*. Reading, MA: Addison-Wesley.

Berman, P., & McLaughlin, M. W. (1978). *Federal programs supporting educational change, Vol. 8: Implementing and sustaining innovations*. Santa Monica, CA: RAND Corporation.

Biddle, B. J., & Berliner, D. C. (2002). Unequal school funding in the United States. *Educational Leadership*, *61*(2), 48–58.

Bidwell, C. E., & Kasarda, J. D. (1980). Conceptualizing and measuring the effects of school and schooling. *American Journal of Education*, *88*, 401–430.

Billett, S. (2002). Workplaces, communities and pedagogy. In M. R. Lea & K. Nicoll (Eds.), *Distributed learning: Social and cultural approaches to practice* (pp. 83–97). New York: Routledge.

Bishop, R., & Glynn, T. (1999). *Culture counts: Changing power relations in education*. Palmerston North, New Zealand: Dunmore.

Bizar, M., & Barr, R. (2001). *School leadership in times of urban reform*. Mahwah, NJ: Erlbaum.

Blase, J. (1993). The micropolitics of effective school-based leadership: Teachers' perspectives. *Educational Administration Quarterly*, *24*, 143–163.

Blase, J., & Anderson, G. L. (1995). *The micropolitics of educational leadership: From control to empowerment*. London: Cassell.

Bogotch, I. E. (2000). *Educational leadership and social justice: Theory into practice*. Revised version of a paper presented at the annual conference of the University Council for Educational Administration, Albuquerque, NM. ERIC document no. ED 452 585.

Bolman, L. G., & Deal, T. E. (1993). Everyday epistemology in school leadership: Patterns and prospects. In P. Hallinger, K. Leithwood, & J. Murphy (Eds.), *Cognitive perspectives on educational leadership* (pp. 21–33). New York: Teachers College Press.

Borko, H., & Putnam, R. (1996). Learning to teach. In D. C. Berliner & R. C. Calfee (Eds.), *Handbook of educational psychology* (pp. 673–708). New York: Macmillan.

Bourdieu, P. (1977). Cultural reproduction and social reproduction. In J. Karabel & A. H. Halsey (Eds.), *Power and ideology in education* (pp. 1–85). New York: Oxford University Press.

Bourdieu, P. (1997). The forms of capital. In A. H. Halsey, H. Lauder, P. Brown, & A. S. Wells (Eds.), *Education*. Oxford: Oxford University Press.

Bowen, W. G., & Bok, B. (1998). *The shape of the river*. Princeton, NJ: Princeton University Press.

Bowers, C. A. (2001). *Educating for eco-justice and community*. Athens: University of Georgia Press.

Bowles, S., & Gintis, H. (1976). *Schooling in capitalist America*. New York: Basic.

Boyan, N. J. (Ed.). (1988a). *Handbook of research on educational administration*. New York: Longman.

Boyan, N. J. (1988b). Describing and explaining administrator behavior. In N. J. Boyan (Ed.), *Handbook of research on educational administration*. New York: Longman.

Boyd, W., Crowson, R., & Gresson, A. (1997). *Neighborhood initiatives, community agencies and the public schools: A changing scene for the development and learning of children* (LSS Publication Series No. 6). *Retrieved February 19, 2003, from* www.temple.edu/lss/htmlpublications/pubs97-6.htm

Braddock, J. H., & McPartland, J. M. (1993). The education of early adolescents. In L. Darling-Hammond (Ed.), *Review of Research in Education* (Vol. 19, pp. 135–170). Washington, DC: American Educational Research Association.

Bransford, J. D., Brown, A., & Cocking, R. R. (Eds.). (2000). *How people learn: Brain, mind, experience, and school*. Washington, DC: National Academy Press.

Bredo, E., & McDermott, R. P. (1992, June–July). Teaching, relating, and learning [Review of *The construction zone* and *Rousing minds to life*]. *Educational Researcher, 21*(5), pp. 31–35.

Bridges, E. (1982). Research on the school administrator: The state-of-the-art, 1967–1980. *Educational Administration Quarterly, 18*(3), 12–33.

Brophy, J. (Ed.). (1991). *Advances in research on teaching: Teachers' knowledge of subject matter as it relates to their teaching practice*. Greenwich, CT: JAI Press.

Brophy, J. (Ed.). (2001). *Advances in research in teaching: Subject-specific instructional methods and activities* (Vol. 8). Oxford: Elsevier Science.

Brophy, J., & Good, T. L. (1986). Teacher behavior and student achievement. In M. C. Wittrock (Ed.), *Handbook of research on teaching* (pp. 318–375). New York: Macmillan.

Brown, A. L. (1992). Design experiments: Theoretical and methodological challenges in creating complex interventions in classroom settings. *Journal of the Learning Sciences, 2*, 141–178.

Brown, A. L. (1994). The advancement of learning. *Educational Researcher, 23*(8), 4–12.

Brown, C. A., & Borko, H. (1992). Becoming a mathematics teacher. In D. Grouws (Ed.), *Handbook of research on mathematics teaching and learning* (pp. 209–239). New York: Macmillan.

Brown, J., Collins, A., & Duguid, P. (1989). Situated cognition and the culture of learning. *Educational Researcher, 18*, 32–41.

Brown, J. S., & Duguid, P. (1991). Organizational learning and communities of practice: Toward a unified view of working, learning, and innovation. *Organization Science, 2*, 40–57.

Brown, K. M., Anfara, V. A., Hartman, K. J., Mahar, R. J., & Mills, R. (2002). Professional development of middle level principals: Pushing the reform forward. *Leadership and Policy in Schools, 1*, 107–143.

Brown, M., Rutherford, D., & Boyle, B. (2000). Leadership for school improvement: The role of the head of department in UK secondary schools. *School Effectiveness and School Improvement, 11*(2), 237–258.

Browne-Ferrigno, T., & Muth, R. (2004). Leadership mentoring in clinical practice: Role socialization, professional development, and capacity building. *Educational Administration Quarterly, 40*, 468–494.

Bruner, J. (1960). *The process of education.* Cambridge, MA: Harvard University Press.

Brunner, C. C. (Ed.). (1999). *Sacred dreams: Women and the superintendency.* Albany: State University of New York Press.

Bryk, A. S., & Driscoll, M. E. (1988). *The school as community: Theoretical foundations, contextual influences, and consequences for students and teachers.* Madison: University of Wisconsin, National Center for Effective Secondary Schools.

Bryk, A. S., Lee, V. E., & Holland, P. B. (1993). *Catholic schools and the common good.* Cambridge, MA: Harvard University Press.

Bryk, A. S., & Schneider, B. (2002). *Trust in schools: A core resource for improvement.* New York: Russell Sage Foundation.

Bryman, A. (1992). *Charisma and leadership in organizations.* Newbury Park, CA: Sage.

Bulkley, K. (2001). Educational performance and charter school authorizers: The accountability bind. *Educational Policy Analysis Archives, 9*(37). Available at http://epaa.asu.edu/epaa/v9n37.html.

Burch, P., & Spillane, J. (2003). Elementary school leadership strategies and subject matter: Reforming mathematics and literacy instruction. *The Elementary School Journal, 103*(5), 519–535.

Burlingame, M. (1988). The politics of education and educational policy: The local level. In N. J. Boyan (Ed.), *Handbook of research on educational administration* (pp. 439–452). New York: Longman.

Burns, J. M. (1978). *Leadership.* New York: Harper & Row.

Burns, R., & Mason, D. (1998). Class formation and composition in elementary schools. *American Educational Research Journal, 35*, 739–772.

Burns, R., & Mason, D. (2002). Class composition and student achievement in elementary schools. *American Educational Research Journal, 39*(1), 207–233.

Cahill, M. (1993). *A documentation report on the New York City Beacons Initiative.* New York: The Youth Development Institute, Fund for the City of New York.

Caine, R. N., & Caine, G. (1997). *Education on the edge of possibility.* Alexandria, VA: Association for Supervision and Curriculum Development.

Cairney, T., & Munsie, L. (1995). *Beyond tokenism: Parents as partners in literacy.* Portsmouth, NH: Heinemann.

Callahan, R. E. (1962). *Education and the cult of efficiency.* Chicago: University of Chicago Press.

Capper, C. A. (1992). A feminist poststructural analysis of nontraditional approaches in educational administration. *Educational Administration Quarterly, 28*(1), 103–124.

Carbonaro, W. (1998). A little help from my friend's parents: Intergenerational closure and generational outcomes. *Sociology of Education, 71*, 295–313.

Carnes, J. (2003, Spring). Editor's note. *Teaching Tolerance Magazine, 23.*

Carnoy, M., Elmore, R. F., & Siskin, L. S. (2003). *The new accountability: High schools and high stakes testing.* New York: Routledge Falmer.

Carpenter, T. P., Fennema, E., Peterson, P. L., Chiang, C., & Loef, M. (1989). Using knowledge of children's mathematical thinking in classroom teaching: An experimental study. *American Educational Research Journal, 26*, 499–532.

Carpenter, T. P., Fennema, E., Peterson, P. L., & Carey, D. A. (1988). Teachers' pedagogical content knowledge of students' problem-solving in elementary arithmetic. *Journal for Research in Mathematics Education, 19*, 385–401.

Carpenter, T. P., & Moser, J. M. (1984). The acquisition of addition and subtraction concepts in grades one through three. *Journal for Research in Mathematics Education, 15*, 179–202.

Carspecken, P. F. (1996). *Critical ethnography in educational research: A theoretical and practical guide.* New York: Routledge.

Cazden, C. (1986). Classroom discourse. In M. Wittrock (Ed.), *Handbook of research on teaching* (3rd ed., pp. 432–463). New York: Macmillan.

Chaskin, R. (2000, December). Lessons learned from the implementation of the neighborhood and family initiative: A summary of findings. *The Chapin Hall Center for Children at the University of Chicago* (Discussion Paper CB-30). Chicago: University of Chicago.

Chrispeels, J. A., Brown, J. H., & Castillo, S. (2000). School leadership teams: Factors that influence their development and effectiveness. In K. Leithwood (Ed.), *Understanding schools as intelligent systems* (pp. 39–73). Stamford, CT: Jai Press.

Clotfelter, C. T., & Ladd, H. E. (1996). Recognizing and rewarding success in public schools. In H. F. Ladd (Ed.), *Holding schools accountable: Performance-based reform in education* (pp. 23–63). Washington, DC: Brookings Institution.

Cobb, P. (1994). Where is the mind? Constructivist and sociocultural perspectives on mathematical development. *Educational Researcher, 23*(7), 13–20.

Cobb, P. (1998). Learning from distributed theories of intelligence. *Mind, Culture and Activity, 5*(3), 187–204.

Cobb, P., Confrey, J., diSessa, A., Lehrer, R., & Schauble, L. (2003). Design experiments in educational research. *Educational Researcher, 32*(1), 9–13.

Cobb, P., McClain, K., Lamberg, T. D. S., & Dean, C. (2003). Situating teachers' instructional practices in the institutional setting of the school and district. *Educational Researcher, 32*(6), 13–24.

Coburn, C. E. (2001). Collective sensemaking about reading: How teachers mediate reading policy in their professional communities. *Educational Evaluation and Policy Analysis, 23*(2), 145–170.

Coburn, C. E. (2002). *How school leaders influence teachers' implementation of instructional policy.* Paper presented at the Fall Conference of the University Council for Educational Administration, Pittsburgh, PA.

Coburn, C. E. (2003). Rethinking scale: Moving beyond numbers to deep and lasting change. *Educational Researcher, 32*(6), 3–12.

Coburn, C. E. (2004). Beyond decoupling: Rethinking the relationship between the institutional environment and the classroom. *Sociology of Education, 77*, 211–245.

Cochran-Smith, M., & Lytle, S. (1999). Relationships of knowledge and practice: Teacher learning in communities. In A. Iran-Nejad & P. D. Pearson (Eds.), *Review of Research in Education* (Vol. 24; pp. 249–306). Washington, DC: American Educational Research Association.

Cohen, D. K. (1988). Teaching practice: Plus ça change . . . In P. Jackson (Ed.), *Contributions to educational change: Perspectives on research and practice* (pp. 27–84). Berkeley, CA: McCutcheon.

Cohen, D. K. (1990). A revolution in one classroom: The case of Mrs. Oublier. *Educational Evaluation and Policy Analysis, 12,* 327–345.

Cohen, D. K., & Ball, D. L. (1999). *Instruction, capacity and improvement* (CPRE Research Report No. RR-43). Philadelphia, PA: University of Pennsylvania, Consortium for Policy Research in Education.

Cohen, M. D., March, J. G., & Olsen, J. P. (1972). A garbage can model of organizational choice. *Administrative Science Quarterly, 17*(1), 1–25.

Cohn, M. M., & Kottkamp, R. B. (1993). *Teachers: The missing voice in education.* Albany: State University of New York Press.

Coleman, J. S. (1966). *Equality of educational opportunity.* Washington, DC: U.S. Government Printing Office.

Coleman, J. S. (1988). Social capital in the creation of human capital. *American Journal of Sociology, 94*(Supplement), S95–S120.

Coleman, J. S. (1990). *Equality and achievement in education.* San Francisco: Westview.

Coleman, J. S., Campbell, E. Q., Hobson, C. F., McPartland, J., Mood, A. M., Weifeld, F. D., & York, R. L. (1966). *Equality of educational opportunity.* Washington, DC: U.S. Government Printing Office.

Coleman, J. S., & Hoffer, T. (1987). *Public and private high schools: The impact of communities.* New York: Basic Books.

Comer, J. (1984). Home–school relationships as they affect the academic success of children. *Education and Urban Society, 16,* 323–337.

Conger, J., & Kanungo, R. (1998). *Charismatic leadership in organizations.* Thousand Oaks, CA: Sage.

Connell, R. W. (1993). *Schools and social justice.* Philadelphia, PA: Temple University Press.

Cook, T. D. (2002). Randomized experiments in education: Why are they so rare? *Educational Evaluation and Policy Analysis, 24*(3), 175–199.

Cooper, B. S. (1993). When teachers run schools. In T. A. Astuto (Ed.), *When teachers lead* (pp. 25–42). University Park, PA: University Council for Educational Administration.

Copland, M. A. (2000, April). *Developing the problem-framing skills of prospective principals.* Paper presented at the annual meeting of the American Educational Research Association, New Orleans.

Cosgrove, D. (1986). *The effects of principal succession on elementary schools.* Unpublished doctoral dissertation, Department of Educational Administration, University of Utah, Salt Lake City.

Cotton, K. (1995). *Effective schooling practices: A research synthesis.* 1995 Update. School Improvement Research Series. Portland, OR: Northwest Regional Educational Laboratory.

Creemers, B. P. M., & Reezigt, G. J. (1996). School-level conditions affecting the effectiveness of instruction. *School Effectiveness and School Improvement, 7*(3), 197–228.

Croninger, R., & Lee, V. (2001, August). Social capital and dropping out of high school: Benefits to at-risk students of teachers' support and guidance. *Teachers College Record, 103*(4), 548–581.

Crosnoe, R., Johnson, M. K., & Elder, G. H. (2004). Intergenerational bonding in school:

The behavioral and contextual correlates of student–teacher relationships. *Sociology of Education, 77*(1), 60–81.

Crowson, R. (2001). Community development and school reform: An overview. In R. Crowson (Ed.), *Community development and school reform* (pp. 1–18). New York: JAI Press.

Crowson, R. (2003). Empowerment models for interprofessional collaboration. In M. Brabeck & M. Walsh (Eds.), *National Society for the Study of Education yearbook: The contribution/interprofessional collaboration and comprehensive series to teaching and learning* (vol. 102, pp. 1–20). Chicago: University of Chicago Press.

Crowson, R., & Boyd, W. (1993). Coordinated services for children: Designing arks for storms and seas unknown. *American Journal of Education, 101*(2), 140–179.

Crowson, R., & Boyd, W. (2001). The new role of community development in education reform. *Peabody Journal of Education, 76*(2), 9–29.

Crowson, R., Guthrie, J., Goldring, E., & Smith, T. (2002). *The reciprocal interactions regarding context and consequences of learning.* Unpublished paper, Department of Policy, Leadership and Organizations, Peabody College, Vanderbilt University, Nashville, TN.

Cuban, L. (1976). *Urban school chiefs under fire.* Chicago: University of Chicago Press.

Cuban, L. (1988). *The managerial imperative and the practice of leadership in schools.* Albany: State University of New York Press.

Cuban, L. (1993). *How teachers taught: Constancy and change in American classrooms, 1890–1980* (2nd ed.). New York: Teachers College Press.

Daft, R. L. (1992). *Organization theory and design* (4th ed.). St. Paul, MN: West Publishing Company.

Daresh, J. C. (2004). Mentoring school leaders: Professional promise or predictable problems? *Educational Administration Quarterly, 40,* 495–517.

Daresh, J. C., & Playko, M. A. (1995). *Alternative career formation perspectives: Lessons for educational leadership from law, medicine, and training for the priesthood.* Paper presented at the annual meeting of the University Council for Educational Administration, Salt Lake City.

Darling-Hammond, L. (1996). Teacher professionalism: Why and how? In A. Leiberman (Ed.), *Schools as collaborative cultures: Creating the future now* (pp. 25–50). Bristol, PA: Falmer Press.

Darling-Hammond, L., & Youngs, P. (2002). Defining "highly qualified teachers": What does "scientifically-based research" actually tell us? *Educational Researcher, 31*(9), 13–25.

Day, C., & Harris, A. (2002). Leading schools in a data-rich world. In K. Leithwood & P. Hallinger (Eds.), *Second international handbook of educational leadership and administration: Part one.* Norwell, MA: Kluwer.

Day, C., Harris, A., Hafield, M., Tolley, H., & Beresford, J. (2000). *Leading schools in times of change.* Buckingham, UK: Open University Press.

Deal, T., & Peterson, K. (1998). *Shaping school culture: The heart of leadership.* San Francisco: Jossey-Bass.

Dei, G. S. (1996). *Anti-racism education: Theory and practice.* Halifax, Nova Scotia: Fernwood.

Delgado-Gaitan, C. (1991). Involving parents in the schools: A process of empowerment. *American Journal of Education, 100*(1), 20–46.

Delpit, L. D. (1990). The silenced dialogue: Power and pedagogy in educating other people's children. In N. M. Hidalgo, C. L. McDowell, & E. V. Siddle (Eds.), *Facing racism in education*. Reprint Series No. 21. Cambridge, MA: Harvard Educational Review.

DeMoss, K. (2002). Leadership styles and high-stakes testing: Principals make a difference. *Education and Urban Society, 35*(1), 111–132.

Design-Based Research Collective. (2003). Design-based research: An emerging paradigm for educational inquiry. *Educational Researcher, 32*(1), 5–8.

Desimone, L. M., & Le Floch, K. C. (2004). Are we asking the right questions? Using cognitive interviews to improve surveys in education research. *Educational Evaluation and Policy Analysis, 26*(1), 1–22.

Dewey, J. (1897). My pedagogic creed. *School Journal, 54*, 77–80.

Dewey, J. (1916). *Democracy and education*. New York: Macmillan.

Dika, S., & Singh, K. (2002). Applications of social capital in educational literature: A critical analysis. *Review of Educational Research, 72*(1), 31–60.

Dillard, C. B. (1995). Leading with her life: An African American feminist (re)interpretation of leadership for an urban high school principal. *Educational Administration Quarterly, 31*(4), 539–563.

Doyle, W. (1983). Academic work. *Review of Educational Research, 53*(2), 159–199.

Driscoll, M. E. (2001). The sense of place and the neighborhood school: Implications for building social capital and for community development. In R. Crowson (Ed.), *Community development and school reform* (pp. 19–41). New York: JAI Press.

Driscoll, M. E., (2004). The sense of place and Conant's legacy: Connecting schools and their communities. In F. Hammack (Ed.), *A future for the comprehensive high school?* (pp. 114–129). New York: Teachers College Press.

Driscoll, M. E., & Kerchner, C. (1999). The implications of social capital for school, communities and cities: Educational administration as if a sense of place mattered. In J. Murphy & K. S. Louis (Eds.), *Handbook of research on educational administration* (pp. 385–404). San Francisco: Jossey-Bass.

Driscoll, M., Nelson, B. S., Sassi, A., & Kennedy, S. S. (2000). *Administrators learn about mathematics education reform: New ideas, new practices*. Unpublished manuscript.

Dryfoos, J. G. (1994). *Full-service schools: A revolution in health and social services for children, youth, and families*. San Francisco: Jossey-Bass.

DuFour, R., & Eaker, R. (1998). *Professional learning communities at work: Best practices for enhancing student achievement*. Arlington, VA: Association for Supervision and Curriculum Development.

Duke, D., Showers, B., & Imber, M. (1980). Teachers and shared decision making: The costs and benefits of involvement. *Educational Administration Quarterly, 16*, 93–106.

Dunkin, M. J., & Biddle, B. J. (1974). *The study of teaching*. New York: Holt, Rinehart and Winston.

Edelson, D. C. (2002). Design research: What we learn when we engage in design. *Journal of the Learning Sciences, 11*(1), 105–121.

Edmonds, R. (1979). Effective schools for the urban poor. *Educational Leadership, 37*(1), 15–24.

Edmonds, R. R. (1979, March/April). Some schools work and more can. *Social Policy*, pp. 28–32.

Educational Research Service. (1998). *Is there a shortage of qualified candidates for openings in the principalship? An exploratory study* (Report prepared for the National Association of Elementary School Principals and the National Association for Secondary School Principals). Arlington, VA: Author.

Edwards, B., & Foley, B. (1997). Social capital and the political economy of our discontent. *American Behavioural Scientist, 40*(5), 669–678.

Educational Evaluation and Policy Analysis. (1990). [Entire issue of journal], *12*(1), 233–353.

Ehrich, L. C., Hansford, B., & Tennet, L. (2004). Formal mentoring programs in education and other professions: A review of the literature. *Educational Administration Quarterly, 40*, 518–540.

Eisenhart, M., & Towne, L. (2003). Contestation and change in national policy on "scientifically based" education research. *Educational Researcher, (32)*7, 31–38.

Elmore, R. F. (1995a). Structural reform and educational practice. *Educational Researcher, 24*(9), 23–26.

Elmore, R. F. (1995b). Teaching, learning, and school organization: Principles of practice and the regularities of schooling. *Educational Administration Quarterly, 31*(3), 355–374.

Elmore, R. F. (1996). Getting to scale with good educational practice. *Harvard Educational Review, 66*(1), 1–26.

Elmore, R. F. (1997). *Investing in teacher learning: Staff development and instructional improvement in Community School District #2.* New York: National Commission on Teaching and America's Future.

Elmore, R. F. (2000, Winter). *Building a new structure for school leadership.* Washington, DC: Albert Shanker Institute.

Elsberry, C., & Bishop, H. L. (1993, November). *Perceptions of first-year elementary principals in three southeastern states regarding principal induction programs.* Paper presented at the annual meeting of the Mid-South Educational Research Association, New Orleans.

Engestrom, Y., & Middleton, D. (1996). Introduction: Studying work as mindful practice. In Y. Engestrom & D. Middleton (Eds.), *Cognition and communication at work* (pp. 1–14). Cambridge, UK: Cambridge University Press.

Englert, R. M. (1993). Understanding the urban context and conditions of practice of school administration. In P. Forsyth & M. Tallerico (Eds.), *City schools: Leading the way* (pp. 1–63). Newbury Park, CA: Corwin.

English, F. W. (1992). *Deciding what to teach and test.* Newbury Park, CA: Corwin.

Epstein, J. (1996). Perspectives and previews on research and policy for school, family, and commununity partnerships. In A. Booth & J. Dunn (Eds.), *Family–school links* (pp. 209–246). Mahwah, NJ: Erlbaum.

Epstein, J. L. (2001). *School, family, and community partnerships: Preparing educators and improving schools.* Boulder, CO: Westview Press.

Epstein, J., Simon, B., & Salinas, K. (1997). Involving parents in homework in the middle grades. *Phi Delta Kappa Research Bulletin*, No. 18.

Eraut, M. (1994). *Developing professional knowledge and competence*. Washington, DC: Falmer.

Erickson, F., & Gutierrez, K. (2002). Culture, rigor, and science in educational research. *Educational Researcher, 31*(8), 21–24.

Etzione, A. (1993). *The spirit of community: The reinvention of American society*. New York: Touchstone.

Etzioni, A. (1999). *The limits of privacy*. New York: Basic.

Evans, P. M., & Mohr, N. (1999). Professional development for principals: Seven core beliefs. *Phi Delta Kappan, 80*, 530–532.

Evers, C. W., & Lakomski, G. (1991). *Knowing educational administration: Contemporary methodological controversies in educational administration research*. Oxford, UK: Pergamon Press.

Fairhurst, G. T., & Sarr, R. A. (1996). *The art of framing: Managing the language of leadership*. San Francisco: Jossey-Bass.

Fairman, J., & Firestone, W. A. (2001). The district role in state assessment policy: An exploratory study. In S. H. Fuhrman (Ed.), *From the capitol to the classroom: Standards-based reform in the states* (pp. 124–147). Chicago: University of Chicago Press.

Farrell, J. P. (1999). Changing conceptions of equality of education: Forty years of comparative evidence. In R. F. Arnove & C. A. Torres (Eds.), *Comparative education: The dialectic of the global and the local* (pp. 149–177). Lanham, MD: Rowman & Littlefield.

Fashola, O., & Slavin, R. (1998). *Show me the evidence! Proven and promising programs for America's schools*. Thousand Oaks, CA: Corwin.

Fennema, E., Franke, M. L., Carpenter, T. P., & Carey, D. (1993). Using children's mathematical knowledge in instruction. *American Educational Research Journal, 30*, 555–583.

Finn, J. (1989). Withdrawing from school. *Review of Educational Research, 59*(2), 117–143.

Finn, J. (2002). Small classes in American schools: Research, practice and politics. *Phi Delta Kappan, 83*(7), 551–560.

Firestone, W. A., & Fisler, J. L. (2002). Politics, community, and leadership in a school–university partnership. *Educational Administration Quarterly, 38*(4), 449–493.

Firestone, W. A., Fitz, J., & Broadfoot, P. (1999). Power, learning, and legitimation: Assessment implementation across levels in the United States and the United Kingdom. *American Educational Research Journal, 36*(4), 759–793.

Firestone, W. A., Schorr, R. Y., & Monfils, L. (2004). *The ambiguity of teaching to the test*. Mahwah, NJ: Erlbaum.

Fiske, E. B., & Ladd, H. F. (2000). *When schools compete: A cautionary tale*. Washington, DC: Brookings Institution.

Floden, R. (2002). Research on effects of teaching: A continuing model for research on teaching. In V. Richardson (Ed.), *Handbook of research on teaching* (4th ed., pp. 3–16). New York: Macmillan.

Ford, M. (1992). *Motivating humans: Goals, emotions, and personal agency beliefs*. Newbury Park, CA: Sage.

Fordham, S., & Ogbu, J. (1986). Black students and school success: Coping with the burden of acting white. *Urban Review, 18*(3), 176–206.

Foster, W. F. (1989). Toward a critical practice of leadership. In J. Smyth (Ed.), *Critical perspectives on educational leadership* (pp. 39–62). London: Falmer.

Foster, M. (1993). Educating for competence in community and culture: Exploring the views of exemplary African American teachers. *Urban Education, 27*(4), 370–394.

Foster, M. (1995). African American teachers and culturally relevant pedagogy. In J. A. Banks & C. A. M. Banks (Eds.), *Handbook of research on multicultural education* (pp. 570–581). New York: Macmillan.

Freire, P. (1983). *Pedagogy of the oppressed* (M. B. Ramos, Trans.). New York: Continuum.

Freire, P., & Macedo, D. (1998). Literacy: Reading the word and the world. *Thinking, 14*(1), 8–10.

Friedkin, N. E., & Slater, M. R. (1994). School leadership and performance: A social network approach. *Sociology of Education, 67*(2), 139–157.

Fuhrman, S., Clune, W., & Elmore, R. (1988). Research on educational reform: Lessons on the implementation of policy. *Teachers College Record, 90*(2), 237–257.

Fullan, M. G. (1991). *The new meaning of educational change.* New York: Teachers College Press.

Fullan, M. (2001). *Leading in a culture of change.* San Francisco: Jossey-Bass.

Fuller, B. (2000). *Inside charter schools.* Cambridge, MA: Harvard University Press.

Fuller, H. L., Campbell, C., Cielo, M. B., Harvey, I., Immerwahr, J., & Winger, A. (2003). *An impossible job? The view from the superintendent's chair.* Seattle: University of Washington, Daniel Evans School of Public Affairs, Center on Reinventing Public Education.

Furman, G. C., & Starratt, R. J. (2002). Leadership for democratic community in schools. In J. Murphy (Ed.), *The educational leadership challenge: Redefining leadership for the 21st century* (pp. 105–133). Chicago: National Society for the Study of Education.

Gage, N. (Ed.). (1963). *Handbook of research on teaching.* Chicago: Rand McNally.

Gage, N. (1978). *The scientific basis of the art of teaching.* New York: Teachers College Press.

Gage, N., & Giaconia, R. (1981). Teaching practices and student achievement: Causal connections. *New York University Education Quarterly, 12*(3), 2–9.

Gagne, R. M. (1968). Learning hierarchies. *Educational Psychologist, 6,* 1–9.

Gamoran, A., Nystrand, M., Berends, M., & LePore, P. C. (1995). An organizational analysis of the effects of ability grouping. *American Educational Research Journal, 32*(4), 687–715.

Garcia, E. E. (1995). Education of Mexican American students: Past treatment and recent developments in theory, research, policy, and practice. In J. A. Banks & C. A. M. Banks (Eds.), *Handbook of research on multicultural education* (pp. 372–387). New York: Simon & Schuster Macmillan.

Gardner, H. (1985). *The mind's new science: A history of the cognitive revolution.* New York: Basic Books.

Gezi, K. (1990). The role of leadership in inner-city schools. *Educational Research Quarterly, 12*(4), 4–11.

Giroux, H. (1992). *Border crossings: Cultural workers and the politics of education.* New York: Routledge.

Goertz, M. E., & Duffy, M. C. (2001). *Assessment and accountability systems in the 50 states: 1999–2000.* No. RR-046. Philadelphia: Consortium for Policy Research in Education.

Goldfarb, K. P., & Grinberg, J. (2002). Leadership for social justice: Authentic participation in the case of a community center in Caracas, Venezuela. *Journal of School Leadership, 12,* 157–173.

Goldring, E. (1990). Elementary school principals as boundary spanners: Their engagement with parents. *Journal of Educational Administration, 28*(1), 53–62.

Goldring, E., & Greenfield, W. (2002). Understanding the evolving concept of leadership in education: Roles, expectations, and dilemmas. In J. Murphy (Ed.), *The educational leadership challenge: Redefining leadership for the 21st century* (pp. 1–19). Chicago: National Society for the Study of Education.

Goldring, E., & Hausman, C. (2001). Civic capacity and school principals: The missing link for community development. In R. Crowson (Ed.), *Community development and school reform* (pp. 193–210). New York: JAI Press.

Goldring, E., & Sullivan, A. (1996). Beyond the boundaries: Principals, parents, and communities shaping the school environment. In K. Leithwood, J. Chapman, D. Corson, P. Hallinger, & A. Hart (Eds.), *International handbook of educational leadership and administration* (pp. 195–222). Boston: Kluwer.

Goleman, D., Boyatzis, R., & McKee, A. (2002). *Primal leadership: Realizing the power of emotional intelligence.* Boston: Harvard Business School Press.

Good, T., Grouws, D., & Ebmeier, H. (1983). *Active mathematics teaching.* New York: Longman.

Gooden, M. (2002). Stewardship and critical leadership: Sufficient for leadership in urban schools? *Education and Urban Society, 35*(1), 133–143.

Goodlad, S. J. (Ed.). (2001). *The last best hope: A democracy reader.* San Francisco: Jossey-Bass.

Gorman, J. C., & Balter, L. (1997). Culturally sensitive parent education: A critical review of quantitative research. *Review of Educational Research, 67*(3), 339–369.

Granovetter, M. (1985). Economic action, social structure, and embeddedness. *American Journal of Sociology, 83,* 1420–1443.

Grant, C. M., Nelson, B. S., Davidson, E., Sassi, A., Weinberg, A., & Bleiman, J. (2002). *Lenses on learning: Instructional leadership in mathematics.* Parsippany, NJ: Dale Seymour Publications.

Green, J. M. (1999). *Deep democracy: Community, diversity, and transformation.* Lanham, MD: Rowman & Littlefield.

Greenberg, J. (2001). Setting the justice agenda: Seven unanswered questions about "What, why, and who." *Journal of Vocational Behavior, 58,* 210–219. [http://www.idealibrary.com].

Greene, M. (1978). Teaching: The question of personal reality. *Teachers College Record, 80*(1), 23–35.

Greene, M. (1988). *The dialectic of freedom.* New York: Teachers College Press.

Greene, M. (1995). *Releasing the imagination: Essays on education, the arts and social change.* San Francisco, CA: Jossey-Bass.

Greenfield, T. (1991). Re-forming and re-valuing educational administration: Whence and when cometh the phoenix? *Educational Management and Administration, 19,* 200–217.

Greeno, J. G. (1998). The situativity of knowing, learning, and research. *American Psychologist*, *53*(1), 5–26.

Greeno, J. G., Collins, A. M., & Resnick, L. B. (1996). Cognition and learning. In D. C. Berliner & R. C. Chalfee (Eds.), *Handbook of educational psychology* (pp. 15–46). New York: Macmillan Library Reference.

Greeno, J. G., McDermott, R., Cole, K. A., Engle, R. A., Goldman, S., Knudson, J., et al. (1999). Research, reform, and the aims of education: Modes of action in search of each other. In E. C. Lagemann & L. S. Shulman (Eds.), *Issues in education research: Problems and possibilities* (pp. 299–335). San Francisco: Jossey-Bass.

Griffiths, M. (1998). *Educational research for social justice*. Buckingham, England: Open University Press.

Grogan, M., & Crow, G. (2004). Mentoring in the context of educational leadership preparation and development—old wine in new bottles? *Educational Administration Quarterly*, *40*, 463–467.

Gronn, P. (1983). Talk as the work: The accomplishment of school administration. *Administrative Science Quarterly*, *28*(1), 1–21.

Gronn, P. (2000). Distributed properties: A new architecture for leadership. *Educational Management and Administration*, *28*(3), 317–338.

Grossman, P. L. (1990). *The making of a teacher: Teacher knowledge and teacher education*. New York: Teachers College Press.

Grossman, P., Wineburg, S., & Woolworth, S. (2001). Toward a theory of teacher community. *Teachers College Record*, *103*(6), 942–1012.

Grumet, M. (1995). The curriculum: What are the basics and are we teaching them? In J. L. Kincheloe & S. R. Steinberg (Eds.), *Thirteen questions: Reframing education's conversation* (pp. 15–21). New York: Peter Lang.

Gudmundsdottir, S. (1991). Pedagogical models of subject matter. In J. Brophy (Ed.), *Advances in research on teaching: Teachers' knowledge of subject matter as it relates to their teaching practice* (pp. 265–304). Greenwich, CT: JAI Press.

Guinier, L. (1994). *The tyranny of the majority: Fundamental fairness in representative democracy*. New York: The Free Press.

Gutman, A. (1987). *Democratic education*. Princeton, NJ: Princeton University Press.

Hale, E. L., & Moorman, H. N. (2003). *Preparing school principals: A national perspective on policy and program innovations*. Washington, DC: Institute for Educational Leadership.

Hall, K. (1999). Understanding educational processes in an era of globalization: The view from anthropology and cultural studies. In E. C. Lagemann and L. S. Shulman (Eds.), *Issues in education research: Problems and possibilities* (pp. 121–156). San Francisco: Jossey-Bass Publishers.

Hallinger, P. (Ed.). (2003). *Reshaping the landscape of school leadership development: A global perspective*. Lisse, The Netherlands: Balkema Publishers.

Hallinger, P., Bickman, L., & Davis, K. (1996). School context, principal leadership, and student reading achievement. *Elementary School Journal*, *96*(5), 527–549.

Hallinger, P., & Heck, R. (1996a). Reassessing the principal's role in school effectiveness: A review of empirical research, 1980–1995. *Educational Administration Quarterly*, *32*(1), 5–44.

Hallinger, P., & Heck, R. (1996b). The principal's role in school effectiveness: An assessment of methodological progress, 1980–1995. In K. Leithwood et al. (Eds.), *International handbook of educational leadership and administration* (pp. 723–783). Dordrecht, The Netherlands: Kluwer Academic Publishers.

Hallinger, P., & Heck, R. (1998). Exploring the principal's contributions to school effectiveness. *School Effectiveness and School Improvement, 9*(2), 157–191.

Hallinger, P., & Heck, R. (1999). Next generation methods for the study of leadership and school improvement. In J. Murphy & K. S. Louis (Eds.), *Handbook of research on educational administration* (2nd ed., pp. 141–162). San Francisco: Jossey-Bass.

Hallinger, P., & Heck, R. (2002). What do you call people with visions? The role of vision, mission, and goals in school leadership and improvement. In K. Leithwood & H. Hallinger (Eds.), *Second international handbook of educational leadership and administration* (pp. 9–40). London: Kluwer.

Hallinger, P., & Leithwood, K. (1994). Exploring the effects of principal leadership. *School Effectiveness and School Improvement, 5,* 206–218.

Hallinger, P., & Leithwood, K. (1996a). Culture and educational administration: A case of finding out what you don't know you don't know. *Journal of Educational Administration, 34*(5), 98–116.

Hallinger, P., & Leithwood, K. (1996b). Editorial: Cultural and educational leadership: An introduction. *Journal of Educational Administration, 34*(5), 4–11.

Hallinger, P., Leithwood, K., & Murphy, J. (Eds.). (1993). *Cognitive perspectives on educational leadership.* New York: Teachers College Press.

Hamilton, M. L., & Richardson, V. (1995). Effects of the culture in two schools on the process and outcomes of staff development. *Elementary School Journal, 95*(4), 367–385.

Hannaway, J. (1996). Comments on the "Allocation of Resources to Special Education and Regular Instruction" (by Hamilton Lankford and James Wyckoff). In H. E. Ladd (Ed.), *Holding schools accountable* (pp. 258–264). Washington, DC: Brookings Institution.

Hannaway, J. (1999). *Contracting as a mechanism for managing educational services* (Policy Brief No. RB-28). Philadelphia: University of Pennsylvania, Consortium for Policy Research in Education.

Hannaway, J., & Carnoy, M. (Eds.). (1993). *Decentralization and school improvement: Can we fulfill the promise?* San Francisco: Jossey-Bass.

Hannaway, J., & Kimball, K. (2001). Big isn't always bad: School district size, poverty, and standards-based reform. In S. H. Fuhrman (Ed.), *From the capitol to the classroom: Standards-based reform in the states* (pp. 99–123). Chicago: University of Chicago.

Hannay, L. M., & Denby, M. (1994, April). *Secondary school change: The role of department heads.* Paper presented at the annual meeting of the American Educational Research Association, New Orleans.

Hart, A. W. (1993). *Principal succession: Establishing leadership in schools.* Albany: State University of New York Press.

Hart, A. W. (1995). Reconceiving school leadership: Emergent views. *Elementary School Journal, 96,* 9–28.

Heath, S. B. (1983). *Ways with words: Language, life, and work in communities and classrooms.* New York: Cambridge University Press.

Heath, S. B. (1995). Ethnography in communities: Learning the everyday life of America's subordinated youth. In J. A. Banks & C. A. M. Banks (Eds.), *Handbook of research on multicultural education* (pp. 114–128). New York: Simon & Schuster Macmillan.

Heck, R. (1993). School context, principal leadership, and achievement: The case of secondary schools in Singapore. *Urban Review, 25,* 151–166.

Heck, R. H., & Hallinger, P. (1999). Next generation methods for the study of leadership and school improvement. In J. Murphy & K. S. Louis (Eds.), *Handbook of research on educational administration* (2nd ed., pp. 141–162). San Francisco: Jossey-Bass.

Heller, M., & Firestone, W. A. (1995). Who's in charge here? Sources of leadership for change in eight schools. *The Elementary School Journal, 96*(1), 65–86.

Henderson, A. T., & Berla, N. (Eds.). (1994). *A new generation of evidence: The family is critical to student achievement.* Washington, DC: National Committee for Citizens in Education.

Henig, J. R., Holyoke, T. T., Lacireno-Paquet, N., & Moser, M. (2001). *Growing pains: An evaluation of charter schools in the District of Columbia, 1999–2000.* Washington, DC: George Washington University, The Center for Washington Area Studies.

Hess, F. M. (2003, Fall). Lifting the barrier. *Education Next,* pp. 12–19.

Hess, G. (1991). *School restructuring, Chicago-style.* Newbury Park, CA: Corwin.

Hiebert, J., & Carpenter, T. P. (1992). Learning and teaching with understanding. In D. A. Grouws (Ed.), *Handbook of research on mathematics teaching and learning* (pp. 65–97). New York: Macmillan.

Hiebert, J., & Wearne, D. (1988). Methodologies for studying learning to inform teaching. In E. Fennema, T. P. Carpenter, & S. Lamon (Eds.), *Integrating research on teaching and learning mathematics* (pp. 168–193). Papers from the First Wisconsin Symposium for Research on Teaching and Learning Mathematics. Madison: University of Wisconsin.

Hightower, A., Knapp, M. S., Marsh, J. A., & McLaughlin, M. W. (2002). *School districts and institutional renewal.* New York: Teachers College Press.

Hirschman, A. (1984). *Getting ahead collectively: Grass-root organizations in Latin America.* New York: Pergamon Press.

Hodgkinson, C. (1991). *Educational leadership: The moral art.* Albany: State University of New York Press.

Hodgkinson, H. L. (1999). *All one system: A second look.* Washington, DC: Institute for Educational Leadership and National Center for Public Policy and Higher Education. (ERIC Document No. ED 440 592).

Hollister, C. D. (1979). School bureaucratization as a response to parents' demands. *Urban Education, 14,* 221–235.

Honig, M., Kahne, J., & McLaughlin, M. (2001). School–community connections: Strengthening opportunity to learn and opportunity to teach. In V. Richardson (Ed.), *Handbook of research on teaching* (4th ed., pp. 998–1028). Washington, DC: American Educational Research Association.

Hoover-Dempsey, K., & Sandler, H. (1997). Why do parents become involved in their children's education? *Review of Educational Research, 67*(1), 3–42.

Hoy, W. K. (1994). Foundation of educational administration: Traditional and emerging perspectives. *Educational Administration Quarterly, 30,* 178–198.

Hoy, W. K., & Woolfolk, A. E. (1993). Teachers' sense of efficacy and the organizational health of schools. *The Elementary School Journal, 93,* 355–372.

Huber, G. P. (1996). Organizational learning: The contributing processes and the literature. In M. D. Cohen & L. S. Sproull (Eds.), *Organizational learning* (pp. 124–162). Thousand Oaks, CA: Sage.

Hunter-Boykin, H. (1992). Responses to the African American teacher shortage: "We grow our own" through the teacher preparation program at Coolidge High School. *Journal of Negro Education, 61*(4), 483–495.

Ingersoll, R. (1999). The problem of underqualified teachers in American secondary schools. *Educational Researcher, 28*(2), 26–37.

Interstate School Leaders Licensure Consortium. (1996). *Standards for school leaders.* Washington, DC: Author.

Jencks, C., Smith, M. S., Ackland, H., Bane, M. J., Cohen, D., Grintlis, H., et al. (1972). *Inequality: A reassessment of the effect of family and schooling in America.* New York: Basic Books.

Jennings, N. (1992). *Teachers learning from policy: Cases from the Michigan reading reform.* Unpublished doctoral dissertation, Michigan State University, East Lansing.

Jermier, J. M., & Kerr, S. (1997). Substitutes for leadership: Their meaning and measurement—contextual recollections and current observations. *The Leadership Quarterly, 8*, 95–101.

Johnson, S. M. (1990). *Teachers at work: Achieving success in our schools.* New York City: Basic Books.

Kaestle, C. F. (1984). Moral education and common schools in America: A historian's view. *Journal of Moral Education, 13*(2), 101–111.

Kaestle, C. F. (1993). The awful reputation of educational research. *Educational Researcher, 22*(1), 23, 26–31.

Kahne, J., & Bailey, K. (1999, Fall). The role of social capital in youth development: The case of "I have a dream" programs. *Educational Evaluation and Policy Analysis, 21*(3), 321–343.

Kaomea, J. (2003). Reading erasures and making the familiar strange: Defamiliarizing methods for research in formerly colonized and historically oppressed communities. *Educational Researcher, 32*(2), 14–25.

Kennedy, M. (1999). *Form and substance in inservice teacher education.* Research monograph no. 13, National Institute for Science Education, University of Wisconsin-Madison.

Kerchner, C. (1997). Education as a city's basic industry. *Education and Urban Society, 29*(4), 424–441.

Kerchner, C. T. (1993). The strategy of teaching. In P. Hallinger, K. Leithwood, & J. Murphy (Eds.), *Cognitive perspectives on educational leadership* (pp. 5–20). New York: Teachers College Press.

Kerchner, C., & McMurran, G. (2001). Leadership outside the triangle: The challenges of school administration in highly porous systems. In R. Crowson (Ed.), *Community development and school reform* (pp. 43–64). New York: JAI Press.

Kincheloe, J. L., & Steinberg, S. R. (1995). Introduction. In J. L. Kincheloe & S. R. Steinberg (Eds.), *Thirteen questions: Reframing education's conversation.* New York: Peter Lang.

Kincheloe, J. L., & Steinberg, S. R. (1997). *Changing multiculturalism.* Philadelphia: Open University Press.

King, J. E. (1991). Unfinished business: Black student alienation and Black teachers' emancipatory pedagogy. In M. Foster (Ed.), *Readings on equal education: Qualitative investigations into schools and schooling* (pp. 245–271). New York: AMS Press.

King, S. H. (1993). The limited presence of African American teachers. *Review of Educational Research, 63*(2), 115–149.

Kirmani, M. H., & Laster, B. P. (1999). Responding to religious diversity in classrooms. *Educational Leadership, 58*(2), 61–63.

Knapp, M. (2003). Professional development as a policy pathway. In R. E. Floden (Ed.), *Review of Research in Education, 27,* 109–158.

Knapp, M. S., & Associates. (1995). *Teaching for meaning in high-poverty classrooms.* New York: Teachers College Press.

Knapp, M. S., Copland, M., Darling-Hammond, L., McLaughlin, M. W., & Talbert, J. E. (2002, April). *Leadership for teaching and learning: A framework for research and action.* Paper presented at the annual meeting of the American Educational Research Association, New Orleans.

Knapp, M. S., Copland, M. A., Ford, B., Markholt, A., McLaughlin, M. W., Milliken, M., et al. (2003). *Leading for learning sourcebook: Concepts and examples.* Seattle: Center for Teaching Policy.

Knapp, M. S., & Woolverton, S. (1995). Social class and schooling. In J. A. Banks & C. A. M. Banks (Eds.), *Handbook of research on multicultural education* (pp. 548–569). New York: Simon & Schuster Macmillan.

Kruse, S. D., & Louis, K. S. (1995). Developing professional community in new and restructuring urban schools. In K. S. Louis & S. D. Kruse (Eds.), *Professionalism and community: Perspectives on reforming urban schools* (pp. 187–207). Thousand Oaks, CA: Corwin Press.

Kruse, S. D., Louis, K. S., & Bryk, A. S. (1995). An emerging framework for analyzing school-based professional community. In K. S. Louis & S. D. Kruse (Eds.), *Professionalism and community: Perspectives on reforming urban schools* (pp. 23–44). Thousand Oaks, CA: Corwin Press.

Kuhn, T. S. (1962). *The structure of scientific revolutions.* Chicago: University of Chicago Press.

Labaree, D. F. (1998). Educational researchers: Living with a lesser form of knowledge. *Educational Researcher, 27*(8), 4–12.

Ladd, H. F. (1996). *Holding schools accountable.* Washington, DC: Brookings Institute.

Ladson-Billings, G. (1994). *The dreamkeepers: Successful teachers of African American children.* San Francisco: Jossey-Bass.

Ladson-Billings, G. (1995). Toward a theory of culturally relevant pedagogy. *American Educational Research Journal, 32*(3), 465–491.

Lagemann, E., & Shulman, L. (1999). *Issues in education research: Problems and possibilities* (1st ed.). San Franscisco: Jossey-Bass Publishers.

Lambert, L. (1998). *Building leadership capacity in schools.* Alexandria, VA: Association for Supervision and Curriculum Development.

Lambert, L., Walker, D., Zimmerman, D. P., Cooper, J. E., Lambert, M. D., Gardner, M. E., et al. (1995). *The constructivist leader.* New York: Teachers College Press.

Lamme, L. L., & Lamme, L. A. (2001/2002). Welcoming children from gay families into our schools. *Educational Leadership, 59*(4), 65–69.

Lampert, M. (2001). *Teaching problems and the problems of teaching.* New Haven, CT: Yale University Press.

Lareau, A. (1989). Parent involvement in schooling: A dissenting view. In C. Fagano & B. Werber (Eds.), *School, family and community interaction: A view from the firing lines* (pp. 61–74). Boulder, CO: Westview Press.

Larson, C. L., & Murtadha, K. (2002). Leadership for social justice. In J. Murphy (Ed.), *The educational leadership challenge: Redefining leadership for the 21st century* (pp. 134–161). Chicago: National Society for the Study of Education.

Larson, C. L., & Ovando, C. (2001). *The color of bureaucracy: The politics of equity in multicultural school communities.* Belmont, CA: Wadsworth.

Lasch, C. (1995). *The revolt of the elites and the betrayal of democracy.* New York: W. W. Norton.

Lave, J., & Wenger, E. (1991). *Situated learning: Legitimate peripheral participation.* New York: Cambridge University Press.

Lawrence, S. M., & Tatum, B. D. (1997). Teachers in transition: The impact of antiracist professional development on classroom practice. *Teachers College Record, 99*(1), 162–178.

Lea, M. R., & Nicoll, K. (2002). Editors' introduction. In M. R. Lea & K. Nicoll (Eds.), *Distributed learning: Social and cultural approaches to practice* (pp. 1–15). New York: Routledge/Falmer.

Lee, V. E., Bryk, A. S., & Smith, J. B. (1993). The organization of effective secondary schools. In L. Darling-Hammond (Ed.), *Review of Research in Education* (Vol. 19, pp. 135–169). Washington, DC: American Educational Research Association.

Lee, V. E., Dedrick, R. F., & Smith, J. B. (1991). The effect of the social organization of schools on teachers' efficacy and satisfaction. *Sociology of Education, 64,* 190–208.

Lehrer, R., & Schauble, L. (2000). Modeling in mathematics and science. In R. Glaser (Ed.), *Advances in instructional psychology* (Vol. 5, pp. 101–159). Mahwah, NJ: Erlbaum.

Leithwood, K. (1994). Leadership for school restructuring. *Educational Administration Quarterly, 30*(4), 498–518.

Leithwood, K., & Duke, D. L. (1999). A century's quest to understand school leadership. In K. S. Louis & J. Murphy (Eds.), *Handbook of research on educational administration* (2nd ed., pp. 45–72). San Francisco: Jossey-Bass.

Leithwood, K. A., & Hallinger, P. (1993). Cognitive perspectives on educational administration: An introduction. *Educational Administration Quarterly, 29*(3), 296–301.

Leithwood, K., & Jantzi, D. (1990). Transformational leadership: How principals can help reform school cultures. *School Effectiveness and School Improvement, 1*(4), 249–280.

Leithwood, K. A., Jantzi, D., & Coffin, G. (1995). *Preparing school leaders: What works.* Toronto, Canada: Ontario Institute for Studies in Education.

Leithwood, K., Jantzi, D., & Steinbach, R. (1999). *Changing leadership for changing times.* Buckingham, UK: Open University Press.

Leithwood, K., & Steinbach, R. (1990). Characteristics of effective secondary school principals' problem solving. *Journal of Educational Administration and Foundations, 5*(1), 24–42.

Leithwood, K. A., Steinbach, R., & Begley, P. (1992). The nature and contribution of socialization experiences to becoming a principal in Canada. In F. W. Parkay & G. E. Hall (Eds.), *Becoming a principal: The challenges of beginning leadership* (pp. 284–307). Boston: Allyn and Bacon.

Levine, D. U., & Lezotte, L. W. (1990). *Unusually effective schools: A review and analysis of research and practice.* Madison, WI: National Center for Effective Schools Research and Development.

Lieberman, A., Darling-Hammond, L., & Zuckerman, K. (1991). *Early lessons in restructuring schools.* New York: National Center on Restructuring Education, Schools, and Teaching, Teachers College, Columbia University.

Lieberman, A., & Miller, L. (1984). *Teachers, their world, and their work.* Alexandria, VA: Association for Supervision and Curriculum Development.

Lightfoot, S. L. (1983). *The good high school.* New York: Basic Books.

Linn, R. L., Baker, E. L., & Betebenner, D. W. (2002). Accountability systems: Implications of requirements of the No Child Left Behind Act of 2001. *Educational Researcher, 31*(6), 3–16.

Little, J. W. (1982). Norms of collegiality and experimentation: Workplace conditions of school success. *American Educational Research Journal, 19*(3), 325–340.

Little, J. W. (1999). Organizing schools for teacher learning. In L. Darling-Hammond & G. Sykes (Eds.), *Teaching as the learning profession: Handbook of policy and practice* (pp. 233–262). San Francisco: Jossey-Bass.

Little, J. W. (2001). *Locating learning in teachers' communities of practice: Opening up problems of analysis in records of everyday work.* Paper presented at the annual meeting of the American Educational Research Association, Seattle.

Lomotey, K. (1989). *African American principals: School leadership and success.* New York: Greenwood Press.

Lomotey, K. (1994). African American principals: Bureaucrat/administrators and ethnohumanists. In M. J. Shujaa (Ed.), *Too much schooling, too little education: A paradox of Black life in White societies* (pp. 203–219). Trenton, NJ: Africa World Press.

Lord, R. G., & Maher, K. J. (1993). *Leadership and information processing.* London: Routledge.

Lortie, D. (1975). *Schoolteacher: A sociological analysis.* Chicago: University of Chicago Press.

Louis, K. S., Kruse, S. D., & Associates. (1995). *Professionalism and community: Perspectives on reforming urban schools.* Thousand Oaks, CA: Corwin Press.

Louis, K. S., Marks, H. M., & Kruse, S. (1996). Teachers' professional community in restructuring schools. *American Educational Research Journal, 33*(4), 757–798.

Louis, K. S., & Smith, B. (1992). Cultivating teacher engagement: Breaking the iron law of social class. In F. M. Newmann (Ed.), *Student engagement and achievement in American secondary schools* (pp. 119–152). New York: Teachers College Press.

Louis, K. S., Toole, J., & Hargreaves, A. (1999). Rethinking school improvement. In J. Murphy & K. S. Louis (Eds.), *Handbook of research on educational administration* (2nd ed., pp. 251–276). San Francisco: Jossey-Bass.

Loveless, T. (2001). *The great curriculum debate: How should we teach reading and math?* Washington, DC: Brookings Institution.

Lugg, C. A., Bulkley, K., Firestone, W. A., & Garner, C. W. (2002). The contextual terrain facing educational leaders. In J. Murphy (Ed.), *The educational leadership challenge: Redefining leadership for the 21st Century, 101st Yearbook of the National Society for the Study of Education, Part I* (pp. 20–41). Chicago: National Society for the Study of Education.

Luhm, T., Foley, E., & Corcoran, T. (1998). *The accountability system: Defining responsibility for student achievement.* Philadelphia: Consortium for Policy Research in Education.

Lundeberg, M. A. (1997). You guys are overreacting: Teaching prospective teachers about subtle gender bias. *Journal of Teacher Education, 48*(1), 55–61.

Macedo, D. (1995). Power and education: Who decides the forms schools have taken, and who should decide? In J. L. Kincheloe & S. R. Steinberg (Eds.), *Thirteen questions* (2nd ed.). New York: Peter Lang.

Macgillivray, I. K. (2001, April). *Implementing school policies that include sexual orientation: A case study in school and community politics.* Paper presented at the annual meeting of the American Educational Research Association, Seattle.

MacKinnon, D. (2000). Equity, leadership, and schooling. *Exceptionality Education Canada, 10*(1&2), 5–21.

Malen, B., & Ogawa, R. (1988). Professional-patron influence on site-based governance councils: A confounding case study. *Educational Evaluation and Policy Analysis, 10*(4), 251–270.

Malen, B., Ogawa, R., & Kranz, J. (1990). What do we know about school based management? A case study of the literature—A call for research. In W. Clune & J. Witted (Eds.), *Choice and control in American education* (vol. 2, pp. 112–132). New York: Falmer.

Mann, D. (1976). *The politics of administrative representation.* Lexington, MA: D.C. Heath.

Marks, H. M., & Louis, K. S. (1997). Does teacher empowerment affect the classroom? The implications of teacher empowerment for instructional practice and student academic performance. *Educational Evaluation and Policy Analysis, 19*(3), 245–275.

Marks, R. (1989). *What exactly is pedagogical content knowledge?* Paper presented at the annual meeting of the American Educational Research Association, San Francisco.

Marshall, C. (2004). Social justice challenges to educational administration. *Educational Administration Quarterly, 40*, 5–15.

Mattingly, D., Prislin, R., McKenzie, T., Rodrigues, J., & Kayzar, B. (2002). Evaluating evaluations: The case of parent involvement programs. *Review of Educational Research, 72*(4), 549–576.

Mawhinney, H. (2001). Schools in the bowling league of the new American economy: Theorizing on social/economic integration in school-to-work opportunity systems. In R. Crowson (Ed.), *Community development and school reform* (pp. 211–244) New York: JAI Press.

Maxcy, S. J. (1995). *Democracy, chaos, and the new school order.* Thousand Oaks, CA: Corwin Press.

Maxwell, J. A. (2004). Causal explanation, qualitative research, and scientific inquiry in education. *Educational Researcher, 33*(2), 3–11.

May, S. (1994). *Making multicultural education work.* Clevedon, England: Multilingual Matters.

May, S. (2000). *Multiculturalism in the 21st century: Challenges and possibilities.* Paper presented at the annual meeting of the American Educational Research Association, New Orleans.

Mayrowetz, D., & Weinstein, C. S. (1999). Sources of leadership for inclusive education: Creating schools for all children. *Educational Administration Quarterly, 35*(3), 423–449.

McCarthy, M. M. (1999). The evolution of educational leadership preparation programs. In J. Murphy & K. S. Louis (Eds.), *Handbook of research on educational administration* (2nd ed., pp. 119–139). San Francisco: Jossey-Bass.

McCauley, C. D., & Van Velsor, E. (Eds.) (2004). *Handbook of leadership development* (2nd ed). San Francisco: Jossey-Bass.

McColl-Kennedy, J. R., & Anderson, R. D. (2002). Impact of leadership style and emotions on subordinate performance. *Leadership Quarterly, 13*, 545–559.

McCoy, A. R., & Reynolds, A. J. (1999). Grade retention and school performance: An extended investigation. *Journal of School Psychology, 37*(3), 273–298.

McGaughey, C. (2001). The role of education in community development: The Akron enterprise community initiative. In R. Crowson (Ed.), *Community development and school reform* (pp. 121–138). New York: JAI Press.

McGough, D. J. (2003). Leaders as learners: An inquiry into the formation and transformation of principals' professional perspectives. *Educational Evaluation and Policy Analysis, 25*, 449–471.

McKnight, J., & Kretzmann, J. (1993). *Building communities from the inside out.* Evanston, IL: Northwestern University.

McLaughlin, M. W. (1987). Learning from experience: Lessons from policy implementation. *Educational Evaluation and Policy Analysis, 9*(2), 171–178.

McLaughlin, M. W. (2000). *Community counts: How community organizations matter for youth development.* Washington, DC: Public Education Network.

McLaughlin, M. W., & Mitra, D. (2001). Theory-based change and change-based theory: Going deeper, going broader. *Journal of Educational Change, 2*, 301–323.

McNeil, L. (2000). *Contradictions of school reform.* New York: Routledge.

McPherson, B., Crowson, R., & Pitner, N. (1986). *Managing uncertainty.* Columbus, OH: Charles E. Merrill.

Mechanic, D. (1962). Sources of power of lower participants in complex organizations. *Administrative Science Quarterly, 7*, 672–678.

Mehan, H. (1979). *Learning lessons: Social organization in the classroom.* Cambridge, MA: Harvard University Press.

Melaville, A., Shah, B., & Blank, M. (2003). *Making the difference: Research and practice in community schools.* Washington, DC: Coalition for Community Schools c/o Institute for Educational Leadership.

Merriam, S. B., & Caffarella, R. S. (1991). *Learning in adulthood.* San Francisco: Jossey-Bass.

Meyer, J. (2000). Reflections on education as transcendence. In L. Cuban & D. Shipps (Eds.), *Reconstructing the common good in American education: Coping with intractable American dilemmas.* Stanford, CA: Stanford University Press.

Miklos, E. (1983). Evolution of administration preparation programs. *Educational Administration Quarterly, 19*(3), 153–177.

Miklos, E. (1988). Administrator selection, career patterns, succession, and socialization. In N. J. Boyan (Ed.), *Handbook of research on educational administration* (pp. 53–76). New York: Longman.

Miles, M. B., & Huberman, A. M. (1994). *Qualitative data analysis: An expanded sourcebook.* Thousand Oaks, CA: Sage.

Miles, R. E. (1965). Human relations or human resources? *Harvard Business Review, 7*, 148–163.

Miller, R. (2002). *Free schools, free people: Education and democracy after the 1960s.* Albany: State University of New York.

Mitchell, A. (1998). African American teachers: Unique roles and universal lessons. *Education and Urban Society, 31*(1), 104–122.

Mitzel, H. E. (1960). Teacher effectiveness. In C. W. Harris (Ed.), *Encyclopedia of educational research* (3rd ed., pp. 1481–1486). New York: Macmillan.

Mohr, N., & Dichter, A. (2001, June). Building a learning organization. *Phi Delta Kappan, 82*(10), pp. 744–747.

Mohrman, S., Wohlstetter, P., & Associates. (1994). *School-based management: Organizing for high performance.* San Francisco: Jossey-Bass.

Moll, L. C., Amanti, C., Neff, D., & Gonzalez, N. (1992). Funds of knowledge for teaching: Using a qualitative approach to connect homes and classrooms. *Theory Into Practice, 31*(1), 132–141.

Moll, L., & Diaz, R. (1987). Teaching writing as communication: The use of ethnographic findings in classroom practice. In D. Bloom (Ed.), *Literacy and schooling* (pp. 55–65). Norwood, NJ: Ablex.

Moll, L. C., & González, N. (1994). Lessons from research with language minority children. *Journal of Reading Behavior, 26*(4), 439–456.

Moll, L., & Greenberg, J. B. (1990). Creating zones of possibilities: Combining social contexts for instruction. In L. C. Moll (Ed.), *Vygotsky and education* (pp. 319–348). Cambridge, UK: Cambridge University Press.

Monk, D. H. (1994). Subject area preparation of secondary mathematics and science teachers and student achievement. *Economics of Education Review, 13*(2), 125–145.

Montecel, M. R. (2002, September). Texas needs diplomas not delusions. *Intercultural Development Research Association (IDRA) Newsletter,* pp. 3–10.

Moore, A., George, R., & Halpin, D. (2002). The developing role of the headteacher in English schools. *Educational Management and Administration, 30*(2), 175–188.

Mortimore, P. (1993). School effectiveness and the management of effective learning and teaching. *School Effectiveness and School Improvement, 4*(4), 290–310.

Mumby, H., Russell, T., & Martin, A. K. (2001). Teachers' knowledge and how it develops. In V. Richardson (Ed.), *Handbook of research on teaching* (4th ed., pp. 877–904). Washington, DC: American Educational Research Association.

Munn, P. (1993). *Parents and schools.* London: Routledge.

Murphy, J. (1999). *The quest for a center: Notes on the state of the profession of educational leadership.* Columbia, MO: University Council for Educational Administration.

Murphy, J. (2001). *Reculturing the profession of educational leadership: New blueprints.* Columbia, MO: National Commission for the Advancement of Educational Leadership Preparation.

Murphy, J. (Ed.) (2002a). *The educational leadership challenge: Redefining leadership for the 21st century. One hundred-first yearbook of the National Society for the Study of Education.* Chicago: National Society for the Study of Education.

Murphy, J. (2002b). Reculturing the profession of educational leadership: New blueprints. In J. Murphy (Ed.), *The educational leadership challenge: Redefining leadership for the 21st Century, 101st Yearbook of the National Society for the Study of Education, Part I* (pp. 65–82). Chicago: National Society for the Study of Education.

Murphy, J. (in press). *Charting the changing landscape of the preparation of school leaders:*

An agenda for research and action. Columbia, MO: University Council for Educational Administration.

Murphy, J., & Beck, L. G. (1995). *School-based management as school reform: Taking stock.* Thousand Oaks, CA: Corwin Press.

Murphy, J., & Datnow, A. (Eds.). (2002). *Leadership lessons from comprehensive school reforms.* Thousand Oaks, CA: Corwin Press.

Murphy, J., & Louis, K. S. (Eds.). (1999). *Handbook of research on educational administration* (2nd ed. pp. 25–43). San Francisco: Jossey-Bass.

Murphy, M., & Prestine, N. A. (2001, October). *A slow, painless death: A study of an urban high school's five-year effort to create professional learning communities.* Paper presented at the Fall Conference of the University Council for Educational Administration. Cincinnati, OH.

Murphy, J., & Vriesenga, M. (2004). *Research on preparation programs in educational administration: An analysis.* Columbia, MO: University Council for Educational Administration.

National Commission on Excellence in Education. (1983). *A nation at risk: The imperative for educational reform.* Washington, DC: U.S. Department of Education.

National Commission on Excellence in Educational Administration. (1987). *Leaders for America's schools.* Tempe, AZ: University Council for Educational Administration.

National Council of Teachers of English, & International Reading Association. (1996). *Standards for the English language arts.* Urbana, IL: Authors.

National Council of Teachers of Mathematics. (1989). *Curriculum and evaluation standards for school mathematics.* Reston, VA: National Council of Teachers of Mathematics.

National Council of Teachers of Mathematics. (2000). *Principles and standards for school mathematics.* Reston, VA: National Council of Teachers of Mathematics.

National Institute of Child Health and Development. (2000). *Report of the National Reading Panel. Teaching children to read: An evidence-based assessment of the scientific research literature on reading and its implications for reading instruction.* Retrieved November 10, 2004, from http://www.nichd.nih.gov/publications/nrp/smallbook.htm

National Research Council. (1996). *National science education standards.* Washington, DC: National Academy Press.

National Research Council. (2000). *How people learn.* Washington, DC: National Academy Press.

National Research Council. (2002). *Scientific research in education.* (R. J. Shavelson & L. Towne, Eds.; Committee on Scientific Principles for Educational Research). Washington, DC: National Academy Press.

Natriello, G., McDill, E. L., & Pallas, A. M. (1990). *Schooling disadvantaged children: Racing against catastrophe.* New York: Teachers College Press.

Nelson, B. S., & Sassi, A. (2000). Shifting approaches to supervision: The case of mathematics supervision. *Educational Administration Quarterly, 36*(4), 513–553.

Neufeld, B. (1997). Responding to the expressed needs of urban middle school principals. *Urban Education, 31*, 490–509.

Newman, D., Griffin, P., & Cole, M. (1989). *The construction zone: Working for cognitive change in school.* New York: Cambridge University Press.

Newmann, F. M., & Associates. (Eds.). (1996). *Authentic achievement: Restructuring schools for intellectual quality.* San Francisco: Jossey-Bass.

Newmann, F. M., King, M. B., & Rigdon, M. (1997). Accountability and school performance: Implications from restructuring schools. *Harvard Education Review, 61*(1), 41–69.

Newmann, F. M., Smith, B., Allensworth, E., & Bryk, A. (2001). Instructional program coherence: What it is and why it should guide school improvement policy. *Educational Evaluation and Policy Analysis, 23*(4), 297–321.

Newmann, F. M., & Wehlage, G. G. (1995). *Successful school restructuring.* Madison: Center on Organization and Restructuring of Schools, University of Wisconsin.

Nias, J., Southworth, G., & Campbell, P. (1989). *Staff relationships in the primary school.* London: Cassell.

Nicolopoulou, A., & Cole, M. (1993). Generation and transmission of shared knowledge in the culture of collaborative learning: The fifth dimension, its play-world, and its institutional contexts. In E. A. Forman, N. Minick, & C. A. Stone (Eds.), *Contexts for learning: Sociocultural dynamics in children's development* (pp. 283–314). New York: Oxford University Press.

Noddings, N. (1992). *The challenge to care in schools.* New York: Teachers College Press.

Noguera, P. (2003). *City schools and the American dream: Reclaiming the promise of public education.* New York: Teachers College Press.

Norris, P. (1996). Does television erode social capital? A reply to Putnam. *PS: Political Science and Politics, 29,* 474–480.

Norton, S. M. (1994, November). *Differences in perceptions of the organizational socialization process among subgroups of beginning principals in Louisiana.* Paper presented at the annual meeting of the Mid-South Educational Research Association, Nashville.

Nye, B., Hedges, L. V., & Konstantopoulos, S. (1999). The long-term effects of small classes: A five-year follow-up of the Tennessee class size experiments. *Educational Evaluation and Policy Analysis, 21*(2), 127–142.

O'Conner, M. C., & Michaels, S. (1993). Aligning academic task and participation status through revoicing: Analysis of a classroom discourse strategy. *Anthropology and Education Quarterly, 24*(4), 318–335.

O'Day, J. (2002). Complexity, accountability and school improvement. *Harvard Education Review, 72*(3), 293–329.

Ogawa, R. T., & Bossert, S. T. (1995). Leadership as an organizational quality. *Educational Administration Quarterly, 31*(2), 224–243.

Ogawa, R. T., Goldring, E. B., & Conley, S. (2000). Organizing the field to improve research on educational administration. *Educational Administration Quarterly, 36*(3), 340–357.

Ogawa, R., & Studer, S. (2002). Bridging and buffering parent involvement in schools: Managing exchanges of social and cultural resources. *Theory and Research in Educational Administration, 1,* 97–128.

Ogbu, J. U. (1995). Understanding cultural diversity and learning. In J. A. Banks & C. A. M. Banks (Eds.), *Handbook of research on multicultural education* (pp. 582–593). New York: Simon & Schuster Macmillan.

Ohde, K. L., & Murphy, J. (1993). The development of expertise: Implications for school administrators. In P. Hallinger, K. Leithwood, & J. Murphy (Eds.), *Cognitive perspectives on educational leadership* (pp. 75–87). New York: Teachers College Press.

Oliver, C. (1991). Strategic responses to institutional processes. *Academy of Management Review, 16*(1), 145–179.

Olson, L., & Viadero, D. (2002, January 30). Law mandates scientific base for research. *Education Week, 21*(20), pp. 1, 14–15. Available at http://www.edweek.com/ew/ewstory.cfm?slug=20whatworks.h21

Orfield, G., & Kornhaber, M. (Eds.). (2001). *Raising standards or raising barriers? Inequity and high stakes testing in public education.* New York City: Century Foundation Press.

Orr, M. (1999). *Black social capital: The politics of school reform in Baltimore, 1986–1998.* Lawrence: University Press of Kansas.

Palincsar, A. S., & Brown, A. L. (1984). Reciprocal teaching of comprehension-fostering and monitoring activities. *Cognition and Instruction, 1*(2), 117–175.

Papa, F. C., Jr., Lankford, H., & Wyckoff, J. (2002). *The attributes and career paths of principals: Implications for improving policy.* Unpublished manuscript, State University of New York, Albany.

Parker, L., & Shapiro, J. P. (1993). The context of educational administration and social class. In C. A. Capper (Ed.), *Educational administration in a pluralistic society* (pp. 36–65). Albany: State University of New York Press.

Parks, S. (1999). Reducing the effects of racism in schools. *Educational Leadership, 58*(2), 14–18.

Paul, J. L., & Marfo, K. (2001). Preparation of educational researchers in philosophical foundations of inquiry. *Review of Educational Research, 71*(4), 525–547.

Pena, R., McGill, C., & Stout, R. (2001). Community based organizations, Title 1 schools and youth opportunity: Challenges and contradictions. In R. Crowson (Ed.), *Community development and school reform* (pp. 65–99). New York: JAI Press.

Pewewardy, C. (2003). 100 Defensive tactics and attributions: Dodging the dialog on cultural diversity. *Multicultural Education, 11*(1), 23–28.

Pfeffer, J. (1981). *Power in organizations.* Marshfield, MA: Pitman.

Phillips, D. C. (1990). Postpositivistic science: Myths and realities. In E. G. Guba (Ed.), *The paradigm dialog* (pp. 31–45). Newbury Park, CA: Sage.

Piaget, J. (1977). *The essential Piaget.* London: Routledge and Kegan Paul.

Pitman, K., & Cahill, M. (1992). Pushing the boundaries of education: The implication of a youth development approach to education, policies, structures and collaborations. In Council of Chief State School Officers (Ed.), *Ensuring student success through collaboration: Summer institute papers and recommendations of the Council of Chief State School Officers.* Washington, DC: Council of Chief State School Officers.

Pitner, N. (1988). The study of administrator effects and effectiveness. In N. Boyan (Ed.), *Handbook of research in educational administration* (pp. 99–122). New York: Longman.

Pittman, T. S. (1998). Motivations. In D. T. Gilbert, S. Fiske, & G. Lindzey (Eds.), *The handbook of social psychology* (4th ed., vol. 1, pp. 549–590). Boston: McGraw-Hill.

Podsakoff, P. M., MacKenzie, S. B., Moorman, R. H., & Fetter, R. (1990). Transformational leaders' behaviors and their effects on followers' trust in leader, satisfaction, and organizational citizenship behaviors. *The Leadership Quarterly, 1*(2), 107–142.

Portes, A. (1998). Social capital: Its origins and applications in modern sociology. *Annual Review of Sociology, 22*, 1–24.

Portin, B. S. (2000). The changing urban principalship. *Education and Urban Society, 32*(4), 492–505.

Pounder, D. G. (1994). Educational and demographic trends: Implications for women's representation in school leadership. *Advances in Educational Administration, 3*, 135–149.

Pounder, D. (2000). Introduction to the special issue. *Educational Administration Quarterly, 36*(3), 336–339.

Prestine, N. A., & McGreal, T. (1997). Fragile changes, sturdy lives: Implementing authentic assessment. *Educational Administration Quarterly, 33*(3), 371–400.

Pribesh, S., & Downey, D. (1999). Why are residential and school moves associated with poor school performance? *Demography, 36*(4), 521–534.

Proefriedt, W. (1985). Education and moral purpose: The dream recovered. *Teachers College Record, 86*(3), 399–410.

Public Agenda. (2001). *Trying to stay ahead of the game: Superintendents and principals talk about school leadership.* New York City: Public Agenda.

Purkey, S. C., & Smith, M. S. (1983). Effective schools: A review. *Elementary School Journal, 83*, 427–453.

Putnam, R. (1993). *Making democracy work: Civic traditions in modern Italy.* Princeton, NJ: Princeton University Press.

RAND Mathematics Study Panel. (2003). *Mathematical proficiency for all students: Towards a strategic research and development program in mathematics education.* Santa Monica, CA: RAND.

Rapp, D. (2002). Social justice and the importance of rebellious, oppositional imaginations. *Journal of School Leadership, 12*, 226–245.

Raun, T., & Leithwood, K. (1993). Pragmatism, participation, and duty: Value themes in superintendents' problem-solving. In P. Hallinger, K. Leithwood, & J. Murphy (Eds.), *Cognitive perspectives on educational leadership* (pp. 54–72). New York: Teachers College Press.

Reavis, C., & Griffith, H. (1993). Feeling the ripples, riding the waves: Making an essential school. In J. Murphy & P. Hallinger (Eds.), *Restructuring schooling* (pp. 32–62). Newbury Park, CA: Corwin Press.

Reese, W. J. (2000). Public schools and the elusive search for the common good. In L. Cuban & D. Shipps (Eds.), *Reconstructing the common good in education: Coping with intractable American dilemmas* (pp. 13–31). Stanford, CA: Stanford University Press.

Reid, K. S. (2001, March 21). U.S. census underscores diversity. *Education Week, 20*(27), 1, 18–19. Available http://www.edweek.org/ew/ewstory.cfm?slug=27census.h20

Resnick, L. (1987). *Education and learning to think. Committee on Mathematics, Science and Technology Education,* Commission on Behavioral and Social Sciences and Education, Natonal Research Council. Washington, DC: National Academy Press. Available http://www.nap.edu. Retrieved February 13, 2003, from http://books.nap.edu/books/0309076390/html/index.html

Resnick, L. B. (Ed.). (1989). *Knowing, learning, and instruction: Essays in honor of Robert Glaser.* Hillsdale, NJ: Erlbaum.

Reyes, P., Scribner, J. D., & Scribner, A. P. (Eds.). (1999). *Lessons from high-performing Hispanic schools: Creating learning communities.* New York: Teachers College Press.

Reyes, P., Scribner, J., & Wagstaff, L. (1999). *A vision for tomorrow: Successful migrant education practices.* Austin: Texas Education Agency.

Reyes, P., Velez, W., & Pena, R. (1993). School reform: Introducing race, culture, and ethnicity into the discourse. In C. A. Capper (Ed.), *Educational administration in a pluralist society* (pp. 66–85). Albany: State University of New York Press.

Reynolds, D., & Teddlie, C. (2000). The processes of school effectiveness. In C. Teddlie & D. Reynolds (Eds.), *The international handbook of school effectiveness research* (pp. 124–159). London: Falmer Press.

Ricciardi, D. (1999, April). *Examining professional training of middle level principals: Responding to a reform environment.* Paper presented at the annual meeting of the American Educational Research Association, Montreal.

Ricciardi, D., & Petrosko, J. M. (2000, April). *Perceptions of first-year administrators: Impact of responsibilities and preparation on professional growth needs.* Paper presented at the annual meeting of the American Educational Research Association, New Orleans.

Richardson, V. (1994). Conducting research on practice. *Educational Researcher, 23*(5), 5–10.

Riehl, C. J. (2000). The principal's role in creating inclusive schools for diverse students: A review of normative, empirical, and critical literature on the practice of educational administration. *Review of Educational Research, 70*(1), 55–81.

Riehl, C. (2004, April). *Feeling better: Finding solace and inspiration in a comparison of recent agitations in medical research and educational research.* Paper presented at the annual meeting of the American Educational Research Association, San Diego.

Riehl, C., Larson, C. L., Short, P. M., & Reitzug, U. C. (2000). Reconceptualizing research and scholarship in educational administration: Learning to know, knowing to do, doing to learn. *Educational Administration Quarterly, 36*(3), 391–427.

Rimer, S. (2002, November 12). Colleges find diversity is not just numbers. *New York Times,* pp. A1, A21.

Rist, R. (1996). Information needs in the policy arena: Linking educational research to the policy cycle. In *Knowledge bases for education policies* (pp. 141–154). Paris: Organisation for Economic Co-operation and Development.

Rogoff, B., Radziszewska, B., & Masiello, T. (1995). Analysis of developmental processes in sociocultural activity. In L. W. Martin, K. Nelson, & E. Tobach (Eds.), *Sociocultural psychology: Theory and practice of doing and knowing* (pp. 125–149). New York: Cambridge University Press.

Romberg, T. A. (n.d.). *Creating a research community in mathematics education.* Unpublished manuscript.

Rorrer, A., & Reyes, P. (2000, March). *Leadership and equity.* Paper presented at the annual meeting fo the American Educational Research Association, New Orleans.

Rosenblum, S., Louis, K. S., & Rossmiller, R. A. (1994). School leadership and teacher quality of work life in restructuring schools. In J. Murphy & K. S. Louis (Eds.), *Reshaping the principalship: Insights from transformational reform efforts* (pp. 99–122). Thousand Oaks, CA: Corwin Press.

Rosenholtz, S. J. (1985). Effective schools: Interpreting the evidence. *American Journal of Education, 93*(3), 352–388.

Rosenholtz, S. J. (1989). *Teachers' workplace: The social organization of schooling.* New York: Longman.

Rosenshine, B., & Stevens, R. (1986). Teaching functions. In M. C. Wittrock (Ed.), *Handbook of research on teaching* (3rd ed., pp. 376–391). New York: Macmillan.

Roth, W., & Bowen, G. M. (1995). Knowing and interacting: A study of culture, practices, and resources in a grade 8 open-inquiry science classroom guided by a cognitive apprenticeship metaphor. *Cognition and Instruction, 13*(1), 73–128.

Rothstein, R. (2000). Equalizing education resources on behalf of disadvantaged children. In R. D. Kahlenberg (Ed.), *A notion at risk* (pp. 31–92). New York: Century Foundation Press.

Rowan, B. (1990). Commitment and control: Alternative strategies for the organizational design of schools. In C. B. Cazden (Ed.), *Review of research in education*, vol. 16 (pp. 353–389). Washington, DC: American Educational Research Association.

Rowan, B. (1995). Learning, teaching, and educational administration: Toward a research agenda. *Educational Administration Quarterly, 31*(3), 344–354.

Rowan, B., Correnti, R., & Miller, R. J. (2002). What large-scale, survey research tells us about teacher effects on student achievement: Insights from the "Prospects" study of elementary schools. *Teachers College Record, 104*(8), 1525–1567.

Rowan, B., Dwyer, D., & Bossert, S. (1982). *Methodological considerations in the study of effective principals.* Paper presented at the annual meeting of the American Educational Research Association, New York.

Roza, M. (2003, January). *A matter of definition: Is there truly a shortage of school principals?* Seattle: University of Washington, Center on Reinventing Public Education.

Rumberger, R. W. (1987). High school dropouts: A review of issues and evidence. *Review of Educational Research, 57*(2), 101–121.

Rusch, E. A. (1995). *Leadership in evolving democratic school communities.* Paper presented at the annual meeting of the American Educational Research Association, San Francisco.

Rusch, E. A. (2004). Gender and race in leadership preparation: A constrained discourse. *Educational Administration Quarterly, 40*, 16–48.

St. Pierre, E. A. (2002). "Science" rejects postmodernism. *Educational Researcher, 31*(8), 25–27.

Sammons, P., Hillman, J., & Mortimore, P. (1995). *Key characteristics of effective schools: A review of school effectiveness research.* London: Office for Standards in Education.

Sanders, M., & Harvey, A. (2002). Beyond the school walls: A case study of principal leadership for school–community collaboration. *Teachers College Record, 104*(7), 1345–1368.

Sapon-Shevin, M., & Zollers, N. J. (1999). Multicultural and disability agendas in teacher education: Preparing teachers for diversity. *International Journal of Leadership in Education, 2*(3), 165–190.

Saxe, R. (1983). *School–community relations in transition.* Berkeley, CA: McCutchan.

Scheerens, J. (1992). *Effective schooling. Research, theory and practice.* London: Cassell.

Scheerens, J. (1997). Conceptual models and theory-embedded principles on effective schooling. *School Effectiveness and School Improvement, 8*(3), 269–310.

Scheerens, J., & Bosker, R. J. (1997). *The foundations of educational effectiveness.* New York: Elsevier.

Scheurich, J. J. (1997). *Research method in the postmodern.* London: Falmer Press.

Scheurich, J. J. (1998). Highly successful and loving, public elementary schools populated mainly by low-SES children of color: Core beliefs and cultural characteristics. *Urban Education, 33*(4), 451–491.

Scheurich, J. J., & Skrla, L. (2003). *Leadership for equity and excellence: Creating high-achievement classrooms, schools, and districts.* London: Sage.

Schifter, D., & Fosnot, C. T. (1993). *Reconstructing mathematics education: Stories of teachers meeting the challenge of reform.* New York: Teachers College Press.

Schneider, M., Teske, P., & Marschall, M. (2000). *Choosing schools: Consumer choice and the quality of American schools*. Princeton, NJ: Princeton University Press.

Schoenfeld, A. H. (2002). Making mathematics work for all children: Issues of standards, testing, and equity. *Educational Researcher, 31*(1), 13–25.

Schön, D. A. (1983). *The reflective practitioner*. New York: Basic Books.

Scott, J. (2000). *Social network analysis: A handbook* (2nd ed.). London: Sage Publications.

Scott-Jones, P. (1984). Family influences on cognitive development and school achievement. In E. Gordon (Ed.), *Review of research in education, Vol. 11* (pp. 227–258). Washington, DC: American Educational Research Association.

Scribner, J. P., Hager, D. R., & Warne, T. R. (2002). The paradox of professional community: Tales from two high schools. *Educational Administration Quarterly, 38*(1), 45–76.

Senge, P. M. (1990). *The fifth discipline: The art and practice of the learning organization*. New York: Currency Doubleday.

Senk, S. L., & Thompson, D. R. (2003). *Standards-based school mathematics curricula: What are they? What do students learn?* Mahwah, NJ: Erlbaum.

Sergiovanni, T. J. (1992). *Moral leadership: Getting to the heart of school improvement*. San Francisco: Jossey-Bass.

Sergiovanni, T. (2001). *The principalship: A reflective practice perspective* (4th ed.). Boston: Allyn and Bacon.

Sfard, A. (1998). On two metaphors for learning and the dangers of choosing just one. *Educational Researcher, 27*(2), 4–13.

Shaker, P., & Heilman, E. (2004). The new common sense of education: Advocacy research versus academic authority. *Teachers College Record, 106*(7), 1444–1470.

Shakeshaft, C. (1999). The struggle to create a more gender-inclusive profession. In J. Murphy & K. S. Louis (Eds.), *Handbook of research on educational administration* (2nd ed., pp. 99–118). San Francisco: Jossey-Bass.

Shavelson, R. J. (1983). Review of research on teachers' pedagogical judgments, plans and decisions. *Elementary School Journal, 83*(4), 392–413.

Shavelson, R., & Towne, L. (Eds.). (2002). *Scientific research in education*. Washington, DC: National Academy Press.

Shavelson, R., Phillips, D., Towne, L., & Feuer, M. (2003). On the science of education design studies. *Educational Researcher, 32*(1), 25–28.

Sheppard, B. (1996). Exploring the transformational nature of instructional leadership. *Alberta Journal of Educational Research, 42*(4), 325–344.

Shields, C. M. (2002). Social justice and academic excellence. *BCAdminfo, 15*(6), 8–10.

Shields, C. M. (2003). *Good intentions are not enough: Transformative leadership for communities of difference*. Lanham, MD: Scarecrow.

Shields, C. M., & Edwards, M. M. (2005). *Dialogue is not just talk: A new ground for educational leadership*. New York: Peter Lang.

Shipps, D. (2003, December). Pulling together: Civic capacity and urban school reform. *American Educational Research Journal, 40*(4), 841–878.

Shirley, D. (1997). *Community organizing for urban school reform*. Austin: University of Texas Press.

Shulman, L. S. (1986a). Paradigms and research programs in the study of teaching: A contemporary perspective. In M. Wittrock (Ed.), *Handbook of research on teaching* (3rd ed., pp. 3–36). New York: Macmillan.

Shulman, L. S. (1986b). Those who understand: A conception of teacher knowledge. *American Educator, 19*(1), 9–15.

Shulman, L. (1987). Knowledge and teaching: Foundations of the new reform. *Harvard Educational Review, 57*(1), 1–22.

Shulman, L. S., & Elstein, A. S. (1975). Studies of problem solving, judgment and decision making: Implications for educational research. In F. N. Kerlinger (Ed.), *Review of research in education* (vol. 3). Itasca, IL: F. E. Peacock.

Sikula, J. (Ed.). (1996). *Handbook of research on teacher education* (2nd ed.). New York: Macmillan.

Silins, H. C., Mulford, W. R., & Zarins, S. (2002). Organizational learning and school change. *Educational Administration Quarterly, 38*(15), 613–642.

Skalbeck, K. L. (1991). *Profile of a transformational leader: A sacred mission.* Ann Arbor, MI: UMI Dissertation Services.

Skrla, L., & Scheurich, J. (2001). Displacing deficit thinking in school district leadership. *Education and Urban Society, 33*(3), 235–259.

Skrla, L., Scheurich, J. J., & Johnson, J. F., Jr. (2000). *Equity-driven, achievement-focused school districts: A report on systemic school success in four Texas school districts serving diverse student populations.* Austin: The University of Texas, Charles A. Dana Research Center.

Skrla, L., Scheurich, J., Johnson, J. F., & Koschoreck, J. W. (2001). Accountability for equity: Can state policy leverage social justice? *International Journal of Leadership in Education, 4*(3), 237–260.

Slater, R. O., & Boyd, W. L. (1999). Schools as polities. In J. Murphy & K. S. Louis (Eds.), *Handbook of research on educational administration* (2nd ed., pp. 323–335). San Francisco: Jossey-Bass.

Slavin, R. E. (2002). Evidence-based education policies: Transforming educational practice and research. *Educational Researcher, 31*(7), 15–21.

Slavin, R. E. (2004). Education research can and must address "what works" questions. *Educational Researcher, 33*(1), 27–28.

Sleegers, P., Geijsel, F., & van den Borg, R. (2002). Conditions fostering educational change. In K. Leithwood & P. Hallinger (Eds.), *Second international handbook of educational leadership and administration: Part one* (pp. 74–102). Norwell, MA: Kluwer.

Smith, G. (2002, April). Place-based education: Learning to be where we are. *Phi Delta Kappan,* pp. 584–593.

Smith, L. T. (1999). *Decolonizing methodologies: Research and indigenous peoples.* New York: Zed Books.

Smith, M. L. (1991). Put to the test: The effects of external testing on students. *Educational Researcher, 20*(5), 8–12.

Smith, M., & O'Day, J. (1991). Systemic school reform. In S. H. Fuhrman & B. Malen (Eds.), *The politics of curriculum and testing* (pp. 233–267). Bristol, PA: Falmer Press.

Smith-Maddox, R. (1999). The social networks and resources of African-American eighth graders: Evidence from the National Education Longitudinal Study of 1988. *Adolescence, 34*(133), 169–183.

Smrekar, C. E. (1996). *The impact of school choice and community.* Albany: State University of New York Press.

Smrekar, C. E., Guthrie, J., Owens, D., & Sims, P. (2001, September). *March towards* excellence: School success and minority achievement in Department of Defense schools (Report to the National Education Goals Panel). Nashville, TN: Vanderbilt University, Peabody Center for Education Policy, Peabody College.

Smrekar, C. E., & Mawhinney, H. B. (1999). Integrated services: Challenges in linking schools, families, and communities. In J. Murphy & K. S. Louis (Eds.), *Handbook of research on educational administration* (2nd ed., pp. 443–461). San Francisco: Jossey-Bass.

Smylie, M. A., Conley, S., & Marks, H. M. (2002). Exploring new approaches to teacher leadership for school improvement. In J. Murphy (Ed.), *The educational leadership challenge: Redefining leadership for the 21st century* (pp. 162–188). Chicago: National Society for the Study of Education.

Smylie, M. A., & Hart, A. W. (2000). School leadership for teacher learning and change: A human and social capital development perspective. In J. Murphy & K. S. Louis (Eds.), *Handbook of research on educational administration* (pp. 421–441). San Francisco: Jossey-Bass.

Smylie, M. A., Lazarus, V., & Brownlee-Conyers, J. (1996). Instructional outcomes of school-based participative decision making. *Educational Evaluation and Policy Analysis, 18*(3), 181–198.

Smylie, M. A., & Miretzky, D. (Eds.). (2004). *Developing the teacher workforce, 103rd yearbook of the National Society for the Study of Education, Part I.* Chicago: National Society for the Study of Education.

Solomon, R. P. (2002). School leaders and antiracism: Overcoming pedagogical and political obstacles. *Journal of School Leadership, 12*(2), 174–197.

Southworth, G. (1998). *Leading improving primary schools.* London: Falmer Press

Spillane, J. P. (1998a). A cognitive perspective on the role of the local educational agency in implementing instructional policy: Accounting for local variability. *Educational Administration Quarterly, 34,* 31–57.

Spillane, J. P. (1998b). State policy and the non-monolithic nature of the local school district: Organizational and professional considerations. *American Educational Research Journal, 35*(1), 33–63.

Spillane, J. P. (1999). External reform initiatives and teachers' efforts to reconstruct their practice: The mediating role of teachers' zones of enactment. *Journal of Curriculum Studies, 31*(2), 143–175.

Spillane, J. P. (2000a). Cognition and policy implementation: District policy-makers and the reform of mathematics education. *Cognition and Instruction, 18*(2), 141–179.

Spillane, J. P. (2000b). *District leaders' perceptions of teacher learning.* CPRE Occasional Paper Series, OP-05. Philadelphia: Consortium for Policy Research in Education, University of Pennsylvania.

Spillane, J. P., Hallett, T., & Diamond, J. B. (2003). Forms of capital and the construction of leadership: Instructional leadership in urban elementary schools. *Sociology of Education, 76*(1), 1–17.

Spillane, J. P., Halverson, R., & Diamond, J. B. (2001). Investigating school leadership practice: A distributed perspective. *Educational Researcher, 30*(3), 23–28.

Spillane, J. P., & Louis, K. S. (2002). School improvement processes and practices: Professional learning for building instructional capacity. In J. Murphy (Ed.), *The educational leadership challenge: Redefining leadership for the 21st century* (pp. 83–104). Chicago: University of Chicago Press.

Spillane, J. P., Reiser, B., & Reimer, T. (2002). Policy implementation and cognition: Reframing and refocusing implementation research. *Review of Educational Research*, *72*(3), 387–431.

Spring, J. (2001). *The American school: 1642–2000* (6th ed.). Boston: McGraw-Hill.

Sprio, R. J., Feltovich, P. J., Coulson, R. L., & Anderson, D. K. (1989). Multiple analogies for complex concepts: Antidotes for analogy-induced misconception in advanced knowledge acquisition. In S. Vosniadou & A. Ortony (Eds.), *Similarity and analogical reasoning* (pp. 489–531). New York: Cambridge University Press.

Stanton-Salazar, R. D. (1997, Spring). A social capital framework for understanding the socialization of racial minority children and youths. *Harvard Educational Review*, *67*(1), 1–40.

Stanton-Salazar, R. D., & Dornbusch, S. (1995). Social capital and the reproduction of inequality: Information networks among Mexican-origin high school students. *Sociology of Education*, *68*(2), 116–135.

Starratt, R. J. (1991). Building an ethical school: A theory for practice in educational leadership. *Educational Administration Quarterly*, *27*(2), 155–202.

Starratt, R. J. (1994). *Building an ethical school: A Practical response to the moral crisis in schools*. London: Falmer.

Stein, M. K., Baxter, J. A., & Leinhardt, G. (1990). Subject matter knowledge for elementary instruction: A case from functions and graphing. *American Educational Research Journal*, *27*(4), 639–663.

Stein, M. K., & Brown, C. A. (1997). Teacher learning in a social context: Integrating collaborative and institutional processes with the study of teacher change. In E. Fenemma & B. Nelson (Eds.), *Mathematics teachers in transition* (pp. 155–191). Hillsdale, NJ: Erlbaum.

Stein, M. K., & D'Amico, L. (1999). *Observations, conversations, and negotiations: Administrator support of literacy practices in New York City's Community School District #2.* Paper presented at the annual meeting of the American Educational Research Association, Montreal.

Stein, M. K., & D'Amico, L. (2000, April). *How subjects matter in school leadership.* Paper presented at the annual meeting of the American Educational Research Association, New Orleans.

Stein, M. K., & D'Amico, L. (2002a). Inquiry at the crossroads of policy and learning: A study of a district-wide literacy initiative. *Teachers College Record*, *104*(7), 1313–1344.

Stein, M. K., & D'Amico, L. (2002b). District as professional educator: Teacher learning in District #2's literacy initiative. In M. Kinapp & M. McLaughlin (Eds.), *School districts and instructional renewal: Opening the conversation* (pp. 61–76). New York: Teachers College Press.

Stein, M. K., Hubbard, L., & Mehan, H. (2004). Reform ideas that travel far afield: The two cultures of reform in New York City's District #2 and San Diego. *The Journal of Educational Change*, *5*, 161–197.

Stein, M. K., & Lane, S. (1996). Instructional tasks and the development of student capacity to think and reason: An analysis of the relationship between teaching and learning in a reform mathematics project. *Educational Research and Evaluation*, *2*(1), 50–80.

Stein, M. K., & Nelson, B. S. (2003). Leadership content knowledge. *Educational Evaluation and Policy Analysis, 25*(4), 423–448.

Stein, M. K., Silver, E. A., & Smith, M. S. (1998). Mathematics reform and teacher development: A community of practice perspective. In. J. Greeno & S. Goldman (Eds.), *Thinking practices in mathematics and science learning* (pp. 17–52). Hillsdale, NJ: Erlbaum.

Stoddart, T. (1993). Who is prepared to teach in urban schools? *Education and Urban Society, 26*(1), 29–48.

Stone, C. (1989). *Regime politics: Governing Atlanta, 1946–1988.* Lawrence: University Press of Kansas.

Stone, C. N., Henig, J. R., Jones, B. D., & Pierannunzi, C. (2001). *Building civic capacity: The politics of reforming urban schools.* Lawrence: University Press of Kansas.

Strike, K. A. (1999a). Can schools be communities? The tension between shared values and inclusion. *Educational Administration Quarterly, 35*, 46–70.

Strike, K. A. (1999b). Justice, caring, and universality: In defense of moral pluralism. In M. S. Katz, N. Noddings, & K. A. Strike (Eds.), *Justice and caring: The search for common ground in education* (pp. 21–36). New York: Teachers College Press.

Talbert, J. E., & McLaughlin, M. W. (1994). Teacher professionalism in local school contexts. *American Journal of Education, 102*, 123–153.

Taylor, D. L., & Bogotch, I. E. (1994). School level effects of teachers' participation in decision making. *Educational Evaluation and Policy Analysis, 16*(3), 302–319.

Teitel, L. (1997). Understanding and harnessing the power of the cohort model in preparing educational leaders. *Peabody Journal of Education, 72*(2), 66–85.

Tharp, R. (1993). Institutional and social context of educational practice and reform. In E. A. Forman, N. Minick, & C. A. Stone (Eds.), *Contexts for learning: Sociocultural dynamics in children's development* (pp. 269–282). New York: Oxford University Press.

Thayer, L. (1988). Leadership/communication: A critical review and a modest proposal. In G. M. Goldhaber & G. A. Barnett (Eds.), *Handbook of organizational communication* (pp. 231–263). Norwood, NJ: Ablex.

Thompson, A., & Gitlin, A. (1995). Creating spaces for reconstructing knowledge in feminist pedagogy. *Educational Theory on the Web, 45*(2), 1–28.

Thomson, S. D. (Ed.). (1993). *Principals for our changing schools: The knowledge and skill base.* Fairfax, VA: National Policy Board for Educational Administration.

Tillman, L. C. (2002). Culturally sensitive research approaches: An African-American perspective. *Educational Researcher, 31*(9), 3–12.

Timpane, M., & Reich, R. (1997, February). Revitalizing the ecosystem for youth: A new perspective for school reform. *Phi Delta Kappan, 78*(6), 464–470.

Townsend, T. (2001). Satan or saviour? An analysis of two decades of school effectiveness research. *School Effectiveness and School Improvement, 12*(1), 115–129.

Tschannen-Moran, M., Firestone, W. A., Hoy, W. K., & Johnson, S. M. (2000). The write stuff: A study of productive scholars in educational administration. *Educational Administration Quarterly, 36*(3), 358–390.

Tucker, M. S., & Codding, J. B. (Eds.). (2002). *The principal challenge: Leading and managing schools in an era of accountability.* San Francisco: Jossey-Bass.

Turner, J. C., & Patrick, H. (2004). Motivational influences on student participation in classroom learning activities. *Teachers College Record, 106*(9), 1759–1785.

Tyack, D. B., & Cuban, L. (1995). *Tinkering toward utopia: A century of public school reform*. Cambridge, MA: Harvard University Press.

Tyack, D. B., & Hansot, E. (1982). *Managers of virtue: Public school leadership in America 1920–1980*. New York: Basic Books.

Ubben, C. G., & Hughes, W. L. (1996). *The principal: Creative leadership for effective schools* (pp. 19–27). Boston, MA: Allyn & Bacon.

U.S. Congress. (2001). *No Child Left Behind Act of 2001*. Washington, DC: Author.

Valencia, R. R. (1997). *The evolution of deficit thinking: Educational thought and practice*. London: Falmer.

Valenzuela, A. (1999). *Subtractive schooling: U.S.–Mexican youth and the politics of caring*. Albany: State University of New York Press.

van de Grift, W., & Houtveen, A. A. M. (1999). Educational leadership and pupil achievement in primary education. *School Effectiveness and School Improvement, 10*(4), 373–389.

Vandenberghe, R. (2003, April). *Beginning primary school principals in Belgium: How they deal with external influences and develop professionally*. Paper presented at the annual meeting of the American Educational Research Association, Chicago.

Van Maanen, J., & Schein, E. H. (1979). Toward a theory of organizational socialization. In B. M. Staw (Ed.), *Research in organizational behavior* (vol. 1, pp. 209–264). Greenwich, CT: JAI Press.

Vygotsky, L. S. (1978). *Mind in society: The development of higher psychological processes*. Cambridge, MA: Harvard University Press.

Wagner, R. K. (1993). Practical problem solving. In P. Hallinger, K. Leithwood, & J. Murphy (Eds.), *Cognitive perspectives on educational leadership* (pp. 88–102). New York: Teachers College Press.

Walberg, H. J. (1984). Improving the productivity of America's schools. *Educational Leadership, 41*(8), 19–27.

Walker, E. M., Mitchel, C. P., & Turner, W. (1999, April). *Professional development and urban leadership: A study of urban administrators' perceptions of what matters most in their professional development*. Paper presented at the annual meeting of the American Educational Research Association, Montreal.

Waller, W. (1932). *The sociology of teaching*. New York: Wiley.

Wang, M., Haertel, G., & Walberg, H. (1992). Toward a knowledge base for school learning. *Review of Educational Research, 63*(3), 249–294.

Wasley, P. A. (1991). *Teachers who lead: The rhetoric of reform and the realities of practice*. New York: Teachers College Press.

Wasley, P. (1995). *Teacher leadership in a teacher-run school*. Providence, RI: Coalition of Essential Schools, Brown University.

Weber, M. (1947). *The theory of social and economic organizations* (T. Parsons, trans.). New York: Free Press.

Wehlage, G., Neumann, F., & Secada, W. (1996). Standards of authentic achievement and pedagogy. In F. Neumann & Associates (Eds.), *Authentic achievement: Restructuring schools for intellectual quality* (pp. 21–48). San Francisco: Jossey-Bass.

Weindling, D. (2000, April). *Stages of headship: A longitudinal study of the principalship*. Paper presented at the annual meeting of the American Educational Research Association, New Orleans.

Weindling, D., & Earley, P. (1987). *Secondary leadership: The first years.* Philadelphia: NFER-Nelson.

Weiss, C. H. (with Bucuvalas, M. J.). (1980). *Social science research and decision-making.* New York: Columbia University Press.

Weiss, C. H. (1993). Shared decision making about what? A comparison of schools with and without teacher participation. *Teachers College Record, 95*(1), 69–92.

Weiss, C. H., & Cambone, J. (1994). Principals, shared decision making, and school reform. *Educational Evaluation and Policy Analysis, 16*(3), 287–301.

Weissglass, J. (2001, August 8). Racism and the achievement group. *Education Week, 20*(43), 49–72.

Wenger, E. (1998). *Communities of practice: Learning, meaning, and identity.* New York: Cambridge University Press.

Westbury, M. (1994). The effect of elementary grade retention on subsequent school achievement and ability. *Canadian Journal of Education, 19*(3), 241–250.

Willinsky, J. (2001). The strategic education research program and the public value of research. *Educational Researcher, 30*(1), 5–14.

Wilson, B., & Corcoran, T. (1988). *Successful secondary schools: Visions of excellence in American public education.* New York: Falmer.

Wilson, J. Q. (1993). *The moral sense.* New York: Free Press.

Wilson, S. M., & Berne, J. (1999). Teacher learning and the acquisition of professional knowledge: An examination of research of contemporary professional development. In A. Iran-Nejad & P. D. Pearson (Eds.), *Review of research in education* (Vol. 24, pp. 173–209). Washington, DC: American Educational Research Association.

Winter, P. A., & Morgenthal, J. R. (2002). Principal recruitment in a reform environment: Effects of school achievement and school level on applicant attraction to the job. *Educational Administration Quarterly, 38*(3), 319–340.

Witte, J. F. (2000). *The market approach to education: An analysis of America's first voucher program.* Princeton, NJ: Princeton University Press.

Wolf, S. A., Borko, H., Elliott, R. L., & McIver, M. C. (2000). "That dog won't hunt!": Exemplary school change efforts within the Kentucky reform. *American Educational Research Journal, 37*(2), 349–393.

Wood, T., & Yackel, E. (1990). The development of collaborative dialogue within small group interactions. In L. P. Steffe & T. Wood (Eds.), *Transforming children's mathematics education: International perspectives* (pp. 244–252). Hillsdale, NJ: Erlbaum.

Wright, P. M., Dunford, B. B., & Snell, S. A. (2001). Human resources and the resources-based view of the firm. *Journal of Management, 27,* 701–721.

Young, M. D., & McLeod, S. (2001). Flukes, opportunities, and planned interventions: Factors affecting women's decisions to become school administrators. *Educational Administration Quarterly, 37,* 462–502.

Yukl, G. (2002). *Leadership in organizations* (5th ed.). Upper Saddle River, NJ: Prentice Hall.

Zederayko, G., & Ward, K. (1999, February). Schools as learning organizations: How can the work of teachers be both teaching and learning. *NASSP Bulletin, 83*(604), 35–45.

About the Editors
and the Contributors

William A. Firestone is professor of educational policy and leadership at Rutgers University, where he also serves as director of the Center for Educational Policy Analysis and principal investigator of the New Jersey Math Science Partnership. His interests include policy implementation, how testing affects teaching, and school improvement. Recent publications include *The Ambiguity of Teaching to the Test* (with Roberta Y. Schorr and Lora Monfils) and "Politics, Community, and Leadership in a School–University Partnership" (with Jennifer Fisler, published in *Educational Administration Quarterly*).

Carolyn Riehl is an associate professor in the Department of Educational Leadership and Cultural Foundations at the University of North Carolina at Greensboro. She is a sociologist of education with special interests in leadership and organizational dynamics in schools and school systems, equity and instructional reform, and public engagement in education. Recent publications include "Educational Leadership in Policy Contexts That Strive for Equity" in the *International Handbook of Educational Policy*.

Albert Bennett is professor of public policy and professor of education and director of the St. Clair Drake Center for African and African-American Studies at Roosevelt University in Chicago. His research interests include leadership, education policy and the politics of school reform, and university and community collaborations. Bennett received his Ph.D. in Institutional Analysis and Policy Studies from the University of Chicago, his M.A. from the University of Chicago, and his B.A. from the University of Illinois, Chicago. Bennett is a former elementary school teacher.

Mary Erina Driscoll is an associate professor and director of the Program in Educational Leadership in the Steinhardt School of Education at New York University. Her research focuses on the sense of place in schools, the connections between schools and their communities, and the ways in which communities can serve as the contexts for student learning. Her publications include "*The Implications of Social Capital for Schools, Communities and Cities: Educational Administration as if a Sense of Place Mattered*" (with C. Kerchner, published in the *Handbook of Research on Educational Administration*) and *The Sense of Place and Conant's Legacy: Connecting Schools and Their Communities*.

Carol R. Fendt is co-director of the Chicago Math and Science Initiative Evaluation Project at the University of Illinois at Chicago. She is also a doctoral student in educational policy studies at UIC. She received her M.A. in educational leadership from Dominican University and her B.S. from the University of Wisconsin-Milwaukee. Fendt has worked as a high school English teacher and principal in schools of the Archdiocese of Chicago.

Gail C. Furman is a professor of educational leadership at Washington State University. Her current research interests include the concept of community in schools and moral leadership. Recent publications include the book *School as Community: From Promise to Practice*; a chapter in the 2002 NSSE Yearbook (with Robert J. Starratt) on "Leadership for Democratic Community in Schools"; and articles in the *Journal of Educational Administration* and *Educational Administration Quarterly*. She won the Davis Award for outstanding article in *Educational Administration Quarterly* for 1998 and served as president of the University Council for Educational Administration (UCEA) in 2000–2001.

Ellen B. Goldring is professor of education policy and leadership at Peabody College, Vanderbilt University. She currently serves as the co-editor of *Educational Evaluation and Policy Analysis*. Her research explores relationships among families, communities, and schools. She also studies school leadership and the link between the practice of school leadership and learning. Recent publications include "Transition Leadership in a Changing Policy Environment" (with Crowson, Laird, and Berk, in *Educational Evaluation and Policy Analysis*), and *We Must Model How We Teach: Learning to Lead with Compelling Models of Professional Development* (with N. Vye, published in *Educational Administration, Policy and Reform*).

Pamela Konkol is Visiting Program Associate and a doctoral student in social foundations of education at the University of Illinois at Chicago. She conducts research on teacher and administrator preparation from practicing educator and higher education perspectives. Konkol received her M.Ed. in Curriculum and Instruction from UIC and her B.S. from Northwestern University. She has served as a member of the Illinois Governor's Council on Teacher Quality and as the director of a high school communications and journalism program. She also works with school districts on issues of educational improvement.

Kenneth A. Leithwood is professor of educational leadership at the Ontario Institute for Studies in Education/University of Toronto. His research and writing focus on school leadership, educational policy, and organizational change. His research has been carried out in many countries, and he has published widely on these themes.

Barbara Scott Nelson is senior scientist and director of the Center for the Development of Teaching at Education Development Center, Inc., Newton, MA. Her current research focuses on school and district administrators' practical judgment, in particular, how administrators' ideas about the nature of mathematics, learning, and teaching affect their administrative practice. Recent publications include "Leadership Content Knowledge" (with Mary Kay Stein) published in *Educational Evaluation and Policy Analysis*, and *Leading Learners: Stories from Administrators' Practice in Instructional Leadership in Elementary Mathematics* (with Annette Sassi), to be published in summer 2005.

Nona A. Prestine is a professor in the Educational Leadership Program at Penn State University. Her research interests are in the areas of school leadership, sociocultural perspectives, and organizational change. Her recent publications include "Disposable Reform? Assessing the Durability of Secondary School Reform" in *Planning and Changing* and a chapter co-authored with Ken Leithwood, "Unpacking the Challenges of Leadership at the School and District Level," in *The Educational Leadership Challenge: Redefining Leadership for the 21st Century, 101st Yearbook of the National Society for the Study of Education.*

Pedro Reyes is associate vice chancellor for Academic Planning and Assessment at The University of Texas System and professor of education policy and administration at The University of Texas at Austin, where he is also a faculty research associate at the Population Research Center. He received his Ph.D. in 1985 from the University of Wisconsin-Madison and has been a member of the faculty at Texas since 1991. His academic work is focused on the sociology of education organizations. Dr. Reyes is the author of *Teachers and Their Workplace: Commitment, Performance, and Productivity*, and co-author of *Lessons from High-Performing Hispanic Schools*. His most recent book is *Resiliency and Success.*

Carolyn M. Shields is professor of educational leadership in the Department of Educational Studies, the University of British Columbia. Her research and teaching interests focus on cross-cultural leadership and leadership for social justice. These interests are reflected in numerous articles and her most recent books: *Good Intentions Are Not Enough: Transformative Leadership for Communities of Difference*; *Pathologizing Practices: The Impact of Deficit Thinking on Education* (co-authored with Russell Bishop and Andre Mazawi); and *Inspiring Practices: Spirituality and Educational Leadership* (co-edited with Mark Edwards and Anish Sayani).

Dorothy Shipps is assistant professor of education at Teachers College, Columbia University. Her research interests include the historical and political policy analysis of urban school reform, work for which she was honored as a Carnegie Scholar in 2000–01. Recent publications include *Reconstructing the Common Good in Public Education: Coping with Intractable American Dilemmas* (with Larry Cuban) and "Pulling Together" (*American Educational Research Journal*, 2003).

Mark A. Smylie is professor and chair of the Policy Studies Area in the College of Education at the University of Illinois at Chicago. His research interests include urban school improvement, leadership, teacher learning and development, and the relationship of school organization to classroom teaching and student learning. Smylie received his Ph.D. in educational leadership from Peabody College at Vanderbilt University and his M.Ed. and B.A. from Duke University. He is a former high school social studies teacher.

James Spillane is professor of education and social policy at Northwestern University. His most recent book is *Standards Deviation*, and *Distributed Leadership* will be published in 2005. Recent publications can be found in *Teachers College Record, Sociology of Education, Elementary School Journal*, and *Journal of Curriculum Studies*.

Mary Kay Stein holds a joint appointment as research scientist at the Learning Research and Development Center and associate professor in the School of Education at the University of Pittsburgh. Her research interests include teacher learning in mathematics and how policy, leadership, and social interaction shape teacher learning. Recent publications include "Leadership Content Knowledge," which appeared in the 2003 special edition of *Educational Evaluation and Policy Analysis*. She is co-author of a three-volume set of cases, *Cases of Mathematics Instruction to Enhance Teaching*, for teacher professional development in mathematics that will be published in 2005.

Lonnie Wagstaff is an emeritus professor of educational administration at The University of Texas at Austin. He received his Ph.D. from the University of Oklahoma and has been a member of the faculty at Texas since 1989. He was also dean of the College of Education at the University of Cincinnati and a member of the faculty at the Ohio State University. He has many years of teaching experience in both public schools and higher education and has won major awards for his teaching and service to the education community.

Index

Accountabilities, 81–100
  bureaucratic, 83, 85–86, 90–91
  conflicts between, 90–91
  external, 83–97
  high-stakes, 108–109, 117–118
  internal, 83, 87–90, 97–98
  market, 83, 86–87
  moral, 83, 88–90, 97–98
  multiple types of, 83–84
  political, 83, 84–85, 90
  professional, 83, 87–88, 90–91
  research methods for, 98–100
  student learning and, 81–100
Ackland, H., 15
Action research, 157
Activity theory, 59
Administrators. *See* Educational
  leadership; Principal leadership
Advances in Research on Teaching
  (Brophy), 33–34
African Americans
  dropout rates of, 3
  as educational leaders, 107–108
  as percentage of school population,
    103
  perspective of, 133
  school culture and, 107–108
  social capital and, 72
Allensworth, E., 23
Amanti, C., 26, 68
American Educational Research
  Association (AERA), 154, 184

American Indians
  as percentage of school population,
    103
  school culture and, 107–108
Anderson, D. K., 52
Anderson, G. L., 109
Anderson, L., 33
Anderson, R. D., 21
Anfara, V. A., 149
Apple, M. W., 119, 123, 125
Archer, J., 175, 176
Argyris, C., 143
Asian Americans
  dropout rates of, 3
  as percentage of school population,
    103
Assessment, accountabilities and, 95,
  108–109, 117–118

Bailey, K., 70–71
Baker, E. L., 86
Ball, D. L., 34, 48
Balter, L., 25
Bane, M. J., 15
Banks, J. A., 128
Banner, D. K., 19
Barber, B. R., 121, 122
Barnard, C. I., 50, 157
Barnett, B. G., 147
Barr, R., 16, 85
Bascia, N., 18
Basom, M. R., 147

Bass, B. M., 140, 141
Baxter, J. A., 42
Beane, J. A., 119, 123, 125
Becher, T., xi
Beck, L. G., 19, 21, 62–63, 120
Beck, M. S., 109
Begley, P., 149
Behaviorist learning theory, 48
Bennett, A., 10, 138–155, 166, 181–
    183
Bennis, W., 20
Berends, M., 23
Beresford, J., 19–20
Berla, N., 25
Berliner, D. C., 2, 123, 170
Berman, P., 159
Berne, J., 60 n. 8, 143
Betebenner, D. W., 86
Bickman, L., 16, 31
Biddle, B. J., 2, 31, 123
Bidwell, C. E., 16
Billett, S., 52
Bishop, H. L., 148
Bishop, R., 133
Bizar, M., 85
Blacks. See African Americans
Blank, M., 67, 75
Blase, J., 109
Bleiman, J., 37
Bogotch, I. E., 18, 123
Bok, B., 102
Bolman, L. G., 43
Borko, H., 18, 29, 36, 39
Bosker, R. J., 15–17, 167
Bossert, S. T., 19, 32, 50
Bourdieu, P., 72, 113
Bowen, G. M., 59
Bowen, W. G., 102
Bowers, C. A., 121
Bowles, S., 119
Boyan, N. J., x, 119–120
Boyatzis, R., 21

Boyd, W. L., 64–65, 74, 173
Boyle, B., 18
Braddock, J. H., 177
Bransford, J. D., 46–48, 65–66, 172–
    173
Bredo, E., 37
Breeder effect (Driscoll & Kerchner),
    114
Bridges, E., 31
Broadfoot, P., 35
Brophy, J., 15, 29, 33–34, 42
Brown, A. L., 38, 46–48, 59, 60 n. 7,
    65–66, 159, 165, 172–173
Brown, C. A., 39, 40
Brown, J., 65
Brown, J. H., 19
Brown, J. S., 19
Brown, K. M., 149
Brown, M., 18
Browne-Ferrigno, T., 147
Brownlee-Conyers, J., 16
Brown v. Board of Education, 103
Bruner, J., 46–47
Brunner, C. C., 144
Bryk, A. S., 23, 24, 34, 57, 89, 176,
    177
Bryman, A., 19
Bulkley, K., 91, 138
Burch, P., 43
Bureaucratic accountability, 83, 85–86,
    90–91
Burlingame, M., 97
Burns, J. M., 14
Burns, R., 16

Caffarella, R. S., 143
Cahill, M., 68
Caine, G., 112, 114–115
Caine, R. N., 112, 114–115
Cairney, T., 62
Callahan, R. E., 46
Cambone, J., 59 n. 1

Campbell, C., 90
Campbell, E. Q., 15
Campbell, P., 16
Campione, J., 60 n. 7
Capper, C. A., 124
Carbonaro, W., 71, 73
Carey, D. A., 33, 60 n. 6
Carnes, J., 104
Carnoy, M., 59 n. 1, 82, 98, 100 n. 1
Carpenter, T. P., 33, 60 n. 6, 172
Carspecken, P. F., 163
Case study approach, 15–16, 99–100,
    164–165
Castillo, S., 19
Catholic schools, 70, 89
Cazden, C., 37
Charter schools, 87, 91
Chaskin, R., 74, 76
Chiang, C., 60 n. 6
Chicago, high-stakes accountability in,
    108–109
Child Development Project (CDP), 54,
    60 n. 7
Chrispeels, J. A., 19
Cielo, M. B., 90
Civil Rights Act (1964), 103
Closed systems, schools as, 62
Clotfelter, C. T., 87
Clune, W., 20, 93
Cobb, P., 34, 38–40, 52, 166, 175–
    176
Coburn, C. E., 15–16, 40, 58–59, 97,
    164
Cochran-Smith, M., 143
Cocking, R. R., 46–48, 65–66, 172–173
Codding, J. B., 138–139
Coffin, G., 147
Cognitive learning theory
    behaviorist theories versus, 48
    mediational paradigms and, 32–34
    tenets of, 47
Cohen, D. K., 15, 35, 47–48

Cohen, M. D., 93
Cohn, M. M., 92
Cole, K. A., 7
Cole, M., 37, 59
Coleman, J. S., 15, 26, 70, 113, 119
Collaborative processes, 22
Collins, A. M., 47–48, 60 n. 3, 65
Comer, J., 63
Communal dimension, of leadership,
    129–130, 136
Communities of practice. *See also*
    Democratic community;
    Distributed leadership; School-
    community relationship
    community-centered approach
        (Bransford et al.), 67
    nature of, 24, 176
    neighborhood community and, 179–
        180
    principals in promotion of, 109–
        110, 114
    professional community, 178–179
    rethinking, 56–58
    student community, 176–177
    as vital to learning, 69
Conger, J., 20
Conley, S., 6, 18, 50, 51, 129, 178
Connell, R. W., 125
Constructivist leadership theory, 129
Constructivist learning theory, 38–39,
    54, 58, 127
Content knowledge
    leadership, 55, 143
    pedagogical, 41–42, 44, 55–56, 57–
        58, 109
Context
    communities and learning, 67, 77–
        78
    contextual dimension, of leadership,
        129–130, 136
    for educational leader development,
        144

Context (*continued*)
  fluid nature of, 79
  integrative role of principal and, 109
  sense of place in community
    development, 73–77
  transfer of student learning and, 66–67
  understanding, 77–78
Conversation as method (Thompson & Gitlin), 133–134
Cook, T. D., 168
Cooper, B. S., 18
Cooper, J. E., 129, 130
Copland, M. A., 19, 48, 68–69, 92, 147
Corcoran, T., 19, 46
Correnti, R., 167–168
Cosgrove, D., 149
Cotton, K., 15
Coulson, R. L., 52
Council of Chief State School Officers, 2
Creemers, B. P. M., 17
Croninger, R., 70
Crosnoe, R., 177
Crow, G., 147, 155 n. 2
Crowson, R., 62, 64–65, 74, 78
Cuban, L., 2, 32, 85, 174

Daft, R. L., 20
D'Amico, L., 12, 36, 40, 55
Danforth Foundation, Program for the Preparation of School Principals, 147
Daresh, J. C., 147, 151
Darling-Hammond, L., 19, 24, 34, 39, 68–69, 88
Dartmouth College, approach to diversity, 102
Datnow, A., 2
Davidson, E., 37

Davis, K., 16, 31
Day, C., 19–20
Deal, T. E., 43, 57
Dean, C., 39–40, 175–176
Declarative knowledge, 143
Dedrick, R. F., 35
Deep content knowledge, 55–56, 109
"Deep" democracy, 121–123, 127–128
Dei, G. S., 26, 124
Delgado-Gaitan, C., 25, 72
Delpit, L. D., 137
Democratic community, 119–123
  concept of, 120–121
  directions for inquiry into, 135
  in ensuring pedagogical focus, 126–128
  frame for, 121–123
  implications for leadership, 128–132
  importance of, 119
  interplay of social justice and, 125
  research agenda for, 132–134
DeMoss, K., 108–109, 117–118
Denby, M., 18
Department of Defense (DOD) schools, 73
Design-Based Research Collective, 59, 77, 166
Design research, 59, 77, 165–167
Desimone, L. M., 167
Developing people, 21–22
  individualized support in, 21
  intellectual stimulation in, 21
  modeling in, 22
Dewey, J., 65–67, 121
Diamond, J. B., 18, 19, 35, 47, 50, 175
Diaz, R., 115
Dichter, A., 53
Dika, S., 70, 71, 77
Dillard, C. B., 24

Distributed leadership, 50–52. *See also*
    Communities of practice
    instructional leadership and, 56
    as leadership beyond the hierarchy, 80
    nature of, 19, 50–51
    professional community and, 178–
        179
    rethinking, 51–52, 176
    theory of, 129
Distributive justice, 125
Diverse student populations, 101–118
    in colleges, 102
    diversity as multidimensional
        concept, 103
    educational leadership for, 22–26
    ethnic minority students, 3, 103,
        106–109, 112–113. *See also*
        names of specific ethnic groups
    integrative role of principals and,
        104–117
    in K-12 schools, 102–103
    nature of diversity, 102
    other aspects of diversity, 103
    research on, 106–109
    research recommendations for, 117–
        118
    school policies surrounding, 102–
        103
    social boundaries in schools and,
        104–105, 109
Dornbusch, S., 72
Downey, D., 71
Doyle, W., 33
Dreeben, R., 16
Driscoll, M. E., 9, 24, 26, 34, 37, 61–
    80, 74–75, 114, 164–165, 166–
    167, 177, 179–180
Dropout rates, 3
Dryfoos, J. G., 25, 64
Duffy, M. C., 46
DuFour, R., 56

Duguid, P., 19, 65
Duke, D. L., 14, 17–18
Dunford, B. B., 140
Dunkin, M. J., 31
Dwyer, D., 32

Eaker, R., 56
Earley, P., 149
Ebmeier, H., 31
Edelson, D. C., 166
Edmonds, R. R., 31, 49, 106, 165
Educational Development Center, 37
Educational Evaluation and Policy
    Analysis (EPPA), 35
Educational leader development, 138–
    155
    capacities for effective educational
        leadership, 140, 141–143
    defined, 139, 151
    effectiveness of means of, 140–141,
        145–150
    processes of, 140, 144
    proposed research agenda for, 150–
        154
    unknowns of, 181–183
Educational leadership. *See also*
    Educational leader development;
    Principal leadership; Teacher
    leadership
    basic leadership practices in, 19–
        22
    capacity-building for, 117
    conflicting accountabilities and, 81–
        100
    dimensions of leadership, 129–130,
        136
    distributed, 19, 50–52, 56, 80, 129,
        176, 178–179
    equity and, 2–4
    expanding understanding of learners
        and leaders in, 52–53

Educational leadership
  (*continued*)
  impact on student learning, 2–4,
    15–17, 22–26, 30–32, 172
  implementing the agenda for, 183–
    184
  implications of democratic
    community for, 128–132
  implications of social justice for,
    128–132
  instructional, 49–50, 56–58, 69,
    174
  mediational paradigms for, 34–37
  nature of, 49–51
  needs for research on, 4–6
  policy environment for, 102–103,
    180–181
  problems of, 5–6
  proposed research agenda for, 6–10,
    183–184
  research-based claims concerning, 6,
    14–27, 30–44
  research methods for studying, 156–
    170
  responses to external accountabilities,
    91–97
  rethinking, 51–53
  school-community relationship and,
    61–80
  in social and and interactive context,
    39–40
  sources of knowledge on, 156–158
  thinking processes of, 42–44
  tranformative, 111, 130, 136
  transformative dimension of, 111,
    130, 136
  types of, 17–19
  working conception of, 13–14
Educational Research Service, 138
Education Leadership Constituent
  Council, 88
Edwards, B., 113

Edwards, M. M., 130
Effective schools movement, 62–63
Ehrich, L. C., 147, 148, 151, 155 n. 1
Eisenhart, M., 161
Elder, G. H., 177
Elliott, R. L., 18
Elmore, R. F., 20, 46, 47, 49, 52–53,
  58, 82, 93, 96, 98, 100 n. 1
Elsberry, C., 148
Elstein, A. S., 41
Empowerment, models of, 74
Engestrom, Y., 52
Engle, R. A., 7
Englert, R. M., 24
English, F. W., 125
Epstein, J. L., 16, 25, 26, 64
Equity. *See also* Social justice
  educational leadership and, 214
  multiple aspects of, 125
Eraut, M., 143
Erickson, F., 161
Ethical dimension, of leadership, 129,
  136
Ethnic minority school leaders
  and school culture, 107–108
  and socialization in educational
    leader development, 148, 151
Ethnic minority students. *See also*
    names of specific ethnic groups
  dropout rates of, 3
  integrative role of principals and,
    104–117
  as percentage of school population,
    103
Etzioni, A., 114
Evans, P. M., 149
Evers, C. W., 158
Experimental research, 16–17, 99–100,
  158–159, 168
External accountabilities
  local responses to, 91–97
  types of, 83–90

Fairhurst, G. T., 20
Fairman, J., 95
Fairness. *See also* Equity; Social justice
  criterion of, 124
Farrell, J. P., 124
Fashola, O., 123
Feltovich, P. J., 52
Fendt, C. R., 138–155, 166, 181–183
Fennema, E., 33, 60 n. 6
Fetter, R., 21
Feuer, M., 77, 166
Finn, J., 23, 25
Firestone, W. A., 1–11, 6, 7, 9, 10, 18,
  35, 81–100, 95, 97, 138, 145,
  156–170, 164, 171–184, 175–
  176, 178, 180, 181
Fiske, E. B., 81
Fisler, J. L., 18
Fitz, J., 35
Floden, R., 45 n. 1
Foley, B., 113
Foley, E., 46
Ford, B., 48, 92
Ford, M., 20
Ford Foundation, Neighborhood and
  Family Initiative, 74, 76
Fordham, S., 73
Fosnot, C. T., 60 n. 8
Foster, M., 23, 107, 108, 110–111
Foster, W. F., 20, 62–63, 130
Fostering a Community of Learners
  (FCL), 38, 54, 60 n. 7
Four-walls-of-the-school tradition
  (McPherson et al.), 62
Franke, M. L., 60 n. 6
Freire, P., 89, 124, 125, 127
Friedkin, N. E., 95
Fuhrman, S., 20, 93
Fullan, M. G., 18, 57
Fuller, B., 87
Fuller, H. L., 90
Full-service schools (Dryfoos), 64

Furman, G. C., 10, 119–137, 120,
  121, 165, 167, 172, 173, 179,
  181

Gage, N., 30, 31
Gagne, R. M., 48
Gagné, T. E., 19
Gamoran, A., 23
Garcia, E. E., 107
Gardner, H., 47–48
Gardner, M. E., 129, 130
Garner, C. W., 138
Geijsel, F., 22
George, R., 20
Gezi, K., 15, 24
Giaconia, R., 31
Gintis, H., 119
Giroux, H., 120
Gitlin, A., 133–135
Glynn, T., 133
Goals, in educational leadership, 20–21
Goertz, M. E., 46
Goldfarb, K. P., 130
Goldman, S., 7
Goldring, E. B., 6, 9, 61–80, 62, 63,
  65, 74, 76, 78, 119, 164–165,
  166–167, 177, 179–180
Goleman, D., 21
González, N., 26, 68, 108
Good, T. L., 15, 29, 31
Gooden, M., 106–107
Goodlad, S. J., 119
Gorman, J. C., 25
Graduation rates, 2–3
Granovetter, M., 73
Grant, C. M., 37
Green, J. M., 121–123
Greenberg, J. B., 115, 123, 124
Greene, M., 89, 124, 128
Greenfield, T., 129
Greenfield, W., 119
Greeno, J. G., 7, 47–48, 60 n. 3, 60 n. 4

Gresson, A., 74
Griffin, P., 37
Griffith, H., 18
Griffiths, M., 132, 133, 135, 137 n. 4
Grinberg, J., 130
Grintlis, H., 15
Grogan, M., 147, 155 n. 2
Gronn, P., 19, 166
Grossman, P. L., 18, 36
Grouws, D., 31
Grumet, M., 127, 131
Gudmundsdottir, S., 42
Guinier, L., 121, 122
Guthrie, J., 70, 73, 78
Gutierrez, K., 161
Gutman, A., 121, 122

Haertel, G., 15
Hafield, M., 19–20
Hager, D. R., 18
Hale, E. L., 138–139
Hall, K., 163
Hallett, T., 18, 35
Hallinger, P., 2, 6, 14–16, 20, 23, 30–
    32, 34, 35, 42–43, 47, 49, 60
    n. 5, 77, 78, 106, 142–143, 158,
    159, 164, 167, 175
Halpin, D., 20
Halverson, R., 19, 47, 50, 175
Hamilton, M. L., 15–16
*Handbook of Research on Educational
    Administration* (Boyan, ed.), 119–
    120
*Handbook of Research on Educational
    Administration* (Murphy & Louis,
    eds.), 119–120
Hannaway, J., 59 n. 1, 86, 87, 94
Hannay, L. M., 18
Hansford, B., 147, 148, 151, 155 n. 1
Hansot, E., 46, 88
Hargreaves, A., 21
Harris, A., 19–20

Hart, A. W., 18, 39, 144, 149
Hartman, K. J., 149
Harvey, A., 72
Harvey, I., 90
Hausman, C., 65, 74, 76
Heath, S. B., 26, 107
Heck, R. H., 6, 14–16, 20, 23, 30–32,
    34, 35, 47, 49, 60 n. 5, 77, 78,
    158, 167
Hedges, L. V., 23
Heilman, E., 4
Heller, M., 18, 178
Henderson, A. T., 25
Henig, J. R., 85, 87
Hess, F. M., 138–139
Hess, G., 63
Hiebert, J., 33, 34, 172
High-stakes accountabilities, 108–109,
    117–118
Hightower, A., 92, 94, 96
Hillman, J., 15
Hirschman, A., 114
Hispanics
    dropout rates of, 3
    as percentage of school population,
        103
    school culture and, 107–108
Hobson, C. F., 15
Hodgkinson, C., 129
Hodgkinson, H. L., 123
Hoffer, T., 70
Holland, P. B., 89
Hollister, C. D., 62
Holyoke, T. T., 87
Honig, M., 64, 68, 72, 78, 79
Hoover-Dempsey, K., 63
Horizontal networks (Putnam), 72
Houston Annenberg Project, 101
Houtveen, A. A. M., 15
Hoy, W. K., 6, 7, 35, 141, 142, 145
Hubbard, L., 40
Huber, G. P., 93–95

Huberman, A. M., 162
Hughes, W. L., 49
Hunter-Boykin, H., 108

Imber, M., 18
Immerwahr, J., 90
Individualized support, in developing
    people, 21
Ingersoll, R., 16
In-service professional development, in
    educational leader development,
    149–150
Instructional leadership
    communities of practice and, 56–58
    nature of, 49–50
    research on, 174
    rethinking, 69
Intellectual stimulation, in developing
    people, 21
Internal accountabilities
    equity and, 97–98
    student achievement and, 97–98
    types of, 83, 87–90
Interpretation, accountabilities
    concerning, 95–97
Interstate School Leaders Licensure
    Consortium (ISLLC), 2, 88, 141–
    143

Jantzi, D., 19–20, 22, 96, 147
Jencks, C., 15
Jennings, N., 35
Jermier, J. M., 19
Johnson, J. F., Jr., 106, 137 n. 3
Johnson, M. K., 177
Johnson, S. M., 6, 7, 88, 145
Jones, B. D., 85
Justice. *See* Social justice

Kaestle, C. F., 158, 172
Kahne, J., 64, 68, 70–72, 78, 79
Kanungo, R., 20

Kaomea, J., 137 n. 4
Kasarda, J. D., 16
Kayzar, B., 25, 77
Kennedy, M., 29, 40
Kennedy, S. S., 37
Kerchner, C. T., 26, 43, 74, 80, 114
Kerr, S., 19
Kimball, K., 94
Kincheloe, J. L., 123–124
King, J. E., 107
King, M. B., 97, 98
King, S. H., 108
Kirmani, M. H., 123
Knapp, M. S., 15, 19, 23, 48, 60 n. 8,
    68–69, 92, 94, 96, 107
Knowledge acquisition, accountabilities
    concerning, 93–94
Knowledge development, 7
Knowledge distribution,
    accountabilities concerning, 94–
    95
Knudson, J., 7
Konkol, P., 138–155, 166, 181–183
Konstantopoulos, S., 23
Kornhaber, M., 86
Koschoreck, J. W., 137 n. 3
Kottkamp, R. B., 92
Kranz, J., 18
Kretzmann, J., 74
Kruse, S. D., 22, 24, 57, 176, 178
Kuhn, T. S., 159

Labaree, D. F., 158
Lacireno-Pacquet, N., 87
Ladd, H. F., 81, 86, 87
Ladson-Billings, G., 23, 103, 108
Lagemann, E., 4, 158
Lakomski, G., 158
Lamberg, T. D. S., 39–40, 175–176
Lambert, L., 117, 129, 130
Lambert, M. D., 129, 130
Lamme, L. A., 123

Lamme, L. L., 123
Lampert, M., 34, 48
Lane, S., 60 n. 6
Lankford, H., 138
Lareau, A., 72
Larson, C. L., 5, 119, 124, 157, 169
Lasch, C., 122
Laster, B. P., 123
Latinos. *See* Hispanics
Lave, J., 38–40
Lawrence, S. M., 26
Lazarus, V., 16
Lea, M. R., 52
Leadership content knowledge (Stein & Nelson), 55, 143
Leadership for America's Schools (National Commission on Excellence in Educational Administration), 2
Learning. *See* Student learning; Teaching and teacher learning
Learning theories
  behaviorist, 48
  cognitive, 32–34, 47, 48
  constructivist, 38–39, 54, 58, 127
Lee, V. E., 24, 35, 70, 89, 176, 177
Le Floch, K. C., 167
Lehrer, R., 7
Leinhardt, G., 42
Leithwood, K. A., 8, 12–27, 14, 17–18, 19–20, 21, 22, 32, 42–43, 96, 98, 106, 142–143, 147, 149, 159, 164, 174, 175, 176
LePore, P. C., 23
Levine, D. U., 15
Lezotte, L. W., 15
Lieberman, A., 34, 37, 39
Lightfoot, S. L., 37
Linn, R. L., 86
Little, J. W., 21, 34, 39, 56, 111
Loef, M., 60 n. 6
Lomotey, K., 107

Lord, R. G., 21
Lortie, D., 21, 37, 92
Louis, K. S., x, 14, 18, 21–24, 53, 57, 119–120, 176, 178
Loveless, T., 4–5
Lugg, C. A., 138
Luhm, T., 46
Lundeberg, M. A., 123
Lytle, S., 143

Macedo, D., 119, 127
Macgillivray, I. K., 103
MacKenzie, S. B., 21
MacKinnon, D., 123, 124
Magnet schools, 63–64
Mahar, R. J., 149
Maher, K. J., 21
Malen, B., 18, 63
Mann, D., 62
March, J. G., 93
Marfo, K., 169
Market accountability, 83, 86–87
Markholt, A., 48, 92
Marks, H. M., 18, 24, 50, 51, 129, 178
Marks, R., 42
Marschall, M., 87
Marsh, J. A., 92, 94, 96
Marshall, C., 140, 145
Martin, A. K., 143
Masiello, T., 59
Mason, D., 16
Mathematics education, 3, 4, 7, 46, 94, 169
Mattingly, D., 25, 77
Mawhinney, H. B., 25, 75
Maxcy, S. J., 120–122
Maxwell, J. A., 161
May, S., 124
Mayrowetz, D., 18
McCarthy, M. M., 146
McCauley, C. D., 140

McClain, K., 39–40, 175–176
McColl-Kennedy, J. R., 21
McCoy, A. R., 23
McDermott, R. P., 7, 37
McDill, E. L., 24
McGaughey, C., 73, 74
McGill, C., 75
McGough, D. J., 144
McGreal, T., 58
McIver, M. C., 18
McKee, A., 21
McKenzie, T., 25, 77
McKnight, J., 74
McLaughlin, M. W., 19, 39, 48, 53, 54, 56, 64, 68–69, 72, 78, 79, 86, 92, 94, 96, 159
McLeod, S., 144
McMurran, G., 80
McNeil, L., 119
McPartland, J. M., 15, 177
McPherson, B., 62
Mechanic, D., 50
Mediational paradigms, 32–37
    research on educational leadership, 34–37
    research on teaching, 32–34
Mehan, H., 33, 37, 40
Melaville, A., 67, 75
Mentoring programs, 147–148
Merriam, S. B., 143
Metacognitive skills, 66
Mexican Americans. *See also* Hispanics
    school culture and, 107–108
Meyer, J., 89
Michaels, S., 38
Middleton, D., 52
Migrant students, 112–113
Miklos, E., 144, 146, 148
Miles, M. B., 162
Miles, R. E., 50
Miller, L., 37
Miller, R. J., 123, 167–168

Milliken, M., 48, 92
Mills, R., 149
Mills v. Board of Education of the District of Columbia, 103
Minority students. *See* Ethnic minority students
Miretzky, D., 140
Mitchel, C. P., 149
Mitchell, A., 107, 108, 110–111
Mitra, D., 53, 54, 56
Mitzel, H. E., 31
Modeling, in developing people, 22
Mohr, N., 53, 149
Mohrman, S., 20
Moll, L. C., 25, 26, 68, 108, 115
Monfils, L., 81, 97, 175–176, 180
Monk, D. H., 15
Montecel, M. R., 123
Mood, A. M., 15
Moore, A., 20
Moorman, H. N., 138–139
Moorman, R. H., 21
Moral accountability, 83, 88–90, 97–98
Moral dimension, of leadership, 129, 136
Morgenthal, J. R., 23
Mortimore, P., 15
Moser, J. M., 33
Moser, M., 87
Mulford, W. R., 177
Multi-frame thinking (Bolman & Deal), 43
Mumby, H., 143
Munn, P., 63
Munsie, L., 62
Murphy, J., x, 2, 19, 29, 42–43, 119–121, 140, 142–143, 145–146, 159, 175
Murphy, M., 56, 57
Murtadha, K., 124
Muth, R., 147

Nanus, B., 20
National Assessment of Educational
     Progress (NAEP), 3
National Center for Educational
     Statistics (NCES), 103
National Commission for the
     Principalship, 141
National Commission on Excellence in
     Education, 2
National Commission on Excellence in
     Educational Administration, 2
National Council of Teachers of
     English (NCTE), 46
National Council of Teachers of
     Mathematics (NCTM), 3, 7, 46,
     94
National Institute of Child Health and
     Development, 160
National Policy Board for Educational
     Administration, 2, 141–143
National Reading Panel, 160
National Research Council (NRC), 3,
     65, 77, 143, 157–158, 160–163,
     169, 170
National Science Foundation, 183
Nation at Risk, A, 2, 30
Native Americans. See American Indians
Natriello, G., 24
Neff, D., 26, 68
Neighborhood and Family Initiative
     (Ford Foundation), 74, 76
Neighborhood community, 179–180
Nelson, B. S., 8–9, 37, 44, 46–60, 55–
     56, 143, 146, 164, 166, 171,
     173–176, 178–179
Neufeld, B., 144, 149
Neumann, F., 66
New accountability, 86
Newman, D., 37
Newmann, F. M., 23, 24, 34, 97, 98
New York City, Community School
     District 2, 36

New Zealand, dominant discourse and,
     133
Nias, J., 16
Nicoll, K., 52
Nicolopoulou, A., 59
No Child Left Behind, 3, 5, 30, 69, 84–
     85, 89, 160
Noddings, N., 89
Noguera, P., 73, 76
Normative research, 157
Norris, C. J., 147
Norris, P., 113
Northwest Regional Laboratory,
     Onward to Excellence Program,
     134
Norton, S. M., 148–149
Nye, B., 23
Nystrand, M., 23

O'Conner, M. C., 38
O'Day, J., 63, 81, 86–88, 91
Ogawa, R. T., 6, 18, 19, 50, 63, 65
Ogbu, J. A., 73, 107
Ohde, K. L., 43
Oliver, C., 97
Olsen, J. P., 93
Olson, L., 5
Ontario Institute for Studies in
     Education, 42–43
Onward to Excellence Program
     (Northwest Regional Laboratory),
     134
Opportunity costs, of social capital, 72
Optimistic education, 124
Orfield, G., 86
Organizational design
     collaborative processes in, 22
     organizational structure in, 22
     school culture in, 22
Organizational structure, 22
Orr, M., 70–72
"Otherist" perspectives, 124

Ovando, C., 119
Owens, D., 70, 73

Palincsar, A. S., 38, 159
Pallas, A. M., 24
Papa, F. C., Jr., 138
Parents
  delegation model of involvement, 62,
    63
  family culture and, 24–25, 115
  involvement in schools, 62–63
  new roles for, 63–64
Parker, L., 108, 110–111
Parks, S., 131
Patrick, H., 176
Paul, J. L., 169
Pedagogical content knowledge
  of administrators, 44, 56
  coherence and consistency of
    pedagogical theory and, 57–58
  deep content knowledge, 55–56, 109
  of teachers, 41–42, 55–56
Pedagogical dimension, of leadership,
    44, 56, 130–131, 136
Pena, R., 75, 107
*Pennsylvania Association for Retarded
  Children v. Commonwealth of
  Pennsylvania*, 103
Performance expectations, in
  educational leadership, 21
Peterson, K., 57
Peterson, P. L., 33, 60 n. 6
Petrosko, J. M., 148
Pewewardy, C., 105
Pfeffer, J., 50
Phillips, D. C., 5, 77, 166
Piaget, J., 46–47, 65
Pierannunzi, C., 85
Pitman, K., 68
Pitner, N., 29–31, 62
Pittman, T. S., 20–21
Playko, M. A., 151

Podsakoff, P. M., 21
Political accountability, 83, 84–85, 90
Portin, B. S., 24, 144
Pounder, D. G., ix, 144
Poverty
  school culture and, 104–105, 107–
    108
  social boundaries in schools and,
    104–105, 109
  social capital and, 70–71
Preexisting knowledge
  family culture and, 24–25, 115
  importance for understanding new
    learning, 65–66
Preservice preparation, for educational
  leader development, 146–148
Prestine, N. A., 8–9, 46–60, 56, 57,
    58, 164, 166, 171, 173–176,
    178–179
Pribesh, S., 71
Principal leadership. *See also*
    Educational leader development;
    Educational leadership
  ability and, 110–111, 116–117
  certification and, 2, 88, 141–143
  communities of practice and, 109–
    110, 114
  effective behaviors in, 34–35, 58–59,
    152
  forms of, 17–19
  integrative role of principals and,
    104–117
  pedagogical content knowledge in,
    44, 56
  professional community and, 178–
    179
  theory-based understandings in, 54–
    55
  understanding of teaching practices
    and, 53
Prislin, R., 25, 77
Problem-based learning, 66, 147

Procedural knowledge, 143
Process-oriented approach, 161
Processual dimension, of leadership, 130, 136
Proefriedt, W., 69
Professional accountability, 83, 87–88, 90–91
Professional community, 178–179
Professional development
  co-participation in, 53
  in educational leader development, 149–150
  principal role in, 111–112
Program for the Preparation of School Principals (Danforth Foundation), 147
Public Agenda, 85
Purkey, S. C., 6, 31, 37, 98
Putnam, R., 29, 36, 70, 72, 109, 113, 114

Quality of educational research, 158–160
  critical question and, 160
  experimental question and, 158–159
  foundational critique and, 159–160
Quantitative research, 16–17, 99–100, 167–168

Radziszewska, B., 59
RAND Mathematics Study Panel, 4, 169
Rapp, D., 119
Raun, T., 43
Real-world contexts for learning, 65, 66–67, 68–69
Reavis, C., 18
Reconstructed knowledge (Thompson & Gitlin), 133–134
Reese, W. J., 89
Reezigt, G. J., 17
Reflective practice, 157
Reich, R., 73
Reid, K. S., 3

Reimer, T., 35
Reiser, B., 35
Reitzug, U. C., 5, 157, 158, 169
Research methods, 156–170
  action research, 157
  case studies, 15–16, 99–100, 164–165
  design research, 59, 77, 165–167
  experimental research, 16–17, 99–100, 158–159, 168
  implications of, 169–170
  National Research Council (NRC) and, 160–163
  normative scholarship, 157
  quality of educational research, 158–160
  quantitative research, 16–17, 99–100, 167–168
  reflective practice, 157
  systematic research, 157–158
Resnick, L. B., 47–48, 60 n. 3, 66
Respect
  in democratic community, 122
  of principals for teachers, 110
Revoicing (O'Conner and Michaels), 38
Reyes, P., 9–10, 23, 101–118, 106, 107, 109, 110, 112–114, 165, 173, 177, 179
Reynolds, A. J., 23
Reynolds, D., 96, 98
Ricciardi, D., 144, 148
Richardson, V., 15–16, 157
Riehl, C. J., 1–11, 5, 8, 10, 12–27, 23, 156–170, 157, 158, 168, 169, 171–184, 174, 176
Rigdon, M., 97, 98
Rimer, S., 102
Rist, R., 113
Ritzug, U. C., 5
Rodrigues, J., 25, 77
Rogoff, B., 59
Romberg, T. A., 6

Rorrer, A., 109, 113
Rosenblatt, Z., 100 n. 2
Rosenblum, S., 14
Rosenholz, S. J., 23, 34, 37, 39, 178
Rosenshine, B., 29, 48
Rossmiller, R. A., 14
Roth, W., 59
Rothstein, R., 125
Rowan, B., 32, 47, 49, 58, 167–168
Roza, M., 138
Rumberger, R. W., 25
Rusch, E. A., 134, 144, 145
Russell, T., 143
Rutherford, D., 18

St. Pierre, E. A., 5
Salinas, K., 64
Sammons, P., 15
Sanders, M., 72
Sandler, H., 63
Sapon-Shevin, M., 123
Sarr, R. A., 20
Sassi, A., 37, 166, 178
Saxe, R., 62
Schauble, L., 7
Scheerens, J., 15–17, 167, 168
Schein, E. H., 143
Scheurich, J. J., 15, 23, 104–106, 108, 137 n. 3, 158
Schifter, D., 60 n. 8
Schneider, B., 89
Schneider, M., 87
Schoenfeld, A. H., 60 n. 6
Schön, D. A., 143, 157
School-centric view, 64
School-community relationship, 61–80
  connecting community services with schools, 64
  evolving perspectives on, 62–65
  methodological challenges for scholars, 77–80
  neighborhood community and, 179–180
  "new science" of learning and, 65–69
  parent involvement and, 62–64
  sense of place and community development, 73–77
  social capital and schools in, 69–73
School culture, 22
  integrative role of principal and, 104–117
  social boundaries in schools and, 104–105, 109
School districts
  accountability demands and, 93–97
  influence on teaching, 92–93
School leadership. *See* Educational leader development; Educational leadership; Principal leadership; Teacher leadership
Schools for Thought (SFT), 54, 60 n. 7
Schorr, R. Y., 81, 97, 175–176, 180
Scott, J., 99
Scott-Jones, P., 25
Scribner, A. P., 23, 101, 106, 107, 110
Scribner, J. D., 23, 101, 106, 107, 110, 112, 114
Scribner, J. P., 18
Secada, W., 66
Senge, P. M., 112, 157
Senk, S. L., 60 n. 6
Sergiovanni, T. J., 89, 106, 112, 129
Setting directions, 20–21
  goals in, 20–21
  performance expectations in, 21
  vision in, 20
Sexual identity, 103
Sfard, A., 38
Shah, B., 67, 75
Shaker, P., 4
Shakeshaft, C., 144
Shapiro, J. P., 108, 110–111
Shavelson, R. J., 5, 41, 77, 166

Sheppard, B., 34–35
Shields, C. M., 10, 119–137, 121, 123, 124, 130, 165, 167, 172, 173, 179, 181
Shipps, D., 9, 81–100, 85, 87, 164, 180, 181
Shirley, D., 75
Short, P. M., 5, 157, 158, 169
Showers, B., 18
Shulman, L. S., 4, 29, 31, 32, 37, 41–42, 48, 157, 158, 173–174
Sikula, J., 140
Silins, H. C., 177
Silver, E. A., 40
Simon, B., 64
Sims, P., 70, 73
Singh, K., 70, 71, 77
Siskin, L. S., 82, 98, 100 n. 1
Skalbeck, K. L., 22
Skrla, L., 104–106, 137 n. 3
Slater, M. R., 95
Slater, R. O., 173
Slavin, R. E., 123, 158–159, 170
Sleegers, P., 22
Smith, B., 23
Smith, G., 75
Smith, J. B., 24, 35, 176, 177
Smith, L. T., 137 n. 4
Smith, M., 63, 81, 86
Smith, M. S., 6, 15, 31, 37, 40, 98
Smith, T., 78
Smith-Maddox, R., 71
Smrekar, C. E., 25, 64, 70, 73
Smylie, M. A., 10, 16, 18, 39, 50, 51, 129, 138–155, 140, 178, 181–183
Snell, S. A., 140
Social capital, 69–73
    emerging questions concerning, 71–73
    expanding amount of, 26
    intervention with high-poverty students and, 70–71
    nature of, 69–70, 113
    research on, 70–71
    social networks and, 113–114
Socialization, in educational leader development, 144, 148–149
Social justice. See also Equity
    concept of, 123
    directions for inquiry into, 135
    education for, 125
    in ensuring pedagogical focus, 126–128
    frame for, 123–126
    implications for leadership, 128–132
    importance of, 119
    interplay of democratic community and, 125
    moral accountability and, 88–90
    multiple meanings of, 124–125
    research agenda for, 132–134
Solomon, R. P., 26
Southern Poverty Law Center, 104–105
Southworth, G., 16, 19–20
Spillane, J. P., 8, 12, 18, 19, 28–45, 35, 40, 43, 44, 47, 50, 52–53, 95, 96, 164, 171, 173–175, 178, 182
Spring, J., 102–103
Sprio, R. J., 52
Standpoint theory, 133
Stanton-Salazar, R. D., 72, 113–114
Starratt, R. J., 120–122, 129, 130
Stein, M. K., 8, 12, 28–45, 36, 40, 42, 44, 55–56, 60 n. 6, 143, 146, 164, 171, 173–175, 178, 182
Steinbach, R., 19–20, 43, 96, 98, 149
Steinberg, S. R., 123–124
Stevens, R., 29, 48
Stoddart, T., 107
Stone, C. N., 74, 85
Stout, R., 75
Strike, K. A., 120, 121
Student community, 176–177
Student culture, 177

Student learning
accountabilities and, 81–100
building powerful forms of teaching
and learning, 23–24
complexity of, 173–176
expanding understanding of learners
and leaders in educational
leadership, 52–53
impact of educational leadership on,
2–4, 15–17, 22–26, 30–32,
172
long-term versus short-term
perspectives on, 79
mediational paradigms and, 32–37
nature of, 47–49
"new science" of, 65–69
opportunities to learn, 68
outcomes of, 67–68
problem-based, 66, 147
qualitative case studies on, 15–16,
99–100
quasi-experimental quantitative
studies on, 16–17, 99–100
real-world contexts for, 65, 66–67,
68–69
reconceptualizing, 79–80
research on teaching and, 28–45
rethinking, 54–56
school-community relationships and,
65–69, 78–79
in social and and interactive context,
37–40
thinking processes of teachers and,
41–44
transferring from one context to
another, 66–67
Students. *See also* Student learning
diversity of, 3. *See also* Diverse
student populations
dropout rates of, 3
graduation rates of, 2–3
Studer, S., 65

Sullivan, A., 62, 63
Systematic research, 157–158

Talbert, J. E., 19, 39, 68–69
Tatum, B. D., 26
Taylor, D. L., 18
Teacher leadership. *See also* Distributed
leadership; Educational leader
development; Educational
leadership
forms of, 17–19
instructional, 49–50, 56–58, 69,
174
and professional community, 178–179
Teaching and teacher learning
accountabilities and, 81–100
complexity of, 173–176
educational leadership and, 29
linking educational practice to
student learning, 30–32
literature on, 143
mediational paradigms for, 32–37
nature of, 47–49
opportunities to teach, 68
processes in, 41–44
professional development, 53, 149–
150
research-based claims concerning,
30–44
research on learning to teach, 35–36
rethinking, 54–56
in social and interactive context, 37–
40
thinking processes in, 41–44
Team learning (Senge), 112
Technical knowledge, 143
Teddlie, C., 96, 98
Teitel, L., 147
Tennet, L., 147, 148, 151, 155 n. 1
Teske, P., 87
Tharp, R., 53
Thayer, L., 20–21

"Thick" democracy, 121–122
"Thin" democracy, 121
Thompson, A., 133–135
Thompson, D. R., 60 n. 6
Thomson, S. D., 141
Tillman, L. C., 137 n. 4
Timpane, M., 73
Tolley, H., 19–20
Toole, J., 21
Towne, L., 5, 77, 161, 166
Townsend, T., 17
Transformative dimension, of
    leadership, 111, 130, 136
Transmissive teaching practices, 127
Trust, of principals for teachers, 110,
    130, 136
Tschannen-Moran, M., 6, 7, 145
Tucker, M. S., 138–139
Turner, J. C., 176
Turner, W., 149
Tyack, D. B., 2, 46, 85, 88

Ubben, C. G., 49
University Council for Educational
    Administration (UCEA), 141–
    142, 154

Valencia, R. R., 105
Valenzuela, A., 107–108, 119
van de Grift, W., 15
Vandenberghe, R., 144, 149
van den Borg, R., 22
Van Maanen, J., 143
Van Velsor, E., 140
Variance-oriented approach, 161
Velez, W., 107
Vertical networks (Putnam), 72
Viadero, D., 5
Vision, in educational leadership, 20
Vriesenga, M., 145–146
Vygotsky, L. S., 46–47, 65

Wagner, R. K., 43
Wagstaff, L., 9–10, 101–118, 110,
    112, 114, 165, 173, 177, 179
Walberg, H. J., 15, 25
Walker, D., 129, 130
Walker, E. M., 149
Waller, W., 177
Wang, M., 15
Ward, K., 53
Warne, T. R., 18
Wasley, P. A., 18, 57
Wearne, D., 33
Weber, M., 50
Wehlage, G. G., 34, 66
Weifeld, F. D., 15
Weinberg, A., 37
Weindling, D., 144, 149
Weinstein, C. S., 18
Weiss, C. H., 59 n. 1, 162
Weissglass, J., 105
Wenger, E., 19, 38–40, 56, 174, 176
Westbury, M., 23
What Works Clearinghouse, 160
Whites
    dropout rates of, 3
    as percentage of school population,
        103
Wide-awakeness (Greene), 124
Willinsky, J., 7
Wilson, B., 19
Wilson, J. Q., 172
Wilson, S. M., 60 n. 8, 143
Wineburg, S., 18
Winger, A., 90
Winter, P. A., 23
Witte, J. F., 87
Wolf, S. A., 18
Women, and socialization in
    educational leader development,
    148, 151
Wood, T., 38

Woolfolk, A. E., 35
Woolverton, S., 107
Woolworth, S., 18
Wright, P. M., 140
Wyckoff, J., 138

Yackel, E., 38
Yerkes, D. M., 147
York, R. L., 15

Young, M. D., 144
Youngs, P., 24
Yukl, G., 141

Zarins, S., 177
Zederayko, G., 53
Zimmerman, D. P., 129, 130
Zollers, N. J., 122
Zuckerman, K., 34, 39